A GEORDIE IN JAPAN

A Geordie in Japan

by

Olga Rutherford Abrahams

The Memoir Club

First published in 2010 by
The Memoir Club
Arya House
Langley Park
Durham
DH7 9XE
Tel: 0191 373 5660
Email: memoirclub@msn.com

British Library Cataloguing in
Publication Data.
A catalogue record for this book
is available from the
British Library

ISBN: 978-1-84104-512-2

Typeset by TW Typesetting, Plymouth, Devon
Printed by J F Print, Sparkford, Somerset

Contents

Chapter 3: Early married life in Shizunai (1954–1957)

Chapter 4: A lovely city – but a struggle (1958–1963)

Chapter 5: Settled and moved again (1964–1968)

Chapter 6: Literature Work, and then another move (1968–1972)

Chapter 9: Retirement (1985 onwards)

List of Illustrations

Foreword

'As I don't believe a word of Christianity, I do not think I should eat your tea.' With this, Olga made her debut at Cambridge University in 1943 at the age of 17, when invited to a Christian tea party. She enjoyed a good argument then and still does! Her parents were strongly socialist and left her free to develop her own ideas. At Girton College the Communists seemed to be more active than the Socialists so she joined them and became their secretary. But she also continued to argue with her Christian friend Helen Roseveare though Helen did not argue back. Finally, reluctantly, Olga argued herself into belief.

This book tells her story. In 1953 she went to Japan with a missionary society. Some people have distorted ideas about missionaries without really knowing what they do. This book tells you! She arrived eight years after the Pacific war ended, and apart from visits back to Britain every 4–5 years, stayed there until she retired in 1985. Her story includes that of her husband Doug and their three children, and it reveals what it meant to bring up a family in a radically different culture on the other side of the world.

They spent most of those years in the north of Honshu, the main island in Japan, and also in Hokkaido where the climate was harsh in winter as the bitter winds and snow swept south from Siberia. The Japanese themselves had only migrated up there a hundred years earlier when they adopted the Manchurian stove for heating. The population was more scattered and churches far fewer than in the south.

Westerners had to grapple with a difficult language and a strong culture which preserved peace and harmony on the surface but buried the tensions out of sight. After the war tall, out-spoken foreigners ignorant of local etiquette could cause great offence. Their mangled language and alien customs demanded great forbearance and patience from the Japanese. The Shinto gods had been discredited by the defeat, Buddhism was mainly concerned with funerals, and a spiritual vacuum lay at the heart of the nation. Communicating across cultural barriers required much grace, patience, forgiveness and love.

As Olga's story unfolds, all these strands are woven together; the mistakes, misunderstandings, struggles and failures, but also the growing love, joy, and laughter as deep friendships grew, and the barriers of culture and language came down.

Fifty years later, one more strand emerges; the growing number of self-supporting churches with their own pastors and buildings in the farming towns of the Tsugaru plain in the north of Honshu and in the fishing villages, mining towns and cities of Hokkaido. These churches are now taking the good news of Jesus Christ to their own people but with less than 1 ½% of the population Christian, they still have a long way to go. The ministry of Doug and Olga has provided one thread in God's tapestry as their lives have been inextricably woven into the lives of hundreds of others.

Valerie Griffiths

Preface

As the heavens are higher than the earth so are my ways higher than your ways and my thoughts than your thoughts.

Isaiah 55: 9

As I have been writing my story I have been overwhelmed by the realisation that God's ways have been higher than mine; so much has been unexpected.

I would like to thank all the friends who have shown such interest and helped so much with the book. In particular I'd like to thank my neighbour Jean Donovan, a writer whose patient help and advice is much appreciated and Freda Richards, editor of the Stanmore Baptist Church magazine *Linklines,* who gave me the opportunity to contribute a monthly article and whose assistance and encouragement has been invaluable. Irene Hope, a fellow missionary who was my husband's secretary and typist for his book *Doug, Man and Missionary,* was a wonderful proof-reader and fact-checker. The Writers Bureau, with my tutor Diane Paul were a great source of help and advice. I do not claim a perfect memory and may have made mistakes, for which I ask your forgiveness.

I would also like to thank all those who have supported, encouraged and prayed for us over the years and, of course, the Overseas Missionary Fellowship. Finally, I'd like to express my thankfulness to God for all His surprises.

Olga Rutherford Abrahams

Introduction

Chat with Win

'It is a wonderful place – only ten minutes walk down the road from here to St Mary's lighthouse – when the tide is out you can cross to the island, but the tide comes in very quickly so be careful not to get caught.' As we bought the caravan, the salesman enthusiastically told us of the attractions of the district. He didn't know that I was coming home, after half a century, encouraged by Doug who knew my longing to be back by the sea and clear air at Whitley Bay.

My old school friend, Win, visited us. We chatted to the background of the plaintive notes of the foghorn out at sea, and enjoyed the quietness of the warmth of the sunshine streaming through the windows of our spacious, comfortable, 'mobile home'.

When I told her of the salesman talk, she smiled. 'Do you remember when we were marooned on the island? We cycled over, walked round the lighthouse and found the tide had come in and cut us off!'

'I certainly do!' I responded, 'I saw the tide racing in, tried to get you to hurry, but you just dawdled. I was mad that you hadn't believed me!'

'I know – we had to wait till the tide came right in and out again. Then it was dark. The coast was guarded at night against the Germans. We were scared.'

'The burly lighthouse keeper was very kind to us. When the tide had gone out enough, he lent you his huge boots to cross to the mainland and carried me across on his back.'

'How did we get past the guard and the barbed wire?'

'We were feeling nervous. When we heard the order 'Halt. Who goes there?' we halted. Two timid teenagers squeaked "Friend".'

'Then we heard "Advance one".'

'You advanced and explained how we had been cut off by the tide. I think the young soldier was as nervous as we were. Anyway he accepted our story – let us pass – and with a sigh of relief we made for home.'

'We had to come back the next day in daylight when the tide was out for our bicycles.'

Our short-term memories were no longer reliable now that we were nearly eighty but together we relived many of the memories of childhood.

We used to go swimming before school starting in the chill of April days.

'We egged each other on in the two-mile cycle ride to the coast.'

We reached the beach, shivering as we plunged into the sea.

'Cycling holidays in Scotland were great with little traffic. There were no road signs – they had been removed so that, if the Germans invaded, they would get lost. I don't know if it would have worked on the Germans but it certainly did on us. We got lost once and were rescued by a contingent of Polish soldiers who got out their maps to show us the way.'

'We had to part company when I went off to Cambridge to study science, a complete atheist.'

'And I joined the A.T.S, a convinced Christian. *You* always had the brains.'

'Then after graduating, God showed me that my thoughts were not His thoughts – His ways higher than mine. I changed from being an atheist to a Christian and took a job in a Christian girls' boarding school.'

'That was a shock to my Presbyterian mother. She wept thinking you had become a nun.'

'Since then I sailed for Japan while you travelled all over the world with your husband to different embassies. Our paths occasionally crossed. We both had the loneliness of leaving our children in boarding schools. Both lost our first child, mine still-born, yours in the prime of life, killed as an officer in the Falklands War. Before I left, do you remember saying earnestly to me, 'It doesn't matter about writing to me but be sure to keep in touch with your mother regularly.'

'I did that and wrote to my mother every week. She kept the letters leaving me a remarkable source of material to write my own story. I want to share it with friends, fellow workers and my children and grandchildren. I'll start by writing to my daughter and then tell others of my experiences abroad.'

CHAPTER 1

Growing up in England (1925–1952)

To my daughter

Dear Gracely,

Have you ever wondered what kind of world your parents and grandparents lived in? I often imagine my father (born in 1863) transported to 2000 and completely puzzled by pictures on TV, noisy lumps of metal flying overhead, motor cars rushing around, etc. His were the days of the penny-farthing bicycle. In his student days in Edinburgh, he enjoyed a pony trip across the Highlands of Scotland with his friend, Edwin Jack. This friend was a publisher and sent me a good book each Christmas. One of the books I passed on to you recently – the animal picture book, coloured plates of the animals one side, a brief description on the other, I often showed you the pictures and read the description to you and Michael. Result – at the age of three – at Sunday School, when the teacher asked 'What did God make?' you outdid the sun, moon and stars answers with 'The duck-billed platypus'.

The other thing my father and his friend did together was to go out into the countryside, and from opposite points on the lakeside, practice projecting their voices so that they could hear each other. There were no mechanical amplifiers. As a public speaker, he was able to judge the acoustics of a room by listening to the chairman's introduction, and could throw his voice to be heard clearly by all. (He never taught me how to do it!) But I never knew his parents, his mother died when he was five and his little sister three. His father had a draper's shop in Sunderland and was Sunday School Superintendent at a Congregational Church – that's all I know and wish I knew more.

But I can tell you more about your grandfather, if you want to know. You never met him either for he died when I was seventeen, in my first term at university. He studied philosophy and theology at Edinburgh University, graduating in 1890 (1st Class) the year my mother was born. He studied theology at Merton College, Oxford, then became minister of Abbey Congregational Church, Stoke Newington (walking distance from CIM headquarters at Newington Green). His parents moved to look after him until he left to go in an LMS (London Missionary Society) caravan in Wales until 1915. Horses left his caravan at a centre, where he stayed for a time in his 'little house'. He spoke Welsh. Unfortunately, his knowledge of the

1

language was not sufficient to stop him inviting visitors into his 'little house'. That was the euphemistic name for the toilet. He seems to have had a conversion experience that led him into the ministry, followed by disappointment that the church was not what God intended. He left the ministry to take up market gardening on the North Tyne; aged over fifty, he could hardly contribute to the war effort, but reckoned that lives were at risk in bringing him food, so he should help in food production. He had remained a bachelor, believing that Jesus never married; that to follow Him was to remain single (handsome man though he was!)

Why he chose Crawcrook as the site of his market garden I will never know. A small village on the North Tyne, where the weather had to be watched to produce crops – rather cold and inhospitable. (But prize leeks are a feature of the area). Nor do I know how he learned the trade of a market gardener. I do know he was skilful, because we benefited from what he grew in our little garden years later. I see him still, sitting on a low stool, peeling and pickling the shallots he had grown, while I removed caterpillars from the cabbages. The front garden was a rock garden, pretty but producing the minimum of weeds with a rambler rose adorning the fence. But what of the market garden in Crawcrook? I imagine him in a comfortable hut, books abounding, tidy, the table set correctly for his meals and visitors to buy his produce. His constant companions were his dog and cat. He trained the male dog to stand aside to let the female cat have first choice from his food bowl. His visitors enjoyed his courtesy and conversation. The life must have been lonely as the years of war continued; 1918 brought the Armistice with the hopes that it was a war to end wars.

A young school teacher often visited. She liked his conversation and companionship, and realised that his wisdom merited more outreach than the garden gave. Her headmaster, Mr Elsey, was a man interested in adult education. Through him my father began lecturing for the Worker's Educational Association (WEA) first in English literature, then psychology and philosophy with occasional preaching engagements. This sounds somewhat factual and uninteresting but the market gardener at fifty-six fell in love with the school teacher of twenty-nine and they were married in 1920.

My mother was the eldest of three girls and three boys. She was born on her father's 21st birthday – that is how my father came to be older than my grandfather.

(Years later I met Mr Elsey, a thoughtful man, and preached in his Chapel. Mr Elsey lost three wives and, after my father had died, asked my mother to marry him but she didn't want to be the fourth wife to die.)

Home near the sea

By the time my parents were married my father was launched on his career as a lecturer for the Workers Educational Association (WEA). At that time evening classes and adult education were uncommon. He particularly enjoyed teaching groups of miners, who tended to be thinkers while he reckoned teachers just received knowledge.

Graham was born in 1921, the same day as his cousin, Reg. Her sister Peggy had told my mother as soon as she was pregnant and was indignant that my mother had not told her – but she had not realised that she was expecting! My father baptized Graham himself.

Four years later I arrived. My father was ill with life-threatening pneumonia. My mother appealed to the doctor concerning my constant crying. 'She's hungry,' he replied. 'Your worry about your husband's condition is limiting your supply of milk. Get her a bottle.' He was right. My father lived. I imagine the difference it would have made to my life if my mother had been left with a four-year-old boy and a baby girl to look after by herself. Also, could my own temperament have been moulded by the anxiety around me at birth?

We moved to Earsdon while I was still a baby. My father had discovered a new housing estate twenty minutes by bus from Newcastle, convenient for travel to his evening classes. After we moved we found that the journey was longer, nearer forty-five minutes – his first journey had been on the infrequent limited express. I have always been glad about that mistake. We were near the sea and not in the city. God's way was higher than ours.

In 1927 the house we bought was a new semi-detached, built so many to the acre to receive a good grant. The builder had left one area in the middle of the estate (reducing each plot a little to do it). My mother was convinced that in twenty years he would build on the plot also. Meanwhile it was made into three tennis courts. From age ten I enjoyed climbing over the fence to play as a junior member, 6/- a year, and got free coaching from senior members. We could play until 7 p.m. and on Saturday mornings. Once I played on the senior team when they needed an extra player. 'Keep your eye on the ball'. 'Don't believe anything is impossible', was the advice. I was small and had a junior racket, about 10 oz, which meant I could handle it with ease. The tennis pavilion served as a place for dancing lessons – ballroom, ballet, tap dancing – conducted by Gwen Redpath, a teacher of imagination and skill in presentation who held a display once a year in the local church hall.

Winters were cold, bedrooms unheated. The boiler for the hot water was at the back of the living room coal fire, the damper adjusted to heat the water or the room. The cold water tank was in the bathroom at the request of my mother to the builder. Although it was an eye sore its position prevented our pipes freezing in the winter. My father got up at 6 a.m. and laid and lit the fire, using wood kindling helped with rolled up newspapers. He said he didn't like getting up but liked being up. He brought my mother a cup of tea after 7 a.m. and we had breakfast together before going off to school. My father's work was teaching WEA classes in the evenings, during winter months and he studied every morning in the study. So our house included back-kitchen with sink, oven, etc., living-room with pantry and fire plus dining-room table. The room was not large but we had a small billiard table that brought along my brother's pals, and a gramophone, introducing me to classical music, which I loved.

The third room downstairs was my father's study. We could not disturb him during the mornings. A large roll-top desk took up a large part of the room but it was a feature, with a mercury controlled pendulum clock on the top of the desk. Upstairs were the bathroom and three bedrooms. When we first move in, four and a half year old Graham went off reluctantly to a private school. He thought he was being thrown out, leaving father, mother and sister together at home. His first impressions of school were 'too much noise, and too much people.'

We were in a mining area – there were no terrific disasters, but occasional comments about injuries in the mines for one family or another. Our neighbour used to come home black with coal from the pit, and sometimes drunk. Apparently, when I was little he and my father were the only two men of whom I was not afraid. We knew who were miners by the heaps of coal outside their houses, delivered free. We used to play outside in the street, unless told off by the local policeman, 'Fatty Moor' whom we feared. We were scared if a ball went into the neighbour's garden. There was a high unfriendly fence between us and the neighbour. Later we discovered that Veronica wanted privacy because she liked to sunbathe naked. Graham and I used to play 'cricket' with a small bat, a washing board for the wicket, along the drive between our two houses.

School days, swimming and cycling

My granddaughter phoned me to ask me questions about my school days, a project for her school. Not easy to answer the questions off the cuff. So

I thought I would now write something down. I don't have much memory of anything before that – playing with my friend Vera and with a doll's pram.

Infant classes at Earsdon Council School were held in the Methodist school room, one teacher responsible for us all. She taught us needlework, knitting, etc., in a very happy atmosphere. My friends were put up into the main school while I was kept down in the infants department. I was unhappy about this – it was years later that I discovered why I was kept down – my mother had wanted me to enjoy the relaxed atmosphere of the infants before going on to the main school where I would have to study. When finally I did go up I just stayed for half a year in that class. I didn't like the teacher because she shouted (not at me). I remember her sending a girl to the head for some misdemeanour. After a while she returned, 'What did he say?' asked the teacher. 'Nothing,' was the reply. She had been too terrified to go to his room.

The next grade I was put into in the middle of the year, and cried a lot. 'Don't worry,' the Head assured my mother. 'She's struggling with the work and she'll cry until she is top of the class.' Mrs C, a widow, the teacher, taught us poetry and singled out one girl to recite for speech day. The poem was Tennyson's, 'Break, break, break, / on thy cold grey stones, Oh sea! / And I would that my tongue could utter / the thoughts that arise in me'. The poem was faithfully recited. I question whether the performer had much idea that it referred to the death of a loved one. I know I didn't, till years later. The top two classes were together in one large room. We prepared for the scholarship (11 +) exam. Eight of us passed to go to high school.

The school itself was a stone building, the toilets in the yard wooden boxes, no flush. The playground was of asphalt, but we enjoyed it. I was greatly embarrassed when one of the boys tried to kiss me in the playground.

On one occasion I came home distressed because the Head had accused me of lying. Without a word my father set off for the school to confront the Head, indignant at the accusation. He affirmed that his daughter did not lie. His own emphasis on truthfulness had rubbed off on me and he knew it.

Walking to school we were required to avoid the main road and use the slightly longer route through streets and a wide clay road known as 'Teapot Close'. If Graham and I were slightly late he would grasp me by the hand

and run with all his might, my feet barely touching the ground. Turning out of 'Teapot Close' on to the main Earsdon Road, he was on the inside and I seemed to be airborne as I held on and swung round the bend. Perhaps it was my training in running. But one morning I was on my way to school, in the rain, with a couple of lads. We paused to cross the road, nothing to be seen, they crossed, I hesitated and then followed. A car came from behind a stationary bus and knocked me down. I was carried into the classroom with bleeding knees, slightly hurt. But my greatest alarm was when the police came to the classroom to investigate. The driver was upset.

We had two regular holidays. In the past the 'Blaydon Races' had been held at that time. The Town Moor (Newcastle) was alive with swings, roundabouts, shows, coconut shires, etc. Race week was a Tyneside holiday week for elementary schools, usually the last week in June. We regularly went away to Rothbury, staying in a house where the landlady cooked the food my mother had bought. Rothbury is a lovely village in the Cheviots, about thirty miles by train for us – but I used to think it was a very, very long way away. As we lived by the sea we chose the countryside for our holiday. We would set off for a walk in the hills and leave my father at some spot where he thought the view was a picture. He would sit down on the grass, or a stone, get out his sketch book and water colours, and sketch the scene. Graham and I would continue our walk with Mother to some pretty place where she would sit down to rest, and Graham and I would play around, perhaps by a mountain stream. I loved the bracken and watching the rabbits. I wanted to catch one. I figured out that, if a rabbit went down a hole, it would have to come out of it. I spent a long time sitting by the hole waiting for it to reappear.

The path through Cragside was a relatively easy climb between masses of rhododendrons in a glorious riot of colour, reds and pinks. It led up to the historic house of Lord Armstrong, the first house in the world to be lit by hydro-electricity, most of the work and inventions of J.S. Swan. Lord Armstrong's engineering prowess was great – the local university, now Newcastle University, used to be Armstrong College. These details were lost on me at the time but the sheer delight of climbing the path through the rhododendron wood remains with me seventy years on. Occasionally we saw a snakeskin on the hillside, a reminder of the one poisonous English snake, the adder. There was little danger unless the snake was curled up in the sun on a rock amongst the heather, well camouflaged. It would not appreciate a foot on its head. Rothbury was our holiday spot until Graham started high school at eleven. Then Race Week was no longer his school holiday. We changed our location to Falstone on the North Tyne, now incorporated into the massive and beautiful Kielder National Park.

We have a lovely photograph of my mother. We were out for a ramble on the hills where she lost her shoe in a bog. Her cries for help were answered by Graham getting out his camera!! Every year, during our summer holidays, my father lectured for two weeks at the WEA residential summer school in Durham. My mother and I would stay with her Aunt Emma in nearby Darlington and visit my father from there. I luxuriated in her home, sinking into the deep feather-bed mattress, eating delicious Yorkshire puddings with gravy served before the roast beef, fresh mackerel caught by my uncle on his fishing expedition to Redcar. I liked to go with Aunt Emma to the market to buy fresh farm products. She would say of cakes or puddings, 'It must be good. It's got an egg in it.'

We also visited relatives at nearby Coatham. My maternal grandfather after retirement ran a pub, the Travellers Rest, previously run by his sister, Aunt Emma. I hated the atmosphere and smell of beer. But a little way down the road was the watermill and post office. Cousin Walter, lean and wiry, was the miller and postman, his wife, Mary, cheerful and chubby, the postmistress, with Uncle George, bedridden with arthritis, an old man with whom I felt nervous. (On one occasion, a locum did not dare give him the suggested prescription of arsenic – it could have been a lethal dose – but he needed it). Cousin Walter was a delight. I would gaze at the massive waterwheel, driven to grind the corn, but he was careful not to let me go too close. Sadly, the owner of the land wanted to divert the river. He set Walter up with electrically driven machinery but the charm of the huge waterwheel was lost. The flour was produced as before but the atmosphere was laden with flour dust because of the dryness of the atmosphere. My mother would buy some of his wholemeal flour to bake delicious brown bread on our return home. Cousin Walter was also the local postman, getting on his bicycle to deliver mail to the surrounding farmhouses. He had to give up when the farmers started to have their newspapers delivered daily by mail. Walter could not go everyday to every farm. Mary was a warm-hearted, energetic postmistress. They had a large garden, largely of fruit and vegetables. A long path through the garden led to the toilet, the 'earth closet', covered regularly with ash.

During my father's two weeks of lecturing we would take the opportunity of visiting him at Hatfield College. Meals were served at long tables in the Old Hall of the Castle. All stood behind their chairs until my father, head of the table, pronounced grace. *Benedictus benedicat* – may the blessed one bless us. This was followed by a clatter of chairs being moved. Occasionally the loud banging of knife handles and forks on the wooden tables would alert the waiters to something missing. Durham is a beautiful city, very hilly with the Cathedral and Castle dominating the landscape. The Cathedral had been built by devoted monks. St Cuthbert's bones had been brought there from Lindisfarne in stages, to escape desecration by the Vikings. He was one of the pioneers of early Celtic Christianity. The pillars are magnificent, the circumference of each equal to its height and intricately carved. The cloisters are quiet and peaceful. I enjoyed the atmosphere of the Cathedral. My father rowed us on the river below the Cathedral and Castle. Childhood memories are deep and to this day I love Durham's steep cobbled streets and Cathedral and Castle. Travelling by train, London to Newcastle, I still hope for a view of the Cathedral and Castle.

I always enjoyed my stay with great Aunt Emma, oblivious of the tensions in the house. Uncle George had two adult daughters by his first wife. Outwardly he was a handsome gentleman, but she knew his cruelty and liking of drink. She separated from him but refused to divorce him, so that he would not inflict his cruelty on another woman. Then she died.

Aunt Emma, not heeding the warning, agreed when he proposed to her and discovered the problem. Her stepdaughters were always very support-ive. She arranged for the midday meal to be served promptly at noon; in this way he could not get to the pubs that opened then. Fishing was his hobby, going for the day to Redcar. I quite liked him. He showed me how to puncture and flatten the blisters on the paint on the outside wooden doors, by pushing a pin through them making two holes. He took me to the cricket match on the pitch just at the top of their road, with a bag of cherries. I went with Aunt Emma to church on Sunday mornings. I remember she passed her prayer book to me during the service, whispering 'I know this one'. It was the Lord's Prayer I had learned at school. (My father did not mind my going to church away from home, but did not want me to attend regularly and accept all the vicar said. He wanted me to think for myself). Aunt Emma would sit in her armchair by the cheery coal fire knitting. She continued knitting until her heart condition limited her. She seemed determined to outlive her husband: several times her heart stopped beating for several minutes, but finally she died before him.

Back in Earsdon life continued uneventfully. We liked jigsaw puzzles and party games, especially at Christmastime, with a large Christmas tree in the bay window, candles lit on the tree. As my birthday is Christmas Eve I had my party, too, around that time. In warmer weather the beach was the attraction, playing with my cousin, Peter (Aunt Flo lived near us) and my brother. The sand dunes at Seaton Sluice were ideal for hide and seek or Cowboys and Indians, the slopes great for just rolling down. There were pony rides during the summer and 'plodging' in the water.

What more can I say? This was all before war threatened, although not before the period of massive unemployment, the Jarrow marchers, and national 'strike' (lock out). Wealthier relatives bought us a wireless set; we could hear the news, cricket commentaries, classical concerts, and the annual Oxford/Cambridge Boat Race. Politically our home atmosphere was socialist.

High school days are much clearer in my mind. I passed the scholarship exam for Whitley and Monkseaton High School for Girls at ten, smallest in the class. I needed a bicycle to travel the two and a half miles to school. Graham warned me that I would have to mend my own punctures – but the first effort, with his help, required a new inner tube! I enjoyed the cycle ride. I came out top of the form in my first year. The boys and girls joined in one school in my second year. The new Headmaster visited our form to enquire who was to receive the form prize – took one look at me and remarked, 'this little shrimp!' The girls were allowed the school hall to dance in during the breaks – so Jeannette, a taller girl in the form, chose me, because of my size, as her partner, and I learned to dance. I began violin lessons in the school group, but never gained confidence. Our orchestra won the prize, beating the other school competing, with the adjudicator's comment, 'the orchestra has some good players'. I had not reached the point of soaping my bow so I wouldn't be heard.

There were rumours of impending war. My mother hated war, but was not happy to see Hitler devouring one country after another, and especially Czechoslovakia with all its arms potential and the persecution of Jews. War was declared in September 1939 (I was thirteen years old, in the fourth form) finally provoked by Hitler's invasion of Poland. Life changed in many ways for us. We were issued with gas masks, and had to carry them wherever we went. Air-raid shelters were put up in the school grounds and in our gardens. Food was rationed – butter, margarine, milk, jam, sugar, eggs, meat, tea, tinned goods, clothing. Blackout was installed.

Our family huddled into the Anderson Shelter in our garden whenever the air-raid siren sounded. I hurriedly donned my 'siren suit' (warm top and trousers) over my pyjamas and either slept in the shelter or knitted in the dark. Twice our windows were blown out by bombs. We saw flames leaping in the air as a sugar factory in Newcastle was hit. A girl in our school was killed in one raid. Although North East England was the nearest point to the German coast, our immediate area was regarded as neutral – i.e. no children were evacuated for safety from the area, nor were any children brought in from more vulnerable parts. Blackout regulations required all windows to be curtained so that no glimpse of light could escape. (Air-Raid Wardens were on the rounds to ensure full observance). Lights on vehicles were dimmed, street lights were put out, barbed wire was placed on the beaches to deter possible invaders.

Very early in the war young men were being called up for military service, some were already in the forces. My brother's best friend was already in the Air Force and due for leave. I shall never forget the scene as we sat down for a meal after school. 'What time is Denis due home on leave?', my mother asked. 'He's not coming,' was the brief reply. 'Why?' 'He's dead'. There had been a raid over Germany, his plane had been hit and on return to Norfolk had crashed. Denis was an only son, his father a merchant sea captain, several times torpedoed. Graham would have liked to join up and fly after leaving school but was prevented from flying by poor eyesight.

A German submarine commander off the coast could see a pub in Blyth 'I'll have a drink there after the war' – I believe he did.

Rationing meant when food was available it was fairly distributed – meat by price rather than weight, tinned goods by the coupon, eggs (at one point one a week). Dried eggs came from the USA and we made scrambled eggs with them and cakes. Those who kept hens were given an allowance of feed for the hens but no egg ration, fish and vegetables were freely available and much effort was put into growing vegetables in our own gardens, allotments, etc. My father worked my uncle's garden also.

At school regular lessons continued but we lost some of our best teachers through the call up. Sports competition with other schools was also limited.

Win and I had many adventures together on our bicycles. We used to cycle down to the sea before school for an early morning swim from April onwards. It was little more than a dip in and out of the water, followed by a hot drink and girdle scones in the Panama Café, glowing after the cold bathe. The café was a delightful place, constructed of wood from an old wreck, the steering wheel on display among other parts of the ship. Unfortunately it was burned down and irreplaceable. The coastguard knew us well and would permit us to go into the sea even if it was rough, knowing we could swim, but we kept between the two flags he had set up to avoid the currents. He told us he could see the currents from the upper prom. We were swimming one day at the edge of the prescribed area when I realised that we were being drawn away from the shore. I used all my strength to get back to safety, within my depth. I watched Win. She was swimming strongly but not moving. I knew I did not have the power to pull her and myself out of the current. Although I was the slightly stronger swimmer she had endurance. At last we were both safe. Years later I learnt that we should have swum parallel to the shore to get out of the current (a rip tide).

Our other favourite spot was 'Table Rocks' a swimming pool formed naturally in the rocks.

On another occasion I was swimming on my own. A large beach ball had been thrown into the sea so I set off to rescue it. Some distance from the shore I realised that, although I was getting nearer, it was floating away more quickly. Regarding my life as of more value than the ball I turned round to swim for the shore. At that point a boat set out to retrieve the ball and had I got into difficulties rescue was at hand. As I stepped on to the beach every eye was on me – it was as though I was in the centre of an arena.

I loved the sea; my earliest memory was of lying on my back in a few inches of water thinking I was floating. My father at seventy was the swimmer. My mother used to take me to the beach and I would splash around in the waves, teeth chattering and lips blue. She would try to persuade me to come out but I just said I loved it.

I learned to swim in the open-air, unheated swimming pool at Tynemouth. The water was naturally changed when the tide came in. I could just stand at the shallow end up to my neck! The instructor was from the *News Chronicle*, a national newspaper that gave reliable news, but due to insufficient sponsorship ceased circulation. Later I was taught to dive in the same pool. Our school inter-house swimming races were also held here.

My first bicycle was to get me to school at eleven. But cycling turned into a hobby. I could get to the sea easily with Win, and we ventured to Plessey Woods to enjoy the countryside. Win (at sixteen) and I (at fifteen) started our youth hostel trips. We naturally cycled at the same speed, enjoyed each other's company and would average a leisurely sixty miles a day by making an early start.

Scottish Youth Hostels charged 6d a night and did not have to be booked in advance. We packed our sheet sleeping bags and the week's rations, cheese, butter, milk, tins, jams, sugar, etc. into our saddlebags and set off in whichever way the wind was blowing. We reckoned it could change direction and we didn't want to face it both ways. Traffic on the roads was sparse, but it was wartime. England feared an invasion, making every effort to prevent invading German soldiers knowing where they were. Every signpost, milestone, place name on shops, etc., telephone directories from call boxes, had been removed or deleted. We were guided by our own maps and the direction of the main roads. On only one occasion did we lose our way. The road to Edinburgh curved to the right, the road straight ahead looked 'main'. We took it and found ourselves lost. Who could we ask? We saw a contingent of soldiers and enquired. The soldiers happened to be Polish, but very kindly and with the help of their maps got us on the right route. It was a longer haul than usual! We reached the welcoming doors of Edinburgh Youth Hostel at 9.30, closing time was 10.00!!

The border moors were ideal for cycling with leisure to enjoy the vast heather-crowned hills. If occasionally we had to push our bicycles up hill at least we had a great time free wheeling down. (Two or three years later, cycling with less experienced college friends, one of them panicked going down hill, skidded and fell off into gravel and was badly grazed. We received help at the nearby manse and she was bundled off from the border in the bus, bicycle and all, to Edinburgh Infirmary, where another college friend looked after her).

But Win and I continued to revel in the Scottish countryside; the Trossacks – an icy cold morning swim in a pool, a mountain stream, with pure clear water; a lovely ferry ride over to Arran via Troon; cycling up the length of beautiful Loch Lomond, amongst, the hills; Ben Nevis towering above. It was idyllic to be among the hills but on a flat road for cycling all the way.

I cannot remember what we ate on our travels. We could buy goods that were not rationed; including 'bridies', a Scottish meat and onion turnover. We were told that at any of the farmhouses we could buy eggs although they were rationed – 'But don't ask on the Sabbath!' At times we were soaked in the rain but did not catch cold. At Coldingham we enjoyed the junket prepared by the warden so the milk would not turn sour overnight before the days of refrigeration. From Coldingham north of Berwick on the Scottish coast to Whitley Bay was our longest ride, more than seventy miles but we were getting home.

What was school like in those days? And how different from today? When I started high school there were two schools in the same grounds with some shared facilities – the girls' school and the boys' school, 120 children admitted each year by tested ability. Thirty was the maximum allowed per class. The sixty girls were divided into two groups according to age. 1B was on average six months younger than 1A, who would therefore be six months younger than 2B. I was the youngest in 1B. We each had our own desk in rows in the classroom, our books kept in it, one form teacher responsible for attendance, etc. Subject teachers came to us, so the need to hump books around the corridors did not arise. The only exceptions were when we used the science labs, art room and cookery (domestic science) room. Text books, provided by the school and remaining school property, we had to back with brown paper within the week, each numbered with the individual number recorded by the form teacher. We had notebooks for each subject and a rough book which had to be appropriately full, no waste of space, before a new one was issued. This was rigidly observed during wartime shortages. Poorer pupils received free school uniform and school meals until wartime conditions resulted in everyone receiving free meals. Homework time was allocated for each subject, Monday, Tuesday, Thursday, Friday – Wednesday none.

We were free to use the sports field after school. I joined in the hockey group immediately, usually free for all, except one evening there were so many of us that an older girl suggested playing positions. She allocated me to the right wing, and, as we started off, admonished, 'Keep your positions girls'. At that stage I had no idea about positions and somewhat bewildered thought I had to stay just where I was! Hours were strictly 9 a.m. to 4 p.m. with one and a half hours' break for lunch. Arriving late for school resulted in a half-hour detention, other misdemeanours an hour's detention, sitting adding numbers called 'tots'. The detentions had to be reported to the form teacher, house mistress and house prefect which was a bit frightening, but could result in leniency. On one occasion when I was house captain a young girl protested to me that she had been unfairly judged: I was able to take up her cause successfully with the staff concerned.

We had to study – maths, chemistry, French, Latin, history, geography, English, art, leading up to the school certificate examination at sixteen. Games, PE, cookery, scripture were extras. I hated the cookery because we had to weigh out at home the quantities needed for the lesson because of rationing. Our teacher was opposed to fur coats, etc., on the grounds of cruelty to animals; two of us suggested that the turnip we were peeling might be hurt!! She wasn't amused.

The two schools amalgamated in my second year. Co-education was becoming more popular, but our year continued separately until the sixth form. The girls' headmistress had just retired; the senior mistress expressed her distain, seriously believing that joining with the boys would lower the girls' school standard.

The advantage for us was that we shared the staff, and some of us were able to study physics for the school certificate with the boys' group.

Our sixth form was more integrated. Most pupils left at sixteen for work; those who hoped to go on to university were few. There were only about twenty girls in our lower and upper sixth form combined.

No way would we have addressed a teacher by his/her Christian name. Respect was there.

Homework was heavy in the sixth although we studied only three or four subjects. Monday to Friday routine was school, homework and bed. I was among those on school sports teams, hockey, rounders, tennis – playing against other schools. Field trips were just not on in wartime conditions. Our tennis court of white cement had to be stained with permanganate of potash (dark purple) because it was too visible from the air. Older boys and girls joined the cadet forces, in preparation for war service. Part of the field was given over to young gardeners.

A close friend wanted to study mathematics at Cambridge. It was a struggle for her as our best qualified maths master had been called up. She wrote for the syllabus and entrance exam papers. I saw the requirements and realised that the subjects suggested were what I was studying – chemistry, physics and maths. So I decided to try also. Chemistry was my first love and my teacher brilliant and helpful so I took the exam and to my astonishment passed. (My friend failed). The senior mistress reckoned I would be wise to spend another year in school but I questioned whether I would pass in a year's time. (Gap years were unknown.) So off I went, aged seventeen, to Cambridge.

Cambridge University, Communist to Christian

October 1943 – Graham was in the Air Force (not flying), assigned to a radar group and posted to Ismalia in Egypt. A small tin trunk that my mother had formerly used containing my clothes, etc., was sent on ahead by rail to Cambridge. My cousin who had also studied at Girton advised taking a warm housecoat, for going into breakfast in hall!! The ration book must not be forgotten.

Of leaving home for the first time strangely I can recall very little. Several of us were homesick the first three weeks – not those from public schools. Our rooms (off the corridors with windows painted blue because of the blackout) were assigned to us and various introductory meetings arranged. Tutors used our surnames, mine, Miss Rutherford, bore the kudos of the famous physicist, Ernest Rutherford. The new students assembled together were asked to give their names and school. Whitley and Monkseaton High School was a new one. What I did hear was one girl after another announcing her name and North London Collegiate (years later I found myself living in Stanmore within walking distance of this prestigious school). The principal told us that we were a relatively large group, 100 first years. When the college was expanding some years previously the then principal, Miss Jex-Blake, had announced a first year of seventy. 'Oh, Miss Jex-Blake' exclaimed an unfortunate student, 'She'll be seventy-three when she gets her degree.'

I had been awarded a radio bursary on condition that I studied electronics, physics and maths as well as chemistry. It was an excellent financial provision but with the condition that I studied those subjects before call up after two years. The award had depended on my exam results, Cs in chemistry, physics and maths. My tutor knew of my greater interest and ability in chemistry and did her best in vain to have the award changed to metallurgy, and suggested taking a college loan to study what I liked, and stay for three years. I stuck to the financial incentive; looking back I reckon it was a mistake. My maths had not included the double maths requirement. Of electronics I knew nothing. The men on the course had played around with radios,. The other radio bursary student at Girton and I were in the same situation. We struggled, but after two years we managed to scrape through the exams. Myra was also seventeen and both of us could have continued for three years if we had not received these bursaries.

In the first week invitations came from various clubs. The Christian Union one included an invitation to tea and RSVP I replied, 'Thank you for your invitation. As I don't believe a word of Christianity, I do not feel I should eat your tea.' This, of course resulted in a personal visit – 'Come along and eat as much as you like.' I went. I thoroughly enjoyed the meeting, arguing my atheistic views to my heart's content. I loved arguing and believed God did not exist.

Politics was important to me. My parents had never actually joined a political party but had definite socialist views – we lived in a coal-mining area, and they had seen the deprivation of unemployment. My mother was especially distressed that local women were relieved to work in the armaments factory because of the desperation of unemployment, but she hated war. The C.W.S. was our bank. The Jarrow unemployed marched to London, peacefully, but the protests were ignored. Graham's two friends used to argue politics in our house – one was a communist, the other a member of the Independent Labour Party. I had absorbed this, so as a first year college student eagerly joined the Labour Club. Cycling back to Girton from the Labour Club meeting, I mentioned to my companion that I felt the students who knew what they were talking about were the communists! I was talking to the secretary of the Student Communist Party so was quickly enrolled, even though under age. She was impressed by my knowledge of politics. And I set about to put the world right!! I embraced the philosophy of class warfare, no God, and science one day being able to explain everything. Discussions and arguments were great fun.

I played hockey; immediately became a member of the College team and in my third year captained the University Women's Team – when we beat Oxford 6–0.

In the chemistry lab a call came, 'Would Miss Rutherford please go and see the Director of Studies immediately'. It was just November. Surprised I answered the summons. A very sympathetic tutor sorrowfully informed me that my father was seriously ill: the doctor wanted me home immediately. I returned quickly to college in tears, packed a few things and took the L.N.E.R. train to Newcastle. Words from the College Bursar to give me hope, while appreciated, were little comfort. What hope could there be for an eighty year old, seriously ill? He was alive, in bed, when I arrived, speaking with some difficulty, his strong lungs keeping his heart going. He spoke of seeing wheels within wheels. Graham received a telegram in Egypt – expecting it was a birthday greeting for 11 November – telling him of his father's death on 10 November. Eighty years was a good age but Graham would never see his father again and there had been little warning. He had been lecturing just the week before. A WEA colleague, also a Methodist lay preacher, conducted the funeral service at Newcastle, Westgate Road Crematorium. I had no Christian hope. I believed that my father would live on through those left continuing to follow his wisdom and teaching. His lifespan had been longer than expected. I had to return as soon as possible to Cambridge as the rules for graduating required residence, rather than attendance at lectures. I knew I would have to stay behind at the end of term to make up the lost days. My mother's sister, Peg, stayed on with her. Back in college I started study afresh and with a new friend, a fellow science student, a Jewish Zionist communist.

Six of us became a close group – two students of science, two of economics, one history, one English. We enjoyed discussing all kinds of subjects. Women had no official status in the University, and no colleges were mixed. This had little effect on the undergraduates; we attended the same lectures as the men and took the same exams, but were not required to wear gowns, nor were we members of the Union. We would receive only titular degrees. It did affect graduates – my own Director of Studies left Cambridge in disgust because of lack of recognition as a woman scientist and returned to Oxford. We did not lack male companionship, which I enjoyed.

The two women's colleges were both residential, our evening meal held formally in hall. Breakfast was provided, self-service, more flexible times. Some of us queued up for our extra milk ration – given to those under eighteen! Those first two years were dominated by the war. Rationing was tight; we were especially affected by coal rationing, allowed a little for the fires in our rooms and often shared rooms to save coal. The corridors were miserably gloomy – the windows had been painted blue because of the blackout but didn't let light in during the day. We heard the 'doodle bugs' flying overhead. These were unmanned, explosive-laden planes. If we heard them pass we knew we were safe. Later the rockets were more nerve-racking. There was no warning. If you heard the explosion you knew it had not landed on you!

Russia was our ally. We wanted to win the war and the Communist Party members were in agreement. I knew nothing of espionage efforts which came to light later. The zeal of the Party members, and knowledge, convinced me that to work towards a socialist state, working with the University Communist group was most effective. (I had a note in my diary to the effect, that on graduation I did not know if I would continue membership.)

For two years we studied, played, argued, danced, walked along the river, punted, canoed. I tried hard to win others to socialist aims, and to convince Christians of their error.

One biochemistry student challenged me. She said, 'I would like to tell you the reasons for my faith, but you must promise me one thing – you will not in the course of argument say you do not exist.' There was one point at which I would have said it, had I not promised not to. She was pretty convincing; a Hungarian Roman Catholic, who returned for a visit to Hungary after obtaining British Citizenship. Her father had been a keen socialist worker but found that accusations were made through unscrupulous fellows putting their hands into other people's pockets and drawing out incriminating documents that had never been there.

Drawing to the end of the two years, victory in Europe came at last. The country was wild with excitement, lights blazed again, for the College meal we dressed in evening dress (borrowed if not possessed). For me it meant I could continue without a break with my third year of study. Disappointment awaited me when I got my results – 3rd Class. But I was able to return and study the subject that gripped me – chemistry – specialising in physical chemistry, and further colloid and surface chemistry. Again I specialised too much, working brilliantly on colloid chemistry. Much discussion by the examiners having to decide how to classify me between ignorance of organic chemistry and first class physical chemistry. They decided again on 3rd Class!

But it had been a great year. I loved the subject. Lecturers in their own special fields were thrilling. I studied alongside an Indian student, Akbar Imam, in the Surface Chemistry and Colloid department. Only the two of us did that course. Rationing continued but expectations of a happy future encouraged us. I took part in canvassing for the local Labour Party parliamentary candidate – he was elected. I was too young to vote. In canvassing, time and again I got the response, 'I vote as my husband does.' One lady cheered me, 'Yes, dear, I agree with you and my husband's coming round this time'.

Our University women's hockey team went from strength to strength, not losing a match the whole season and beating Oxford 6–0. Some of us also played for the county team. This was how I met Helen Roseveare. In goal, nothing could pass her. As captain I had to put her on the university team, even though my own college captain was a goal keeper (stopping a goal on one occasion with her forehead!!).

Together at an inter-county tournament, we talked non-stop on politics or Christianity – except when the warden of the hostel said, 'We've had enough from you two'. Helen and I were as different as chalk and cheese. I had visited her home – her mother apologised for the lateness of the tea, she had been having tea with the Queen. Helen had arranged for three of us poorer students to stay in a Girls' Friendly Society Hostel, rather than in the hotel used by the other players. On our way I said to Helen, 'I don't believe in what they stand for, I don't feel I should stay there.' 'Don't you?' she replied. 'I do. Don't let it worry you.' That was the start of our discussions.

I was impressed by the consistency of her life. Unable to counter my arguments she simply would reply, 'I don't know the answer to that but I do know that Jesus Christ, God's Son, came to this earth to die on the Cross to reconcile you to God, and rose again.' I was an atheist. I believed that Jesus was an historical character but if God did not exist He could not have a son. I recognised that were this statement true it was of paramount importance.

She told me that she didn't *believe* in Jesus, she *knew* Him. She was a medical student, not without intelligence. It was possible to believe all kinds of imaginary things but not possible to know someone who doesn't exist. She told me that if I believed I would know. 'Yes, I replied, if I know, I will believe.' Stalemate!

My philosophy of life was watertight. I believed that someday science would explain all, I had a purpose in life (political). I regarded Christians as hypocrites or at least wasting one day in seven. I was not completely satisfied but regarded satisfaction as undesirable, resulting in apathy. The only thing I could not explain away was Helen's assurance of *knowing* Christ and the importance of the message. Back in Cambridge the third student in our hockey group came to know Christ herself, although in our discussions she had agreed with me. Her comment was, 'It's like a hunch, but more so.'

I graduated with a miserable third class degree (although I had finished a possible five-year course in three) but was invited back to work in the colloid department, the only woman. I had a short stay in digs, but my landlady objected to my cooking meals over the one gas-burner in my room. (I never liked eating out, neither the food nor the expense). She also took exception to the helpful group of noisy young men who assisted me to move in. They knew of a young lady working at the Arts Theatre Box

Office needing a companion, as her friend had just moved away. So I moved there. Downstairs was the kitchen with a concrete floor. A rickety staircase led through a trap door to the upstairs room with an uneven floor, and a large divan-type double bed in one corner. The property was condemned. It was a cheerful Bohemian style life.

It was here that I became a Christian.

How did it happen?

I had been brought up not to go to church or Sunday School, because my father wanted me to think for myself. I did learn Bible stories from scripture lessons at school: we always had a school assembly – hymns, Bible passage and prayer. There was much discussion on all topics in the home. My father was a strong advocate of the truth. I concluded there was no God. For me, the question of faith was whether the message was true or not, not whether or not I liked it, or would satisfy me, etc. Was it true that Jesus Christ was God's Son and had died to reconcile me to God and risen again? If so, I was mistaken, and would have to follow fully.

On my return to Cambridge, I wanted to play hockey again but my kit had not arrived. I could think of no-one from whom I could borrow other than Helen. She was delighted to have this renewed contact with me.

The Christian Union was having a special week's mission to the University with Dr Barnhouse of America. Helen came along to the laboratory where I was working to invite me to the evening meeting. 'I'm sorry,' I said, 'but I have a previous engagement.'

'OK,' she replied, 'I'll come back for you.' Half an hour later the person I was going out with apologised that he couldn't make it. Helen returned for me. I went with her on three nights.

Dr Barnhouse energetically preached the Gospel, but I remembered only his final appeal. 'You may not know everything about Christianity, but if you have the slightest desire to do so, pray with me, "As best I know how, I receive Jesus Christ as my Saviour".'

What was going through my mind consciously or subconsciously as I listened to this earnest appeal? All my arguments, thoughts, scientific training, political aspirations and discussions with Christians had made me convinced that God did not exist. I had a purpose in life, enjoyment and felt no need of a faith. Eva, my Roman Catholic college friend had been very persuasive (P14) and Jessie, the third member of our hockey group (P15) had shaken me when she turned to Christ and put her trust in Him with conviction. Could they be right after all? If God did exist He could not be ignored. Truth was important for me. I needed to know and could never be agnostic. If God existed, I would have to follow Him wholly, even though I felt this as an atheist. The message was important: 'Jesus Christ, God's Son had come to earth to die on a cross, to reconcile me to God and rose again.' I could not dismiss Helen's statement that she knew Him. If I could not disprove her assertion I would have to accept that Christ did exist. The only way to know was not through argument, logic or desire but simply through belief.

With this background I listened to Dr Barnbouse's appeal, 'If you have the slightest desire to do so please pray with me, "As best I know how I receive Jesus Christ as my Saviour".' I did have a slight desire to join in this prayer. I did not know how to receive Christ but I could pray as best I knew how. This I prayed as I stood silently in the pew. What happened? God Himself had heard my silent prayer and Jesus the Saviour had entered my life although I sensed no immediate change.

To Helen I said, 'You told me that if I believed I would know. To the best of my ability, I have believed but I do not know. If I do not know within the next few days I will consider it an experiment proving you wrong and I will have no further interest in Jesus Christ.'

She must have got her friends praying fervently! In the next few days I knew convincingly that the message was true, the Bible that I had previously pulled to bits, now pulled me to pieces: and I had power to stop smoking, something I had previously tried in vain. I was miserable. All I had based my life on suddenly was gone. I returned home for the Christmas holiday, and my twenty-first birthday, now a Christian but those who knew me said, 'What has happened to Olga? We have never seen her so miserable'. (Later I felt comforted with the realisation that Paul was blind for three days after meeting Jesus – not much joy then). I had not experienced a flashing light or a voice, like Paul on the Damascus Road, but as with Paul God had turned my thinking upside down and I needed time to work through my new belief and experiences.

I received a Christmas present: a calendar, Scripture Union badge, Membership Card and Notes, from Helen with a letter saying, 'The calendar is a present. The rest will cost you 3/6d. If you don't want them send them back.'

So I started on regular Bible reading, the Notes designed for a five-year complete study of the Bible starting at Genesis. I couldn't accept the beginning of Genesis then. Helen's room-mate was very helpful saying,

'Don't worry, you will.' She was right: I found that I was reading God's word: that spoke to me. Back in Cambridge, I told Helen I wanted to be baptized. She took me to Nottingham where she had been baptized the previous month, so that I would have Christian surroundings. As I listened to the preacher I wondered if I could possibly live up to the challenge of a life following Christ. After the baptism I was filled with unspeakable joy, the sense of the close presence of the Lord. I had declined to give my testimony, never having heard one, and not knowing what it meant. Hearing the girl who had been baptized that same night made me realise that I could do it. Nobody asked me again, although six people felt they should!

Reactions of friends were interesting. One communist fellow research student did all in his power to persuade me back to reason. First he tried straight argument, then ridicule, then attempted to get me to fall in love with him, and finally decided to provoke me to jealousy by attracting my room-mate.

The party secretary visited me, assuring me that there were Christians in the Communist Party. (My membership had lapsed from the time of Helen's witness.) When I told him of my faith he declared, 'Oh, that is different. It's mysticism! That is dangerous.'

I was starting on a new path.

Should a Christian be involved with research involving war weapons? At the time my answer was, 'No'. I felt I should change direction, move towards teaching, although the Lord was impressing upon me that He wanted me to become a missionary. Helen had been asked to look after Aida Desta, granddaughter of the Ethiopian Emperor, a first-year student at Newnham College. Her sisters and cousins were at Clarendon School, Malvern, with Miss Swain, the Headmistress as official guardian. Through Princess Aida, Helen heard that the school was looking for an assistant matron. Meanwhile, unexpectedly I was invited to take the position of Assistant Matron at Clarendon Girls' Boarding School, then in Malvern. I was there for about six months before returning to Cambridge for post-graduate teacher training. It was an experience. Nearly all the girls knew much more about the Lord than I did. Sorting laundry, etc. was not my strongest interest but I was asked also to teach post-higher chemistry and physics to two of the girls looking for university entrance, one to Cambridge, one to Dublin. Later I took over from the junior maths teacher who had to go back home on account of her mother's health. The atmosphere was out of this world – no words of complaint were heard amongst the staff. If I ever had a daughter, I thought, I would send her to Clarendon, only if, I was out of the country. Twenty years later, I did!!

Clarendon at that time was housed in a residential area of Malvern, with fantastic views from the hills towards Worcester, the mist in the morning giving a magical view of the cathedral. The children had to be more than naturally quiet because of neighbours. I had an attic room in one house, next to Miss Kobrak, the German teacher. She had come to England as a refugee from Hitler with her sister, both Christians and Jewish. She had been wanting news of her parents when a letter at last arrived. The staff members waited anxiously and prayerfully for her news. Her parents had been killed in a gas chamber!! Miss Pike then gave her the scripture verse in the Syriac translation, 'You will keep him in perfect peace whose imagination stops at you.' Miss Kobrak did just that, not allowing her imagination to dwell on any but her Saviour and Lord. This was the grit of my immediate neighbour who would not give up teaching duties although in pain. One morning she said to me, 'I hope I didn't keep you awake last night with my groaning.'

She thought she had sciatica. At the end of term when she finally got medical treatment, she discovered the problem was a slipped disc. Grace at Clarendon learned German from her, twenty-five years later.

Many children of missionaries attended the school, including those who had been interned in China under Japanese occupation. Some were in a dormitory above the sitting room of two elderly sisters. The sisters were startled as they were enjoying a quiet evening, by bodies from the dormitory above them hurtling past their window on to the lawn below. A sedate girls boarding school was a far cry from the rigours of an internment camp!

My sojourn at Clarendon was bewildering to my mother who was perplexed as to what had happened to me and what I was doing. Win's mother actually wept because she thought I had entered a convent!

At the end of the summer term, Clarendon hosted a China Inland Mission Conference. I was not attracted. 'Yes, Lord,' I said, 'I will go to China, but never with the CIM.'

Through this Conference a former CIM missionary to China approached me to join in the special summer beach mission held in his church in Weston-super-Mare. This was my introduction to children's evangelism. I stayed in the vicarage, enjoying the family – grandparents and children. Grandad had produced huge pumpkins – my first taste. The words on the vicar's study wall impressed me and have remained with me. 'Not I, but Christ.' The vicar spoke of his thankfulness, and tears, when he first managed to hear the base notes of music from his gramophone. by placing his ear on the Chinese ground. For his wife, the dirt and squalor they faced in inland China had been more than she could cope with, so they had left China and continued serving the Lord in the Anglican ministry, in England, continuing their prayer for China.

Back in Cambridge I was different and Cambridge was different. The teacher training college students were all graduates from a variety of universities. The war was over though rationing continued for several months. Men were returning from the forces, experienced, mature, from the front-line, not just from school.

A Cambridge 'rag' was a yearly feature. A warning had been issued that the students were going to burn a bus in the market square. The police were on the alert as a solemn procession of students marched to the square, produced a paper bus, struck a match and set it alight. An old car was seen on the pinnacle of one of the college buildings. Only trained engineers could have got it up there.

The Christian Union was strong: in that year women were at last given full university status, and the Cambridge Women's Christian Union and the Cambridge Inter Collegiate Christian Union were amalgamated. Men and women could pray together. Individual Colleges had their Christian Unions with prayer and Bible Study, the large Saturday Evening University Bible Study meeting was led by the invited speaker for the CICCU evangelistic Sunday evening service (the speaker being informed of his subject). There was a daily prayer meeting. In all I had a spiritual feast which I appreciated after my years of atheism. Talking to others about the Lord presented no difficulty.

Increasingly I felt convinced that the Lord was calling me to serve Him in China, a factor that prevented any firm attachment to young men who either had no missionary call or a call to a different country. Eden Baptist Church sent out an appeal to CICCU for Sunday School teachers. Two of us responded. It was a small friendly church.

Missionary speakers were often invited to the Christian Union. I asked one China missionary, Mrs Maddox, what use chemistry could be in China. Her reply was wise, 'There may be no direct use, but whatever you have God uses.' (Looking back I can see the truth of this, but the greatest value was through teacher training.)

As the teacher training year drew to an end, we all searched the *Times Educational Supplement* for vacancies in high schools. A science teacher was required at Bedlington Grammar School. I applied and was accepted.

Teaching at Bedlington Grammar School

Bedlington Grammar School was about ten miles from my home in Earsdon. To get there I needed two buses and a train. Once or twice I cycled, but that was too strenuous. Then a friend offered to sell me her motorbike. It was a two-stroke, 125 cc model adequate for the journey, but I had to learn to ride it and particularly to start it. (I was allowed petrol coupons because I needed the bike for work.) I wrapped up in an airman's flying suit, looking like a 'Michelin tyre' advertisement, and made sure I was early at school so that the pupils would not see me walking along the corridors. Occasionally I had to beg the assistance of one of the masters to get me started for the journey home. I did not have the strength to kick-start the bike.

I had visited a fellow teacher in her home near Newcastle one frosty night. The sign 'halt, major road ahead' was a problem to me. The major road was at the top of a slight rise. The road was too slippery for me to get any grip with my feet to start off again after I had 'halted'. I can't remember how I eventually got away but I continued nervously. Reaching Newcastle town centre I faced the problem of passing a stationary car!! The road at that point was of wood blocks plus tramlines. Travelling at the great speed of about 10 mph, I swerved slightly to cross the tram lines and came off. The lights automatically went off when the engine stopped. I was surrounded by a group of anxious observers. The policeman arrived exclaiming, 'Oh! It's the girl'. They got me on my feet and the bike upright. One helpful man suggested I should have a drink before going on. My tone of voice on refusal produced his response, 'It's all right dear! You can have lemonade if you want'. I decided to go on but I think he had been right. I wasn't hurt but I was shaken.

My teaching assignment was very agreeable. As I was just out of college I had the sixth form for chemistry, physics and maths. Sixth forms were always small and consisting of young people really interested in their subjects. Coming to school on a motorbike gave me some standing with the boys. I enjoyed the subjects.

I also had a lively second form (twelve–thirteen year olds) for R.E. The

R.E. senior mistress had succeeded in teaching the subject so that it had become accepted as worthwhile.

'We have a lad in school now who is going to go a long way in football.' I heard. That was Bobby Charlton.

While back in Earsdon I lived with my mother. Also I became a member of Whitley Bay Baptist Church. I had no particular church background – my mother had been C of E, my father Congregationalist, but had not had any church allegiance after marriage. I visited various churches. It was at the Baptist church that there was always a word from the Lord for me, although at the time there was no minister and the meeting was in the church hall as the sanctuary had not been repaired after the bomb damage.

My appearance at the church came as a shock to Enid, one young member of the congregation. She had been in the first form of Whitley & Monkseaton High School when I was in the sixth. My atheistic, communist views were known throughout the school. She could hardly believe the change. Her parents had both been much involved in Christian activities including encouraging several young people into missionary service at home and abroad. After a long illness, however, her mother died when Enid was twelve. By the time I arrived on the scene her father, a railway clerk, had remarried and I found a warm welcome on many occasions in her home. Enid was at that stage a day student in the local teacher training college so many Sundays saw us walking home together from church engrossed in deep discussion often theological, sometimes on poetry, and our footsteps became slower and slower as we walked. We also restarted a Christian Endeavour group excellent for training in Bible study, prayer and fellowship.

Enid and I taught in the church Sunday School, enjoyed the outings and picnics, anniversaries (when she conducted the singing) and the Christmas parties. One good friend we had as fellow teacher was Stan Ward, back from the forces and united with his family. I can still see him performing a 'forfeit', jumping round a circle saying, 'I'm my mother's great big bubbly bairn.' The Wards also became great friends. We constantly complained about his obnoxious pipe. When he attempted to quit his wife could not tolerate his bad temper.

Enid's father was a great gardener with immaculate lawn, flowers, fruit, vegetables and trees, as well as being a church deacon. He housed a missionary prayer meeting for years. He had prayed from her birth that Enid would become a missionary. His prayer was fulfilled when Enid went off to the Bible Training Institute in Glasgow and to Nigeria to serve with

S.U.M, in particular she helped design the T.E.E. (Theological Education by Extension) courses, using her expertise as a teacher.

While I was in Cambridge, Graham married Margaret, a German girl, whom he met in France. At first he thought she was French – fluent in French, German and English, but at their civic wedding service she was addressed as 'Frau'. We learned that her first marriage had been an arranged one, not consummated. After my brother's death in 1995 we discovered that she had had two children!! She and Graham remained childless. They lived with us for a short period. I welcomed her as a sister, but was too naïve to recognise that a sister-in-law needed independence. They moved to rooms nearby where the German immaculate cleanliness showed itself. My friend, Win, commented that hers was the only carpet where her little boy could crawl without getting grubby. We had many discussions on Christianity. She realised, as I had not, that my changed life had not helped my mother, especially as I no longer joined her in her visits to the theatre. She made a bargain with me that if I would go to a play with my mother, she would come to church with me. She sat through the service, listened intently to the sermon, and then asked me how the minister had known all about her! But she did not put her trust in Christ. Later she had a dream, Christ appeared to her warning that if she did not trust in Him He would take Graham away from her. It was many years later that they separated. Knowing that I was planning on going to China as a missionary, she said,

'Aren't there enough heathen in this country for you to convert?'

I replied, 'I've been talking to you and Graham long enough and it has made no difference.'

'Don't be so sure' she answered. 'We discuss a lot what you tell us.'

She and Graham went off to Karachi in India; he was working as an electronics consultant, I think with the Indian army. She especially insisted on sailing first class and borrowed money whenever she could for dress, etc., mostly not returned. Later he worked for Marconi in Beirut. When the firm decided to move to Africa, Graham decided to stay, working independently until the political situation made it impossible, his house burnt down.

Towards China and missionary training

During my teaching year I could not escape the insistent call of the Lord to take the Gospel to China. My college friend, Helen Roseveare, invited me to a weekend conference in Oxford for Christian graduates. I chugged along from the north on my little 125 cc two stroke James motorbike, against a headwind. It was too much for the little chap and the engine seized up halfway. A very kind landlady looked after me, gave me a meal and sleep, while the garage mechanic decarbonised the machine. (It is inadvisable to use machinery of which one understands nothing, but I've never learned the lesson.) I set off again and finally arrived dishevelled, late for the start of the conference. Bible readings were challenging and refreshing. Miss Nixon, the gracious graduate fellowship leader was approachable. I told her of my sense of call to China, and that I was planning on going to visit the Baptist Missionary Society in London after the conference.

'Why don't you call on Mrs Fraser of the China Inland Mission while you are in London?' she suggested.

Mrs Fraser was the women's candidate's secretary of the CIM, a saintly lady. She had been widowed in China when her husband, a pioneer missionary to the Lisu tribe of SW China had died of typhoid, leaving her with two young daughters and an unborn baby. She battled on courageous-ly. The Japanese invaded China and interned foreign nationals, including the CIM school. Mrs Fraser among those interned gave herself unstintingly to others in the camp especially the children. She was thin, with a bird's appetite, but a woman of prayer and compassion.

I kept my appointment with the representative of the BMS. She was gracious, frank and understanding and recognised my call to China, a country she knew well.

'China is closing to missionaries,' she explained. 'We are not sending anyone there now. There are opportunities to work in India. We could consider sending you there.'

My sense of call to China was too strong to change to India. Nor did I feel that the BMS was the place for me.

I continued with Helen's help to visit Mrs Fraser. Helen probably telephoned ahead. We entered the gates of the China Inland Mission. 'Jehovah Jireh' – 'God will supply' and 'Ebenezer' – 'Hitherto hath the Lord helped us' were inscribed in Chinese on the posts of the archway. We knocked at the door of the Women's Training Home. Mrs Fraser invited us in. She was taken aback by my introductory words. 'I don't know why I've come but Miss Nixon sent me.'

Later she told me that she had looked on Helen as a likely candidate but that I was most improbable.

We sat in the spacious lounge. I said little but drank in the atmosphere: the whole room was permeated with the presence of the Lord. This, I was convinced, was where I should come and prepare for China.

Mrs Fraser suggested, 'Go to Bible School, read the story of Hudson Taylor (founder of CIM), attend the CIM Whitsuntide Conference in Swanwick and then apply to the CIM if God is then leading you in that direction.'

I had no idea what a Bible School was but could follow the other instructions.

The Swanwick Conference was my opportunity to hear the stories of missionaries back from China, to learn of the state of the country, to meet the enthusiastic candidates about to sail to China. Reports of Chinese coming to Christ were thrilling but the shadow of Mao Tse Tung creeping across the country was ominous. Communism was triumphing. I learned of the financial provision through prayer and not through appeals for funds, and the joy in the Lord for all His goodness.

Among the CIM leaders that I met were Mr George Scott and Mr Norman Pateman. George Scott was assistant Home Director of the CIM, tall, thin and hard of hearing, passionately interested in books. When it was known before the conference began which books he was going to review a large supply had to be brought in. Mr Pateman with a puckish sense of humour was CIM secretary, ready with the announcements (or intimations). I told Mr Scott 'I have lost my purse.'

'What was it like?' he asked.

'A small cream coloured purse with a pagoda on the outside and a pink elephant on the end of the zip.'

It was found and handed to Mr Scott. I approached him again.

'Yes', he said 'I received your purse, and handed it to Mr Pateman. He won't let you have it back till he has made that announcement.'

He did, exactly as I had worded it. It was greeted with laughter. I don't know if anyone believed him.

I happened to meet Doug here for the first time, a lively young candidate with dark curly hair, already trained at All Nations Bible College and looking to China – quite attractive but I was expecting to remain single if I went to China. There were two women to one man in CIM.

Back in Earsdon I sent off my application. The senior mistress of the school agreed to be a referee but her Methodist church background left her a little puzzled by some of the questions on the form she was required to fill in. We walked round the playing field while I explained the questions. I was accepted for two years' training with the CIM but my application had been late, so I started in January 1950.

The physics master questioned my change in occupation. 'Does this mean an increase in salary?' he asked.

My mother was amazingly supportive when a small group challenged me. She volunteered, 'Well, the Bible says "Go into all the world and preach the Gospel".'

It was difficult for her once again on her own but she never put any hindrances in my way.

Open doors closing

The No. 73 double decker bus to Stoke Newington from King's Cross L.N.E.R. station pulled up outside the headquarters of the China Inland Mission. I walked into the compound through the red brick imposing archway and turned left to the Women's Training Home.

I nervously joined the other young women who were training to go to China as missionaries that year, or a year later. All of us were under thirty for CIM's policy was not to send any one out over thirty; we were single, being required to remain so until we had been two years in China and passed the basic language exams. Betty, the wee Scottish lass, was already engaged, the other fourteen of us single, of whom eight never married. We were also joined by students from Norway, Switzerland, Denmark, Sweden, here to learn English to study Chinese from English later. We had varied occupations – civil service, teaching, secretarial, nursing, etc.

We each had our own small room on the first floor, with bed, desk and chair; common washrooms and meals together downstairs round a long narrow table in the dining room. I was a slow eater but did not have a small appetite, a combination that had disadvantages. Miss Bental, a support for Mrs Fraser, was the caterer; she also observed us as we cleared tables and washed up. It was she who first noticed the unsuitability of one of the students, ultra-spiritual, but her over-enthusiasm even as she washed up, put the rest of us on edge. We had a trolley to remove the dishes to the kitchen and I often wondered why others took the dishes from the table to the trolley and I was the only one to take the trolley to the table.

We had a time of prayer and Bible study in the lounge at 7.30 a.m. before breakfast, with Mrs Fraser in charge. The students took turns in leading but Mrs Fraser generally gave us a devotional word. Her saintliness, prayerfulness, close walk with the Lord, inspired us all, to the point for some of almost worshipping her. Her depth of Christian experience, suffering in China and knowledge of the word, moved us deeply. She would implore us, 'Hold on to your quiet time'. 'Beware of drifting, like a boat which has broken its tether.' (She prayed regularly for all the young missionaries in China whom she had helped to train.)

In the holidays her children came home from boarding school. I had taught Eileen, her second daughter, in Clarendon School, and knew that she was one who had jumped out of the upstairs window on to the lawn at school. (See page 23.)

(Eileen wrote the book, *Mountain Rain*, her father's biography.)

We joined the weekly CIM prayer meetings, open to all prayer supporters, held in the large prayer room opposite the training home. A huge map of China showing all the provinces dominated the room, as well as the plaque with the names of the fifty-seven CIM missionaries who had been martyred during the Boxer rising of 1900. We watched as week by week, red spread over the map, indicating the advance over the whole country of Mao Tse Tung's communist army.

Our lecturers were all outstanding men of God. David Bentley-Taylor led us through the whole Bible giving us questions on each book to be discussed the following week. Alan Stibbs expounded 1 Peter in depth – unfortunately at 4 p.m. on a warm afternoon after tennis. This prevented us from gaining its full benefit. Fred Mitchell, Home Director, taught us homiletics. We learned Chinese choruses and the history of Christian work in China and its geography. We cycled to the London Bible College (LBC) in Baker Street and studied under Dr Ernest Kevin. We were having spiritual feasts.

For practical experience we were assigned to different churches and engaged in house to house visitation. Mine was in the East End, Victoria Park Baptist Church. I called regularly on Miss Saint, a pathetic soul, caring for a mentally disabled brother. Her memory of her childhood was of a drunken father coming home and smashing all the furniture. 'My mother used to sweat her guts and eyeballs out.' Her most frequent words to me were, 'You can't understand, you've never been through it'. I told the Lord, 'Any experience I may have, even if it is only to understand someone else, will be worthwhile and from You.'

One street where I visited showed friendliness and a greater willingness to talk about Christ than elsewhere. I asked Sister Mabel of the church whether any one in that street would be praying.

'Yes,' she replied. 'I will introduce you.'

Two elderly ladies, one a spinster the other a widow, lived together. They had not been able to go abroad as missionaries as they had hoped, so resolved that this particular street would be their mission field. Constant prayer had not resulted in anything they could see, but I was acutely conscious of the effect of those prayers on the whole street.

We were free to play tennis in the afternoons. I was enthusiastic. Doug had fallen for me so learnt to play tennis to meet me on the tennis courts. Both with a call to China, we got to know each other better. I met Doug's family and attended his church, West Green Baptist. Doug visited Earsdon, met my mother and my friends at the Baptist Church. We got engaged and looked forward to a life together serving God in China.

We all continued to study and pray, all of us having an overwhelming sense of God calling us to China: but the door for Christian work in China was slowly closing. We saw missionaries returning from China, some having had difficulty in getting out of the land. Hong Kong was the stepping point to escape. By the end of our academic year, it was clear that no more workers could be sent to China and no new candidates were accepted. The British leaders decided we should continue our training for the required two years but the Women's Training Home and the Men's Training Home should join as one. We lost the care and direction of Mrs Fraser but gained that of David Bentley-Taylor. Fred Mitchell explained that the mission could not hold on to those who finished their training and they were free to pursue any leading the Lord gave them. (Doug got a job packing lamp shades until he was appointed as Minister at Longfleet Baptist Church, Poole.)

What of the future?

The interim

Our course finished in July 1951 with the future still uncertain.

Doug was in Poole, planning a children's summer programme. The church elders were a little nervous about the project but agreed to give hospitality to the helpers he invited. June and I prepared to leave London for Poole but finances were getting low. I went along to the bank to withdraw my last £2. 10/- to cover our train fares. Children flocked to

'Sunshine Corner' and responded enthusiastically. On the last day a friend of Doug's invited us to lunch and called Doug back after the meal. He rummaged in his pocket and handed him £5 to be shared between June and me. We were going on from Poole to the Keswick Convention. I opened the letter my mother had forwarded to me. 'I haven't bothered with the rest of the mail but I noticed this was from the bank, so thought you might need it.'

'You have overdrawn by £2. 9/-. I was surprised. I had carefully kept my accounts for six months, usually withdrawing £5 at a time, but had left £2. 10/- to the last. Now I could return £2. 10/- thanks to the gift of Doug's friend. But where had my arithmetic failed? The bank kindly explained. A cheque had been cashed over six months after I had written it. God himself had provided for my needs through an overdraft, even though on principle I wouldn't go into debt. I felt embarrassed paying back the debt at the Keswick P.O. I was among many from the convention who had been challenged by the Lord through the messages to pay back what they owe.

Fred Mitchell spoke clearly on the book of Revelation; he called it a 'tract for the times', showing how the Chinese church could find great comfort in this book during severe persecution.

I returned to Earsdon, penniless and jobless, to my old home. My mother was busy supply teaching and understood my problems. I spent some time coaching mathematics in a small private school and later a very satisfying post as supply chemistry teacher at Blyth Grammar School. I remember my first day there. It was raining. I was wearing a leaf green cape and hood. Not knowing the route I asked the conductress for a ticket to Blyth Grammar School. She clicked my ticket, looked at me again and said,

'You did want a half fare, didn't you?' To my denial, she hesitated and said, 'I've clicked it; take it anyway.'

I made my way to the women's staff room. One teacher was there. She was the daughter of the lighthouse keeper at Whitley Bay. The lighthouse is cut off from the mainland at high tide, so she had come early to cross to the mainland when the tide allowed it and was early.

'Good morning', she greeted me. 'I presume you are the new student teacher.'

I assured her I wasn't but that I had come up in the world since getting off the bus.

It was a good school. The headmaster, a classicist was a strict and fair disciplinarian. The previous chemistry master had been exceptionally good.

From fourth form upwards (fourteen year olds) the pupils could choose their subjects, so the chemistry group was unusually large. Teaching a large group in the chemistry lab could have problems. From the raised bench in the front I explained that when they were doing experiments it was inevitable that they should talk but there could be danger. So when I banged on the bench with the bunsen burner I required instant silence. They responded and listened.

On one occasion, I had a cold and lost my voice. I asked a small boy to stand beside me. I whispered the instructions to him and he told the class.

The sixth form was particularly enthusiastic resulting in a lot of preparation and marking for me. I tried to follow the pattern of my predecessor.

In order to be ready at any time to sail to the Far East I had not applied for a permanent job which would have required three months' notice, supply teaching required only two weeks.

Doug and I were asked whether we would be willing to go to Japan. We prayed about it and discussed the possibility. We were unhappy about going under the shadow of American troops but concluded that the Japanese had a right to hear the Gospel for 'there is no other name given under heaven among men by which you must be saved'. We simply could not see any reason why we should not go.

Doug was asked to go ahead of me. The reason was simply that of the CIM missionaries already in Karuizawa studying the language the number of single women was disproportionately high. One young man, David Hayman from Australia would be a companion for Doug. He sailed in May 1952: I followed in October. The delay was disappointing. With the requirement of two years' language study before marriage, we had a four and a half year engagement.

Where next for the CIM?

China was rapidly changing. The Communist government under Mao Tse Tung ruled the land, ridding the country of all imperialistic personnel and all Christians. We could not go to China, we could pray for it, and especially the Christians, and that the remaining missionaries would be free to leave.

Those of us half way through our missionary training, four women, three men, continued in the first co-ed CIM training home in Highbury New

Park. David Bentley-Taylor, inspiring speaker and leader, sat at the head of the long dining room table, his wife, Jessie, serving the food at the other end, and scattered along both sides the seven candidates, plus Mrs Moore (Jessie's mother), four Bentley-Taylor boys and their governess. They had spent time in China.

David Bentley-Taylor would spend time on busy street corners giving out Gospel tracts. Jessie was burdened for the local women, bringing some to the Lord; she would give out foreign stamps to eager urchins who came to the door (at her instruction). One evening, two lads appeared asking for Mrs Bentley-Taylor.

'Sorry,' they were told. 'She's busy bathing the boys.' There was a pause. 'That's not true,' they expostulated. 'It's not Friday!'

The others from the training homes were scattered, waiting for the next step. Doug worked packing lamp shades until his pastor suggested he apply to become a Baptist Minister. He was welcomed to Longfleet Baptist Church, Poole, at a starting salary just covering board and lodgings. Betty and Peter were advised to marry, as no CIM future was in sight. Some helped Mary Wong in the Chinese Church.

Missionaries returned from China, often exhausted and bewildered. Some resigned. Some went to other lands, and some into home ministry. Much prayer was made for those under house arrest or in prison in China. Was there any future for the CIM, a mission committed specifically to the evangelism of China? Did we no longer have any reason to continue? Some felt we should close down completely.

Yet, we were a structured organisation with a history of God's faithfulness. There were Chinese communities in most countries of the Far East – Thailand, Hong Kong, Singapore, Malaya, Indonesia, etc. Perhaps we should go to those new open countries, and perhaps not only to the Chinese there. But what about Japan? Grave doubts were expressed as some CIM missionaries were guarantors for Christians in China whose lives would be at risk if the missionary behaviour was suspect by the Chinese authorities – evangelising Japan would be frowned upon. But there were those who felt the Lord calling them on to Japan.

The mission leaders in conference were discussing Japan when they had a coffee break. The chairman opened his mail.

'Please accept this cheque of £500, half towards the conference expenses, and half for work in Japan.'

'Our mission has always had a vision for Japan but unable to fulfil it.

Should CIM decide to send workers to Japan, please accept this gift of £1,000.'

Surely God was casting His vote in favour of CIM in Japan.

Of our group, finally six went to Thailand, four to Malay, one to Indonesia, one to Taiwan, two to Japan.

The way to what we termed the 'new fields' opened slowly; those approaching thirty were sent out first.

Fred Mitchell based his talk on Acts 16, where Paul and Silas had attempted to go into various regions but were prevented until the Macedonian call. Was God calling the CIM into different fields?

Interlude

Letters home from the ship to Japan

Mediterranean Sea

20 October 1952

Dear Mam,

I am starting this in good time for posting in Port Said. Mr and Mrs Edwards (Doug's church secretary in Poole) and Mrs Pilgrim (whose ancient husband Doug had buried) saw me off from the quay side. They had obtained special passes to get right on to the platform and quay so I had about an hour and a half with them. I expect Mrs Edwards will have phoned you. Then I went in and discovered the flowers. Thank you very much. They were a complete surprise because I did not even know it was possible to receive them on board. I think the whole party has been very thrilled with flowers. I think there were some with each one of us and they make things gay and cheerful.

You know I was sharing a two-berth cabin with Mary. We had the best cabin in the tourist section (there are only two classes). There is a first class cabin above us. We are next to the dining room and have two portholes; many cabins have none.

As you may or may not be able to make out from the diagram, the cabin is in a sense jutting into the dining room. We could not be more central. There are no dealings between the classes. It is the race segregation system and the first class passengers are not allowed on the tourist deck. The cabin is very roomy and comfortable and the most suitable place for our morning CIM prayer meeting. Needless to say, the tourist section of the boat is about half missionary and extremely interesting in personalities. Many will be leaving us at Bombay. One is going to Bangalore. She had retired after working in India for the YWCA and returned to England but has been ordered back to Bangalore for her health's sake.

The cabin stewards are all from Goa, south of Bombay and are Portuguese Indians and Roman Catholic. Ours is very obliging; most concerned about our health and general well being. Sometimes tending to talk too much and come in at awkward times but always ready to give advice. On the subject of cures for seasickness and the efficacy of Kwells. You will have to use your imagination for the intonation and gestures but the advice was something like this. 'Pills, they no good. They disturb stomach (grimace and shake of the head). Wee drop brandy (nod of the head). Neat, no water, like in England, just spoonful, that OK. Pills no good.' Mary had already found the Kwells some good for her. The second day out I was seasick but very comfortably and without really feeling it. I missed no meals and now I am really enjoying them. Turbot, duck, chickens, frozen peas, veal, ices, roast beef, liver, frittered brains, etc., etc. I always seem to be last at our table in finishing but not just because of quantity. On the whole the missionary section seems to have longer appetites.

21 October

Yesterday we passed Gibralter at 10.45 a.m. after our cabin steward had got me up on false pretences that we were passing it at 6.30 a.m. Still the deck was almost deserted at the time and the view still and lovely. The view of Gibralter was ideal. We were far enough away from the rock to be able to see the whole of it, not just a cliff face. It seems incredible that so many people should live in such a bare place and it looks impregnable. The Mediterranean has been as blue as its reputation and as calm. The North African coast rising steeply out of the sea is somewhat reminiscent of the mountains rising from the Scottish Lochs. The temperature is ideal for summer clothing and sunglasses are essential on deck.

We are due to be in Colombo overnight so it looks as though I shall have a chance of meeting Ray and I hope Graham will come to Colombo rather than Bombay if he is able to come at all as we just have a few hours at Bombay. It is there that the stewards get drunk as they meet their old friends and drink all the wine they have saved up on the voyage. This ship certainly illustrates the 'superiority' of the British race who are so obviously without question in possession of authority here. I have had some conversation with the ship's electrical engineer. He tells me that we will be allowed to visit the engine room but that, very often, the engineer chooses the hottest day of the trip in order to discourage the passengers. The engine room is cooler than the decks on the way down but I shall be able to say more when I have been down. Today's trip should bring us in sight of Malta but there is mist around, visibility is not good. Ships games are underway in the hands of a sports committee.

The journey from now to Port Said should be uneventful, only sea to be seen until we come in sight of Alexandria. We only have about three hours in Port Said, just time for me to buy a suitcase.

Much love, Olga

Port Said
28 October 1952

Dear Mam,

As we arrived in Port Said at 6 a.m. I was up to see us approach the town, and it looked lovely in the early morning sun with an ideal temperature. I caught my first glimpse of palm trees, surprisingly enough looking just like their pictures. As we arrived we watched the pilot take over and the different authorities come on board. We were then contacted by the salesmen in their boats with their wares displayed. Anything you wanted to buy was sent up in a basket on a rope and either returned or the money instead, after a good deal of bargaining. They are very quick to notice the slightest interest shown in any of the goods. I put my head out of the port hole to have a look round later on and was greeted after a while by one of the men as 'Miss Macaroono'. He had a strange pitched voice and his 'hello' was somewhat difficult to resist. There were two men who dived for coins; again their skill rewarded them. They were very quick to see where the coin had fallen and kept all their treasures in their mouths. We went ashore for a short time and I bought another suitcase, because of the extra things I had gathered on the way. We visited a mosque; at least we can say that we had been in but it is so bare inside that it was hardly worth while. The guide showed us nothing. The Greek Orthodox Church was indeed ornate and incense abounded. One very clever picture looked like a blank face until a light was moved just underneath and then Mary's face showed up. I was able to understand a little of the writing as it was in Greek instead of Egyptian. The 'gully-gully' men, or conjurers were very clever, but prepared to get money in any way. They use chickens a lot; one man approached us in the street; he asked us if we had seen the gully-gully men and produced a chicken. We assured him we had already seen one. 'Very clever'. 'Yes' we said. 'Too clever'. With that he gave a wicked smile as much as to say 'You've been had before' and went away.

From Port Said we went down to the Suez Canal, I must have passed Ismailia in the dark. We had a greeting from English voices on the shore, asking us who we were and where we were going. We saw one camel. It was not a particularly exciting region – just sand all around. The view from the Red Sea was rather different. We saw the Arabian Coast, and the mountain ranges which included Sinai, on the Sunday morning. The view was beautiful; the mountains looked almost like clouds coming out of the sea, a sort of golden, fairy like colour. A camera might have helped in some ways but we really need colour photos to do justice to the views.

Much love, Olga

Aden to Bombay
31 October 1952

Dear Mam,

At Aden we visited the tanks which Graham mentioned. They were well worth the visit. Five of us shared a taxi and we were able to see the harbour from fairly high up. The tanks possibly dating from Solomon's time were quite empty. Their capacity must be enormous but it so rarely rains that they are for long periods in disuse. The strange appearance is in the number of green shrubs which grow out of the seemingly barren rock: where they get the moisture is a complete puzzle for sometimes there is no rain to fill the tanks for as long as seven years. We had an excellent guide who insisted on presenting the ladies with pieces of flowering white jasmine. They also had some of the purple shrub beginning with B that you cannot stand but the flower in the case was red. Aden is one of the few places I have seen where the houses look better than the surrounding countryside.

1 November 1952

Aden is utterly barren apart from the houses and trees amongst the houses. It is surprising that anyone should decide to live there. We saw camels pulling carts along the road and goats littering the streets. The native quarters by the seaside look like shacks just pushed together and fitting in with the barrenness of the rock and dust. The men were very gaily attired but I saw only about three women during the whole of our stay. The people looked happier than those in Port Said yet we were somewhat depressed, and relieved to get back to our fellowship on board. Although most of our time since Aden has been spent with a view of the sea it has not been uninteresting. We saw a whale surface twice. One of the stewards told me that the whales are quite common here and that, on one occasion, the boat had hit one. Whale bones thought to have been brought from Abyssinia are visible at Solomon's Wells. This morning we saw a bird which might have been of the albatross variety. It has a very large wingspan. Yesterday we caught sight of many flying fish. They are not easy to distinguish but look like a small flock of birds flying, anything from one to ten yards along the water and splashing in again. One of the passengers with whom we had had some conversation is a Hindu who seems to pick the best out of all religions. I was interested in his outlook: he was the first Easterner to whom I had talked who had demonstrated the Eastern insularity. He finds no difficulty in accepting the resurrection or miracles but was prepared to accept all Christ's teaching except that about his own person. I have succeeded in doing something else I cannot remember having done before, that is to sprain my ankle. I succeeded in reaching the finals of women's doubles and singles at deck tennis but in the final in the second game of the doubles I went over on my ankle. I hadn't realised how bad it was until after the match when it started swelling but I was surrounded by doctors and nurses and strapped until this morning so that I was able to play the singles. It is still somewhat swollen and bruised but, as you can gather from my being able to play, it is not at all serious. I have had continued enquiries from all sorts of passengers as to how it is.

On Monday we reach Bombay in the early hours of the morning and lose several of our passengers with whom we have become very friendly in the last fortnight and others will be joining the ship at Bombay. We have a very short time there but I am going on the official tour which guarantees that we are back in time.

Love, Olga

Bombay and Colombo
4 November 1952

Dear Mam,

Although Graham was not able to see me at Bombay my present to him should arrive safely this time as it is being personally conveyed into India. One of the missionaries, who bound my foot for me, is going in that direction and there were at least three passengers going to Bangalore. Graham's advice to me was to see Bombay from a deck chair on the ship but I am very glad I did not. That would be about the worst view of it. It is a city of islands joined by causeways and land reclaimed from the sea. Places that had been formerly on the shore are now well back. Unfortunately, we had only two hours on shore but two of us took advantage of the bus tour (hardly coach) arranged by the League of Mercy for Destitute Women. It was expensive but then not used for private profit. Bombay is so obviously much wealthier than other places we visited but the bazaar area and the native quarters here were as scruffy as ever. The mixed saris and colourful dresses were gay. In one area the veils spoke of Muslim areas, in another the coloured dots on the foreheads of Hindu women and the shaggy, wild looking quite unshaven men Sikhs. A snake charmer tried to get us to watch showing us his little mongoose first but the snake was too repulsive for the majority. We passed palaces of various maharajas and had a glimpse of the Parsee burial ground. It was difficult to make it out. They leave the bodies for the vultures to devour and the bones fall through a grid into a lime pit. The Parsee's have to wash and change completely before entering their temple. I was very disappointed in the famous Gateway to India. It is as useless as the Marble Arch but more ornate. Perhaps it gives a little shelter from the sun. The hanging gardens on Malabar Hill were well worth the visit. The growth is in two and a half feet of earth in one park used to cover a reservoir. Shrubs were cut out in the shape of animals.

Love, Olga

Bombay to Penang
7 November 1952

Dear Mam,

We are now in the Indian ocean and noticing the heat and dampness which most of us have found quite exhausting. We had an amazing sight yesterday watching lightning in a cloud as it was getting gradually darker. I suppose normally when we watch lightning we are in the cloud ourselves but, in this case, there was no indication of a storm or any rain. It was simply that the cloud, looking rather like a mountain coming out of the sea, was every now and then lit up showing the shape and 'hills' on the cloud. We could not but be reminded of the story of Mount Sinai.

I had written to my school friend, Ray, from Aden and the letter had arrived on 3 November in the morning. She sent a letter to the agent and I received her message about half an hour after we arrived at Colombo. Mary and I had supper with her and Nihal, her husband. They met us by car and took us on a general tour of the town. It is so much pleasanter than the others we visited although it was dark shortly after our arrival. This did not make their house in the setting of palm trees and moonlight any less attractive. Nihal was very interesting and informative. It is surprising how different Ceylon is from India, both in general prosperity and vegetation. One of the greatest problems they have is in preventing illegal immigration from India. The coast line is too vast to be watched closely. Living conditions are preferable in Ceylon but most outbreaks of disease in Ceylon have been traced to these illegal Indians. Ceylon is celebrating 21 years of universal suffrage. Nihal says, that to his knowledge, Ceylon is the only land that gave votes to men and women at the same time. They have a sweet little daughter, Moeena, 14 months old but she, of course, says little. We saw the little lizards come in through the open windows at night. They are excellent insect killers. Colomo temperatures are usually very tolerable and there is little need for elaborate furniture.

They gave us a very enjoyable Singhalese meal all curried but the curry was not hot. Rice, fish, egg, banana, pickles as first course. The fruit eaten fresh has a very different flavour, very much more tasty but, of course, it can't be sent. The bananas we obtained in Bombay were quite soft yesterday. Ray gave us mangos. They tasted something like a melon but are very difficult to eat elegantly.

Evidently, Ceylonese is the term given to all the inhabitants of the island

and Singhalese given to a particular racial group. Nihal is, himself, Singhalese. Penang is our next port of call and said to be the loveliest spot of all the ports.

Love, Olga

Singapore
13 November 1952

Dear Mam,

This is our third day in Singapore. We had a grand time in Penang. One of the girls had Chinese friends there and they entertained us lavishly. They met us at the boat and took us to see the Sunday School in action. We then went to the Chinese service where the speaker and interpreter were present. Most of the service was in Mandarin and interpreted into the Hokkien dialect but an occasional English sentence was put in. Needless to say, I did not understand much. Then they gave us a wonderful Chinese dinner including chicken in jelly, vegetables, fish.

near Hong Kong
16 November 1952

Dear Mam,

I am writing this on deck as portholes have been closed because of waves and spray and the sea is as rough as it has been since the Bay. It is windy and cool. We are due to sail from Hong Kong on 30 November. There is an earlier boat but it will cost us less to stay in a hotel in Hong Kong for the fortnight. This will give us a chance of seeing Hong Kong. The ship's barber has had a go at my hair. It is now very short, needing neither clips, combs or curlers, but how long I shall be able to keep it like this I don't know.

The boat has changed again since Singapore and is now more than half Asiatic. It has been an excellent trip in every way, in company, food, weather, trips ashore, etc. You would enjoy the ice cream. It has been somewhat wasted on me. I obtained a coconut in Singapore and had the pleasure of the milk but was rather disappointed with the rest. It tasted like ordinary desiccated coconut. I haven't space for all details of Singapore and Penang but I should mention that we visited the Tiger Balm Gardens. Tiger Balm is an ointment in such use that the founder appears to be a multimillionaire Chinese. The gardens in Singapore were completely in concrete but set out rather like a zoo with fish-like, animals and nursery characters. Chinese legends, etc., were all in brightly coloured concrete. Some pictures were, indeed, gruesome but I was fascinated by the detail and life-likeness of so much of the work, the tigers look as though they were about to jump. The mermaids, too, were quite convincing.

Love, Olga.

Hong Kong
25 November 1952

Dear Mam,

I am writing this on Hong Kong island looking across very blue water to purple hills beyond and a green slope nearby. Oh to be able to draw. I am sure Graham would enjoy these parts. We are sitting in the shade, the temperature is just right, there are no flies and we have just finished our picnic lunch. There is a little fishing boat in the background and junks with red and black sails behind.

It really is a beautiful scene and ideal setting and requires an artist with paintbrush to produce the right effect. Boats between Hong Kong and Japan are somewhat unpredictable as typhoons tends to hold them up. We are due to go on board tonight and sail tomorrow morning, landing at Kobe. We should then proceed to Tokyo and then change for Karuizawa. This means that we shall have a good view of Fuji on our way. Indeed if this trip had been organised as a pleasure cruise and the weather ordered in advance it could not have been better. Today we are enjoying the last bit of warmth we can expect for some time but I expect by this time you will be having the fire piled high and glad to see the sun occasionally. We have had rain but only at nights. This warmth compensates for about the loss of eight hours on the journey out but I have just slept and slept much more than at home. We are having a week instead of a fortnight here. We spent one night in one of the refugee camps. The journey there was again one of breathtaking beauty, with no chimneystacks to mar the beauty. In this particular camp there must be about 8,000 people, families living in very small areas in shacks which are little protection from the rain. Usually it is fairly warm so there is no undue suffering from cold. Most of those who live there have been from well to do families, often accustomed to having servants. The women are usually addressed by the title 'taitai' meaning 'lady' rather than plain 'Mrs'. Making ends meet is a real problem. They are given 20 cents for embroidering a blouse front, the fastest workers could do one in an hour; it costs us 2 dollars to cross in a boat to the camp. The refugee problem in Hong Kong is acute, very much greater than any in Europe. We have been told that it is as though the whole population of France and Germany moved into England in two years.

We went up in the little cliff railway to Hong Kong peak and, again, had the grand view of the harbour. The cliff is about 1,000 ft up almost straight from the water. We saw the sunset and then lights in the town. There is a great variety of colouring and the whole lowland area is so completely built up that the view is of a mass of sparkling colour and reflections of the colour in the water. The sea is so still that it seems more like a picture than real life.

More anon. There seems so much to describe and ordinary language cannot convey it. The present scene is so peaceful and away from the hurry and bustle of traffic.

Much love, Olga

CHAPTER 2

A New Country and Language (1952–1954)

Karuizawa

AUGUST 1945 HERALDED THE END OF THE war in Japan. American forces occupied the land. The emperor, who had been worshipped, declared that he was not God – he had carefully stated that he was not the Creator, but asked permission to go and report the surrender of his country to his ancestors at the Imperial shrine, indicating that he was descended from the sun goddess. The country was left poor and with a spiritual vacuum. The American occupiers gave much material aid to the country, and General McArthur appealed for missionaries to come to Japan. Many Americans responded, as well as others who had worked in Japan before the war. The influx continued for several years.

Karuizawa was a wooded mountain area, 3,000 ft high, dominated by Mount Asama, 8,000 ft, an active volcano. Tiger lilies grew in profusion: red and pink azaleas blossomed on the slopes of the volcano in the spring. But the trees in the winter, bereft of their leaves, presented a breathtaking fairy-land scene when each branch and twig was encased in frost. The town was very busy in the summer, when residents of Tokyo escaped the oppressive heat of the plain for the cool comfort of the mountains.

Karuizawa had been chosen by American missionaries and CIM for initial language study. OMF had arrived in 1951 direct from China. When I arrived in December 1952 only a few missionaries had moved to pioneer work on the northern island of Hokkaido. Most of us were engaged in language study. We were housed in two buildings. The larger one had been the Swiss Embassy, with a circular central room suitable as a dining room and a meeting room. Two corridors led off in opposite directions with a number of separate rooms. The married couples and three single men occupied one wing, single ladies the other.

Canadian Leonard Street and his wife were in overall charge. They had come from the bleak and difficult area of Kansu, NW China, a largely Muslim area, and watched as the communist army mowed down the opposition troops. American Hubert and Mary Fisher had come direct from

China, just mid-term there. They had looked after Gladys Aylward for six months when she had been in need and not well. Mary was originally from Kelso, on the English-Scottish border, and in 2005 was over 100. Many miscarriages but no successful births, while a disappointment to them, brought them to conclude that the Lord had a work for them to do which would be impossible with children. Bessy and Arthur Kennedy (English and Australian) were the business managers. Ben (Swedish) and Agda (US) Halgren, a very practical and capable couple. Arthur and Joy Reynolds, with whom Doug had travelled, had not come direct from China. He was exceptionally fluent in Chinese. Canadian Lee and Louise Little were younger workers. A fear that all Asia, including Japan, would soon become communist, dominated the minds of several of the older workers. Time was short.

The three young men were new workers. Australian David Hayman, son of CIM missionaries, had been at school in China. His father had been captured and taken for six months on the long march of the Red Army of Mao Tse Tung. He had been thought dead, a funeral service arranged, then he was released. David himself had been returning to school by ship when the ship was captured by pirates. This caused great anxiety to the parents, but adventure for the children. David and Doug arrived in Japan within two weeks of each other. Steve Metcalf joined them in December. Steve was born in SW China, had witnessed for the third time bandits capture and beat his father, and also observed his parents' selfless lives as they gave themselves to the Lisu tribal peoples. Later he was interned by the Japanese with the rest of his school in China. Hatred for the Japanese turned to love as he prayed for them, and a longing to reach them for Christ.

The occupants of the ladies' wing included Miss Eileen Singleton who was the housekeeper, Monica Hogben the doctor, Mary Weller with whom I had travelled and some of the 'forty-niners' – forty-nine young missionaries had gone to China in 1949 but had never been able to get beyond the language school. Japan was open to the Gospel so a number came direct to Japan.

Ruth and Walter Searle were in charge of the smaller house with Bill and Dorothy Pape. Bill was so moved by what he observed in China that it resulted in a nervous breakdown. But both Bill and Dorothy were extremely capable people, Dorothy writing the first CIM book on Japan *Captivities of the Mighty* and Bill *Introduction to the 'New Fields'. Japan Fields for Reaping*. I appreciated discussion at the meal table. Mary Nicol was with us – she had come to teach the children of six missionary couples.

Roslyn Ormiston was also in this house, in a very cold room. Her face cloth was frozen each morning as the wind came in through the floorboards. She became a close friend. She was a fully qualified brilliant doctor but her burden was to reach the Japanese for Christ. Her ancestors had come to Australia with Captain Bligh of the Bounty. Her father, a dentist, showed his concern for others during the depression by over-employing and over-paying his workers. Roslyn inherited her father's generosity. She was vivacious and attractive, although she had recalled the comment of the Vicar's on first seeing her 'I suppose every family has to have one ugly duckling.'

Roslyn's brother in the Australian Air Force had been killed during the war.

We were all together learning the language and the culture of the Japanese people.

Language study

We were a motley group of OMF missionaries, from different countries, different experiences and ages. Most had been in China, learning Chinese. Now in Karuizawa we were together learning the language and the customs of Japan.

There was a sense of urgency. Now was the time to spread the Gospel. We spent six hours a day, Monday to Friday, studying the language from a text book designed for the American Forces. Two hours were with a teacher who would ask us questions and correct us: though no Japanese believed foreigners would ever speak the language perfectly. (This was much better than the early workers of the nineteeth century they were reluctantly allowed teachers by the government but those teachers had been instructed to teach in such a way that the foreigners would never be able to speak Japanese.) We also learned a number of religious sentences.

Saturday was a free day. Doug and I ventured into the neighbouring town of Ueda by train; and practised our Japanese. We had learned the sentence 'Where is the Post Office?' We decided to make enquiries at a local shop; the proprietress was sitting far back at the 'cash desk'. I approached her, while Doug stood at the entrance and asked,

'Where is the post-office?'

She looked at me thoughtfully and then answered, 'Ah! The honourable toilet. Yes, yes. I'll show you.' She escorted me to the toilet and left me. I simply used it and thanked her. We needed more language study.

The Japanese language is reported as being very difficult, but it does have some advantages in the spoken language, even though the written language is almost impossible.

There are only five vowels a, i, u, e, o and no diphthongs, two vowels together being pronounced separately, e.g. 'aa' is twice as long as 'a' alone. Uu could be written ū, indicating a long vowel. It is difficult for us to distinguish the difference. I asked an astonished friend, 'Do you need snow to give out tracts?' Yuki = snow. Yuuki = courage.

Plurals are almost non-existent. A suffix can be added to some words, but we would do well to learn nouns as plurals, e.g. ringo = apples, rather than apple.

Going to the Post Office to buy a stamp I thought I asked for a 10-yen stamp.

'How many?' asked the clerk.

I should have said, '10-yen stamps, one.'

When the pastor asked me to bring the hymn books, I took him a hymn book.

'Where are the rest?' he asked.

Further, there are no articles.

'I am the way, the truth and the life' can be understood as 'I am a way, a truth, a life.'

And there are no genders and no cases, no problem of making the adjective agree with the noun. Yes, Japanese is simpler than German.

Concerning pronunciation. Japanese is not a tonal language like Chinese; there can be an alteration of pitch. To master this is not easy, but most words can be understood without it. Using English pronunciation would sound foreign but again generally understood. There is no 'l', and 'r' is more like a 'd', never rolled.

The language can be written in the form of *Hiragana* and *Katakana*, two alphabets, the first largely for words of Japanese origin, the second for foreign words and names. Our name is 'A bu ra ha mu su', each sound being represented by one kana, and not a combination of consonant and vowel. I wish we could have used this form of Japanese writing from the start, instead of the Romanised form, even if our progress would have been initially slower. I would have been less likely to mix the words *ka bu ru* (wear on the head) and *ku ba ru* (distribute), and ask my tract distributing friend, 'Do you wear the tracts on your head?' instead of, 'Do you distribute tracts?'

Studying the characters, 1800 of them in order to read and write is a long process. They were introduced into the Japanese language from the Chinese, and each may be read in more than one way. Some are simple, e.g. '人' meaning a person can be read in the Japanese way as *hito*, or the Chinese way, *nin* or *jin*. (This led to the sermon on God's love of carrots, which is *ninjin* instead of mankind, *ningen*.) Each character has to be learned accurately; some have as many as 20 strokes; the correct order of the strokes must be observed. We later felt that our older workers would have done better to have learned Japanese from the Chinese.

There are differences in men's and women's language (and children's) e.g. that is so. Men's language – *Só da*.

General polite – *Só desu*.

Ladies language – *Sayó de gozaimasu*.

The ladies' language gives us longer to think about what has been said. Other words vary according to the speaker, e.g. *kanai* = my wife,

   okusan = your wife, his wife, etc.

   chichi = my father, our father

   otosan = your father, etc.

Then, of course, there is no need for the personal pronoun. The Japanese use the personal pronoun as little as possible.

The verb to eat depends on who is eating.

   kuu = an animal eats,

   taberu = I eat

   meshiagaru = you eat.

There are words for older brother or sister, younger brother or sister, yours or mine, but no word for brother or sister.

And so I could go on.

The two words to warn a child to stop I have continued to use even in England. When we say 'No', the child may react 'I am going to do it anyway.' The Japanese say either *da me* meaning that's naughty or *abunai* meaning it's dangerous. The psychological effect of *abunai* is clear, the English 'it's dangerous' is too long.

So I'll stop. Except for 'Yes'.

The dictionary gives *hai* – first meaning 'Yes', second meaning 'No'. That is not too difficult as it answers a negative question 'Aren't you going?' – Yes (I'm not going). But it can simply mean I have received your question, e.g. 'will you do the washing up?' 'Yes' means I know you want me to wash up. I haven't said I would do it. This simple word can cause much confusion, especially when a Japanese answers 'Yes' in English with the Japanese meaning.

A famous shrine, Nikko

'Don't say "it's fine" until you have seen Nikko' – Japanese saying.

Our language teachers wanted us to see the famous Shinto shrine at Nikko with its magnificent scenery. They arranged our travel and accommodation at a Japanese inn. We learned the terms *yadoya* and *hoteru*. *Hoteru* would give Western style facilities: the *yadoya* Japanese style.

Five of us went with five of the teachers and Janet Pape (aged seven). It was a six-hour train journey, yet we could see Mt Asama, the volcano towering 5,000 feet above the 3,000 foot Karuizawa plateau. Nikko is designed to attract all kinds of tourists. We arrived at our *yadoya* and, according to custom, left our shoes at the entrance and donned the heel-less slippers provided by the hotel. The kimono clad young maids guided us as we flopped along the wooden corridors. There is an art in 'flopping', but an even greater art in getting upstairs without losing a slipper. Not all of us were successful. They introduced us to our rooms – two rooms, each with six tatami mats (each mat one yd × two yds) that could be made into one room by sliding back the partition between. We stepped out of our slippers on to the tatami mats; no shoes or slippers are ever worn on tatami. The only furniture in the room was a small table, a mirror and the recesses from the rooms called *tokonoma*. In the centre of the room were low tables: the maids served us green tea immediately; the kettle was kept hot on the *hibachi*, a small portable charcoal fire. We sat on cushions on the floor, but not for long in the approved fashion. (Evidently on visiting a Japanese house, one kneels on the cushion, crossing the feet at the instep, and then sits back on one's feet, until being invited to be at ease. The women are then allowed to sit to one side, the men to cross their legs.)

We left the hotel to visit the temple precincts. We had to pass under the *torii*, the cleansing gates at the entrance of all Shinto shrines. Foreigners are charged for admission to the temple, but we were loath to contribute to the 'gods'. The gods at the entrance were ugly but the colours bright. The row of 300 year old cedars impressed us – their height too great to photograph.

Back at the hotel, the maids invited us to take a bath. They had laid out the two kimono each for us; the cotton one for sleeping in and the wadded one as a dressing gown. Both had to be worn men's fashion, closed left to right. Only a corpse is fitted right over left. We undressed in the changing room, left our clothes there, and proceeded to the bathroom. This particular bath was big enough for three of us; Mary swam a stroke. Following the custom, we washed down with water only stepped into the bath and knelt down up to the neck, got out, washed with soap, rinsed down and got in again and soaked up to the neck. The water is being heated all the time: it is fortunately possible to add cold, but the water is never changed during the evening. As water is added, the bath overflows (and takes any scum with it) and drains out through a hole in the floor. The Japanese regard this type of bath as a necessity but it is definitely a pleasurable relaxation. They may spend up to three-quarters of an hour in the hot water and can bear the water very hot. (I was reminded of the threat in *The Mikado* – 'Boil them in boiling oil'. Would boiling water be too cool?) We dressed in our pyjamas as well as the supplied kimono. Whether it was due to use or the figure, that the Japanese could keep their kimono closed at the bottom at all times while it was just not possible for us.

When all had bathed and dressed in kimono the maids brought in the supper. Our rooms were surrounded on three sides by wooden corridors, the fourth with glass facing the outside. The supper came on individual trays that could be stood on the floor, the other tables having been cleared away.

The girls brought the trays, stacked one on top of the other, along the outer corridor, opened the door from low down, removed their slippers before stepping into the room and bringing in the trays. Rice was served separately. I have very little memory of what we did eat. The Japanese are fond of egg dishes of all kinds, and on this occasion we were not faced with the delicacy of raw fish, but the tastier kind fried in batter. After the meal they removed all the trays. (I tried to give a demonstration of the maids bringing our food – opening the door from as low a position as possible (knees bent), removing my slippers, stepping over the threshold and dropping down again. They were constantly up and down, but when I tried I was told I looked like a thief.)

We had our own Bible reading in alternate languages. When we were ready, the maids brought in the futons and sheets, making up the beds on the floor. It was comfortable for most of us, but a little difficult for the tallest (Dorothy Pape).

In the morning when we were dressed, the maids rapidly removed the bedding, swept the floor and then brought the breakfast by 7 a.m. We set out for the famous beauty spot borrowing umbrellas from the hotel – quite a colourful show and publicity for the hotel. We travelled some distance by electric railway, held up for some time through an electricity cut. From the end of the line we took the cable car, rising steadily through the area of heavy rain to the snow. We were denied the view of the famous waterfall because at the time of our visit there was no water in it. A beautiful view of the lake was also obscured by mists. We returned to a meal in Nikko itself without further excitement. Later we learned that the next day there had been a landslide and an accident to that same cable car.

And so back to Karuizawa.

Designated north

Karuizawa days gave us enriching experiences – knowing our fellow OMF members from different countries, meeting with enthusiastic young American couples, sampling Japanese food, enjoying the changing seasons, combating unpleasant summer insects, and understanding more of the spiritual battle.

The older CIM missionaries straight from China were valiant warriors with much experience of the Lord, struggling with a new culture. They had known privation, provision for their needs and witnessed the suffering of Chinese Christians. Bill had broken down in watching the suffering, unable to help. Arthur had been faced with having to get a group of school children out of China. An American plane appeared to be available, but the crew sadly informed him that they could not get it started.

'I'll have a go,' volunteered Arthur.

The crew looked doubtful, but had nothing to lose. Sure enough in a short while Arthur did get it going – he was an electrical engineer.

We became friendly with an American couple from another mission. They invited us out for the evening. We had our tea as usual, but found that they had prepared a large roast meal for us – delicious but too much. So the next time another couple invited us out we were careful not to eat beforehand. They gave us a hot drink and piece of cake later in the evening. Our OMF friends explained we could have known what to expect by the timing of the invitation.

We were alerted to the spiritual battle on two fronts. Early on, Doug and I were enjoying our Saturday ramble through the wooded countryside, climbing the hills. We came across a patch where there had have been charcoal burners working. Parasitic coils of ivy coiled round the trunks of the trees. A willow tree drooped its branches. I shuddered. There was a sense of evil. Returning to base I was unable to pray. Doug simply read aloud Isaiah 35 and I was freed from bondage. Was even the countryside under the control of evil powers?

Several of us were involved in direct ministry including English Bible classes. When pupils or teachers showed interest in Christ, attendance fell or the school authorities limited the classes.

Our whole group was called upon to decide how we should work and what form of government the churches we aimed to plant should take. We were from a variety of churches, compounded by the sending countries having different views on 'co-operation' and 'compromise'. The final decision was to aim at self-governing independent churches. Some felt that the Japanese 'national' church had compromised with Emperor and Ancestor worship in the war years. The buzz word was forming 'indigenous' churches. Looking back I think we failed to realise that the Japanese pattern was to follow the teacher, rather than to work out the form of church government, with every one from the most experienced to the newest convert making the decision.

We were by this time committed to work in Hokkaido, the most northerly island where there were few Christians. Two of the senior men felt the need to work with Bible Schools in the Metropolis, Tokyo itself – they themselves had a worthwhile ministry in that field.

Our superintendent, Mr Street, spoke to Doug and David, suggesting they go to the unchurched town of Kutchan in Hokkaido in September. To my surprise he asked me to move, almost the same time although I had had only nine months language study, to the NE city of Kitami where a veteran China missionary, Margrit, was stationed; her fellow worker was needed for another town. Margrit was working with a Japanese Presbyterian church. Mr Street asked me whether I was willing to go there. I questioned,

'Do I have any choice, as a new worker?'

'Yes,' he replied, 'it is a Presbyterian church and you are a Baptist.'

I was in fact delighted at such a designation as ideally I wanted to work with a Japanese church rather than be independent.

Mr and Mrs Street were themselves moving to the main city of Hokkaido, Sapporo, and I was to travel with them.

But meanwhile we had a delightful holiday – serendipity.

A lovely holiday – Takayama

Bill and Dorothy Pape invited us to go on holiday with their children to a farmhouse near the sea, a place recommended to them by their teacher.

We had to take everything for the holiday, bedding, mosquito nets, cooking utensils, etc., not being quite sure of the living conditions. The trunks were sent on ahead by train.

We arrived safely and 'set up camp'. The tatami mats had been removed, apparently because of the probability of their housing fleas. We slept on our futons on the wooden floor, protected from the mosquitoes by the nets. During the day we could use a burning coil to keep them away.

Dorothy was a skilful cook – pressure cooker and all. We found that to keep milk and butter cool we had to let them down into the well outside, from which we also obtained our water. Behind us were cultivated hills; in front we looked out on green paddy fields, noisy with frogs in the evening and the Pacific Ocean beyond.

The next morning, Bill took the children to the sea and returned very excited.

'It's a lovely beach,' he enthused. 'But there are lots of foreigners there.'

This was Takayama that we had come across without realising. On either side of the clean, safe bay were two hills with pine trees and numerous chalets owned by missionaries or missionary societies. A chapel had been built on one of the hills.

To us it was a fantastic holiday; over the years it became our summer holiday spot. That first year, meeting with experienced Christian workers, sharing their experiences, joys and problems – their advice as to how to live and witness in Japan was invaluable.

What do you do when you are new to an area?

Answer. Just live there for two years.

One missionary told us of the encounter with a demon-possessed boy. She cast the demon out of the boy but omitted to send it to the abyss or to Jesus himself. The demon attacked her that evening. She was able to send it away but had received a shock.

It was our first visit to Takayama but by no means the last. Bill bought his own chalet. Later he became Mayor of the community. The water was warm, ideal for swimming and body surfing. The bay was safe, although the adjoining beach, beautiful with miles of golden sand, was dangerous for swimmers. One drowning a week was reported – largely teenage boys who were strong swimmers, going out of their depths into currents.

We walked along the cliff on a narrow path between prickly plants. We called them 'ows'. We reached a natural, ten ft deep pool, to swim and dive. On the rocks around were pools filled with brilliant sea anemones and mother-of-pearl shells of abalones. The brilliant sunshine brought out the colours. Hills behind, rocks easy to manoeuvre, the blue Pacific beyond, all to ourselves for the most part.

To reach the pool we had to pass a disused Shinto temple. Discarded little idols were on the ground. One of our missionaries took one as a souvenir, only to find later that he had picked up a 'demon' which oppressed him. Prayer and discarding the idol finally released him.

'The nearby village of Hanabuchi,' I wrote to my mother, 'is a shopping town with a shore not unlike that of Cullercoats, but with houses coming right down to the shore and more shops. Our swimming beach reminds me more of the Haven at Tynemouth and then beyond us a long stretch of sand more like Seaton Sluice. We are looking for a trip round the islands tomorrow but the weather has not been too fine. Doug has been thoroughly sunburned red although the sun did not even break through the clouds.'

We did get our hoped for trip to Matsushima. *Matsu* means 'pine trees', *shima* means islands. The bay is filled with small islands, every one with at least one pine tree. We had a luxurious two-hour trip on a small boat from Hanabuchi (see above) but did not reach the full ocean. We were taken to see the 'oyster beds'. They consisted of a series of long bamboo poles from which shells are hung and oyster eggs laid on these shells. Once a year Matsushima is the scene of a magnificent firework display associated with a Shinto legend.

The holiday season is July/August. Rain in July, typhoons in August hinder enjoyment. We returned year after year for holidays in Takayama, not in the farmhouse but renting one of the many chalets.

Journey to North East Hokkaido

Hokkaido is the most northerly island of Japan developed from 1871, partly as a defence against Russia. Dissident political activists were exiled to Hokkaido, and samurai who had lost their lords developed the roads under cold conditions with few facilities, sometimes with loss of life. These folk populated the island resulting in less ancestral tradition, and also standard Japanese language throughout the island as opposed to distinct dialects in many parts of Japan. Hakodate on the SW tip was one one of the first ports to be opened to foreign trade in 1858, the terminal of the ferry from the mainland, and a thriving city until taken over by the present principal city of Sapporo. The aboriginals of Japan, the *Ainu* (pronounced Inoo), were slowly subjugated, largely through drink. The journey from Karuizawa to Kitami was a long one. I travelled with Mr and Mrs Street who were on their way to Sapporo to take over at his request, from Mr Chapman, a Presbyterian missionary. We took the train to Tokyo, staying overnight at the TEAM (American Missionary Society) home, then on to Aomori, about seventeen hours by train to Aomori, the most northerly port of Honshu, then a rush with the crowd on to the ferry, four hour crossing to Hakodate. The voyage is sheltered by land until the central point of the straits. Then another five-hour journey to Sapporo. Doug was already in Kutchan, two hours west of Sapporo; I had another six-hour train ride east to Kitami

Margrit had previously sent me a welcome letter with the words, 'Magnify the Lord with me and let us exalt His name together.' (I had asked the Lord for a word beforehand. He gave me Romans 15 v 1. 'We who are strong ought to bear with the failings of the weak . . .' 'But Lord', I said, 'should that not be a verse for Margrit, your experienced older servant, rather than for me, just starting.' The Lord reminded me of my time with two strong men, both afraid of spiders. In that situation I was strong, they were weak.) We were to share our rented house.

It was a spacious two-storey wooden house, owned by a dentist friend of Dr Togasa. The downstairs consisted of two rooms with tatami matting, a kitchen, a toilet (a small enclosure with a tin box let into the floor), and an outside well for our water supply. Upstairs were two fairly large bedrooms and one smaller room. Tatami had been removed for health reasons. The sash windows on two sides of my room gave magnificent views of the hills, but in a gale the curtains moved as though the windows were open. My desk and bed were in the room but the main attraction was the 'Rumpen stove' (sketched below). It was filled ready for use with coal almost to the top and kindling on the top.

It was fitted to the chimney pipe that went out through the wall or window. The bottom draught was closed, the top opened and the kindling on the top lit. After a few minutes the top draught was closed, the bottom opened, and if we heard the rush of air through the stove we knew the coal had been fired.

The bottom draught controlled the rate of burning and the heat. We closed it down at night, the stove remained alight but burned very slowly from the top down to the bottom. We opened it up again in the morning.

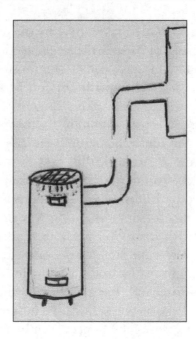

I found I could use a stick from my bed to open the draught and get the room warm before I got up. When the coal was burned there was still heat in the ash Then we replaced the whole stove with another already prepared. (I was told that the name 'Rumpen' was given because there was always one idle stove.) I changed the stoves in the middle of the day. Each burned for over twenty hours.

Kitami could be cold. Margrit often used to say 'It's a healthy cold.' Warm winds reminded her of unhealthy damp winds from Italy in Switzerland. The snowfall in winter was not heavy, but too cold to make snowballs, lying rather like brown flour. Margrit had been an expert skier in Switzerland, but gave it up when she found it was becoming more important to her than the Lord. Regretfully, she didn't teach me to ski and I never learned.

Kutchan had more snow than Kitami. Doug spoke of children skiing from the roofs of the houses. A path had to be dug from the front door to the street daily in the winter. Kitami was simply colder.

Kitami

I was delighted at my designation to work with Margrit Bahler and the Presbyterian Church in Kitami.

Margrit was Swiss, spoke English, German, Chinese and now was learning Japanese. When she recounted her experiences in nearly perfect English, her slight accent enhanced her story. Perhaps our imperfections in Japanese could be an advantage. Returning to her station in China by a small river boat, she awoke in the night to feel water under her, realised that the boat was sinking and escaped. The boatmen, having stolen her property, had decided to sink the evidence. She had lost everything and had to borrow clothing to continue her journey (she was tall but a gentleman's Chinese gown fitted her) but was rejoicing that her life had been spared for a purpose in God's kingdom.

Being forced out of Mao's China, she had felt humiliated by being subjected to search, especially having to let down her long hair to prove she was not hiding anything. She came directly from China to Japan; after the initial language study she came to Kitami at the invitation of Dr Togasa, to the Presbyterian church. She stayed at his home before moving to the present house with a fellow worker.

The Presbyterian church had been founded before the war by Presbyterian missionaries, Mr and Mrs Pearson. They travelled by horseback through rough mountains in Hokkaido to reach Kitami; their efforts were acknowledged by the town in naming a street after them.

A group in the town trusted the Lord and were baptized, the first by the missionary and then by fellow believers. Unfortunately, a subsequent pastor insisted that baptism could be administered only by a fully ordained pastor. Those who would not submit to this had to leave the church, although they held on to their faith. Dr Barnhouse of America had given considerable assistance to the church. I was especially interested in this as it was under Dr Barnhouse's preaching that I had become a Christian.

Dr Togasa's family had been helped; he wanted missionaries to come and help in his church. Pastor Sasaki also welcomed us. During the war many believers were afraid to attend church. Dr Togasa had come to the Lord through the death of his five-year-old little girl and declared his faith by holding a Christian funeral. He and two others were the only ones who remained during the difficult war years. Prescriptions he wrapped in paper that had a Bible text on it. Towards the end of the war, the military police called on him.

'Who is greater? the Emperor of Japan or Jesus Christ?'

'Jesus Christ,' replied Dr Togasa unhesitatingly.

So he was led off to prison.

The warders knew he was no criminal. They also discovered that he was an expert at Kendo, a kind of fencing. Would he teach them, please?

So in prison he had the relief of hitting the warders' heads with long wooden poles (emotionally satisfying) and of getting exercise. The prison term was short-lived, as the war ended.

He was an unusual man, a great help to us, excellent in English and fond of puns. He referred to Margrit as a language Department Store.

Three doctors

Shortly after my arrival I met the three doctors, Dr Ando, Dr Togasa and Dr Aoba. Although they were brothers they had different names. Dr Ando was the eldest and had the family name. The other two were adopted into their wife's families, which had no male heirs. Dr Togasa we got to know very well as he looked after us, was good at English and wanted to practise it. He managed puns, enjoyed tongue twisters. 'Are you copper-bottoming 'em my man'. 'No, I'm aluminiuming 'em mum'. (Try it, it baffled him). He had arranged for us to go to his house three times a week for a 'bath' as we had none in our house. The 'bath' was a tiled cube, water about eighteen inches deep, heated by a boiler outside the bathroom. There was no means of cooling the water. We soaked up to the neck in the approved fashion and boiled. On one occasion Mrs Togasa looked at a very pink Margrit after we came out, asked us if the water was too hot with the comment 'you look like a boiled lobster'. On further occasions it wasn't quite so hot. We sat down in their living room, often too hot, because courtesy required them to heat up the stove for us. The iron stove was literally red-hot. As we arrived and entered the bathroom, Dr Togasa would send his retainer to his field to bring back corn on the cob. It was immediately boiled, ready for us as we emerged. I still relish the flavour of that fresh-cooked corn on the cob. (The Japanese word for it is different in Hokkaido and the rest of the country.) Apart from being a doctor with his own private hospital, he was an expert at Japanese poetry, fencing, catching butterflies, was a church elder and held a Christian meeting for the nurses of his hospital.

Dr Aoba (who enjoyed football) was drawn to Christianity and reckoned he would find happiness in it. His wife believed that happiness would be found in satisfying all selfish purposes. It was he who organised our visit to the forest early one morning to collect mushrooms. The variety was known as 'child of the tree', found under the trees and were bright red and green in colour. I would not have dared touch them without the assurance of the others. Margrit was familiar with the species in Switzerland. They were delicious.

Dr Ando slowly moved towards faith, studied his English and German Bibles because they were easier to understand than the classical Japanese translation. But one day he came to us in great excitement. He had been desperate. The tax inspector had informed him of the amount he owed. It was impossibly high. He remembered the verse of scripture he had been studying. Psalm 50 v 15: 'Call upon Me in the time of trouble. I will deliver you and you will glorify Me.' It was certainly a time of trouble so he called upon the Lord. The next day the inspector looked at his accounts again. 'Yes', he agreed, 'that amount was mistakenly high.' What Dr Ando had to pay was reasonably possible. To us he declared exuberantly. 'This is a miracle. Such a thing does not happen in Japan.' He would say to us, 'I can understand duty, but I can't understand love.'

The three doctors studied the German Bible regularly with Margrit. I joined them; German conversation was beyond me but I could take my turn in reading the Bible, as German is phonetic, and I knew the stories well enough to follow Margrit's teaching. When we came to the story of John the Baptist jumping in Elizabeth's womb on Mary's greeting, I wondered how they would receive it. They nodded, 'Six months, that is just the time the baby would move.'

One evening we were invited to a meal provided by Mrs Aoba, with ourselves and the three brothers. It was a sumptuous meal, beautifully arranged. Wine was offered, Margrit and I declined. This posed a problem for Dr Togasa, for Christians in Japan don't drink. As he passed a large plate of salad across the table to me, he held it, despite its weight with his thumb and three fingers while his little finger moved rapidly to tip over the wine glass. It was not refilled.

This is the translation of Dr Manabu Togasa's testimony as he wrote it:

The fact that Manabu was always very big for his age, may have made some impression on his schoolmates and friends. This was probably the reason that, in about his third year at primary school, he was chosen to be a member of the secret society which had as its aim the rectifying of all injustices in the class. The society was called the Ten Heroes. Among its members was a boy named Takeo, the son of the local pastor. Takeo was too tender-hearted to be considered a hero, but as a consequence was very obedient to others, especially to Manabu. In order to strengthen their courage, the boys often practised jumping down from a ten-foot embankment at the back of the school. At such times, Takeo, closing his large eyes, was always first to jump, in obedience to Manabu.

One day Takeo took Manabu with him to the Sunday School in the church of which his father was the pastor, where Takeo's father, a grey-haired old man with a very tender face just like his son's, received Manabu warmly. Thus it was that Manabu attended Sunday School for about three years, that is until his sixth year in school. On Christmas Eve of that year he sang an English hymn as a solo, and the next day left the church.

One autumn evening, after failing the entrance examination of the First High School (a well-known college) in Tokyo, Manabu sat on the seat of a tram-car pressed in on all sides by the crowd. He was very tired after the day's study in the library and, as he sat staring vacantly at the evening scenery of the Tokyo street, his pre-occupied whistling was suddenly interrupted by a very angry voice exploding in his ear, saying, 'Stop!' It was a policeman. He, too, looked very tired and Manabu stood up instantly, offering him his seat. The policeman took it shamefacedly and at that time Manabu recalled what he had learned in the Sunday School.

By the time Manabu had received his medical degree and was taking a laboratory course, he and his wife, a former pupil of a Mission school, were the parents of a five-year-old daughter. During that summer, Manabu was responsible for conducting the Buddhist ceremony on the thirteenth anniversary of the death of his father. That night he was so tired that he slept soundly all night without knowing that his beloved daughter was ill with a very high temperature. By morning it was too late. When they found the little girl was suffering from a virulent form of dysentery, there was no hope of recovery.

Every now and then, in her delirium, the five-year-old girl sang hymns she had learned in her beginners' class at Sunday School. Each time she heard the song, the mother could not restrain the tears. The parents were sitting together at the bedside when suddenly the mother stood up and said, 'I'm going to the church,' and went out into the darkness of the night. In a short time she was back, followed by the pastor and his wife who quietly entered the room. Manabu recognised them both at once, having previously attended the church two or three times with his wife. As the minister prayed at great length, the father found that he, too, was weeping. At that time, with a most earnest expression on her face, his wife asked him if he would agree to having their daughter baptized. Though so near death, the beloved child seemed happy and while she was being baptized asked in her delirium 'Where is the butterfly? Where is the butterfly?' Before the child had drawn her last breath, the mother too had been baptized.

The day before the funeral, for the evening ceremony, an American lady missionary together with the pastor came to the house. They sang hymns very loudly and happily and thanked God for what He had done.

At the funeral itself there were very few present because almost all of the relatives and friends disliked the Christian Church. As far as Manabu was concerned, however, the Christian funeral had served to show his colours. Whenever his thoughts turned towards heaven, he found that unbearable grief of separation had been marvellously taken away. On Christmas Eve of that year, he too was baptized.'

(Note: The Christian funeral and baptism are significant declarations of faith in Buddhist Japan).

Day by day

Before I left England, Win had said to me, 'It doesn't matter about writing to me but, whatever else you do, be sure to write regularly to your mother.' I took her advice: my mother and I both wrote every week: the excellent airmail service usually took four or five days. She could share my life, and through her I knew what was happening at home, and concerning my brother in India. Other friends who were looking after her also wrote to me. Douglas and I wrote regularly to each other. Other personal letters were limited by the pressure of language study, visitors, meetings and church.

This was our weekly programme:

Sunday	8.30 a.m.	Sunday School. I attended but did not take part.
	10 a.m.	Morning Service. Margrit played the organ. I understood very little of the sermon. About fifty congregation.
	7 p.m.	Evening Service – meant to be evangelistic but very poorly attended.
Monday		Margrit visited neighbouring houses with tracts and a Japanese helper.
Tuesday		I visited with tracts and Miss Kambara's help.
	7 p.m.	The elders were planning to study the Westminister Catechism fortnightly.
Wednesday		Young People's Bible study – run by the YP, usually interpreting the difficult language of the old Bible into understandable modern Japanese.
	7 p.m.	Bible study and prayer meeting, poorly attended.

Thursday	7 p.m.	English Bible class – Margrit and I took turns using simple English.
Friday	7 p.m.	German Bible class – Margrit with the three doctors – I attended using my vocabulary *Ja* and *Nein*.
		(Later another gentleman joined. He had seen the notice outside the church, 'Kindergarten', knew it was German, so had asked if there was a German Bible class he could attend).
Saturday	7 p.m.	Nurses' meeting at Dr Togasa's hospital, with about nine nurses, Dr Togasa, the Pastor, Margrit and me taking turns in speaking.

Monday to Friday we have two hours' language study with our teachers, followed by English Bible study for them and then study on our own.

We read the Bible most days with our house help.

We take a bath at the Togasa's house three times a week. We shop and cook, etc. The fishmonger used to tell me not only the names of the fish but also how to cook them.

An unfortunate incident occurred one snowy evening. We must have surprised a thief on our return. The downstairs window was open, a small amount of money had been taken from Margrit's desk, but most of the money in the house was untouched. When Dr Togasa later informed the police, the Kitami 'Sherlock Holmes' was upset that we had not been in touch sooner. The footprints outside the window were largely obliterated by fresh snow. No doubt the thief had watched us as we regularly went out. Discussion with Dr Togasa and the Pastor resulted in a general consensus that we should not both go out together. This turned out well for us: we had been expected to attend all meetings, now one of us was always excused. We had been finding the programme exhausting.

One day a beggar visited us while Dr Togasa was in the house. Dr Togasa railed at the little man. 'How dare you come here begging from foreign guests. You, a Japanese, should be ashamed of yourself'. He left sheepishly.

A lively Christian lady whose husband was opposed to her faith used to visit me. She brought her twelve-year-old daughter who has never forgotten me. I offered her a bowl of sweets and, as she hesitated, I took one and gave it to her. Later I learned that she had expected to receive the whole bowl. Years later I discovered a related custom. If visitors come for a meal it would be normal to give them to take home food that was still on the table (doggie-bag?)

Another mistake we made when Dr Togasa came for a meal. We had managed to buy and cook an ox tongue, enough for large portions per person. Dr Togasa commented, 'This is the cheapest meat, isn't it'. Per pound that was so, but the amount was large. The Japanese would buy the most expensive.

Giving gifts was another problem. We had learned that if we received a gift we should return something slightly less valuable. Dr and Mrs Togasa showered gifts on us. If we gave anything in return, they would then increase their giving to us. We had to give up. The one group of people who are not expected to return gifts are pastors and teachers like ourselves. Pastor Sasaki is able to exist on a small salary because it is augmented by frequent gifts from the congregation.

Broadcasting

The local radio station asked us for interviews for school broadcasts. They wanted us to describe school life in England and Switzerland and say why we were here. Dr Togasa compared the different characteristics of Margrit and myself in response to the request. The recording was made in our house. I was enthusiastic when I heard about the project but nervous when it came to the day; Margrit was hesitant at first, but completely confident on the day. Church friends were very encouraging and supportive. The interviewers brought us a wireless to listen to the recording. I was clearer because I had been closer to the microphone. We could listen in: unfortunately our Kitami friends were unable to receive the station.

Cherry blossom

We joined the crowds visiting the park to admire the cherry blossom. At the entrance we were followed by a young man insisting on sketching us. Folks were very friendly, inviting us to join their groups. Some were dancing, singing and decidedly drunk. They have a proverb *Hana yori dango* meaning the food and drink are better than the flowers. We didn't stay long. The local people seemed to find us more interesting than the flowers.

Post

The postal system kept us well in touch with home news. Japanese letters have the address of the sender on the envelope. (We have on occasion lost an address simply by throwing away the envelope while keeping the letter.) When a letter has insufficient postage attached it is returned to the sender for postage due, if it is for overseas. If it is inland, the letter is delivered and the receiver pays. Each way is to the advantage of the Japanese GPO. Any letter sent to Kitami is likely to reach us as we are the only foreigners here. Sending parcels abroad is difficult for the Post Office is not used to customs' forms.

Language exams

I had to travel to Tokyo and Karuizawa, a thirty-six hour journey for two language exams.

The first in February was the final of the two Yale volumes. I would probably have completed them before moving from Karuizawa if I had had the full year there instead of nine months. Pastor Sasaki kindly arranged my travel, 2nd not 3rd class in the train. We always took 2nd class on long journeys. The 3rd class was very crowded and the seats too small for Western figures. I was fortunate in having two seats to myself, enabling me to do last minute revision, to sleep, and to be kept from talking to a neighbour on the train, as was my custom. Five of us passed the exam successfully.

The second exam was on the first volume of the Naganuma course, including Japanese writing and stories. With Rinya's help I rushed through it in four months. Our yearly mission conference was being held in Karuizawa in June, so if I could take the exam then it would save me the two thirty-six hour journeys from Kitami and back. I took the exam and passed if not brilliantly. While in Karuizawa, Doug and I were able to make some arrangements for our wedding. He had had the operation on his knee. Its condition had been worse than the doctors had expected but the operation more successful than they had anticipated. It never was 100 per cent. We travelled to Hokkaido together. I left him at Mori to spend Sunday with my missionary friends, including Mary Weller (with whom I had sailed), and Ruth White. Ruth planned to have her holiday in Kitami with me in July when Margrit would be away for her two week holiday. I was especially pleased because Ruth is a good tennis player. Mori itself is a small town on the western coast of Hokkaido. It had been a prosperous fishing village, but with over-fishing the fish had disappeared. I went on alone to Kitami where Dr Togasa met me in his new car. He had bought it and learned to drive, not very common in those days.

Sitting on the floor

My mother had written asking whether I still studied sitting on the floor with papers around me and the chair as a desk. Yes, I still did; our house-help catching me like that was impressed that I was conforming to the Japanese pattern.

The Church

Pastor Sasaki was a quiet man. He gave us a welcome. He was always open to suggestions, but seemed to keep his thoughts very much to himself.

The church membership was around eighty, about fifty present on Sunday mornings, but few in the evening. Margrit played the small organ. If she played at her normal speed she would finish two bars ahead of the congregation. Japanese hymn-singing was at a funereal pace. During my whole year in Kitami I could not follow the Pastor's sermon unless he told me beforehand what he was going to preach about. We were told they were very intellectual. (Later we learned that the Japanese did not expect to understand the sermon, reckoning that if they did it was too simple and the Pastor had not prepared sufficiently. They found it easier to understand the missionary, and accepted greater simplicity on the grounds that effort was required for the missionary to speak in Japanese.) The Wednesday evening Bible study was much easier to follow.

I found it physically difficult to sit on a hard bench, not being permitted to cross my legs (which could be hard to do for ladies wearing kimono) and not understanding an hour's sermon. Coats are never worn indoors and the church was not warm. I managed an unobservable compromise. I wore a grey woollen dress and instead of a coat I put over it my grey costume. The church was heated by two stoves. We sat as near as possible in the winter. I was away from Kitami on the very cold Sunday ($-25°C$) when the Pastor broke custom by wearing his coat in the pulpit. He was puzzled by seeing a white powder falling on his Bible. It was his breath freezing.

He had a meeting for a few believers in the neighbouring town of Bihoro, a town without a church, and a good group in the Sanatorium.

Tuberculosis was rife in Japan and patients had long stays in the Sanatorium. Church members took turns in the ministry there.

We were invited to the Pastor's house to celebrate a New Year's meal with his family. I did not realise at the time what an honour this was – New Year's Day is normally a private family celebration. The meal is fairly standard, glutinous rice balls in a red-bean soup is usual. The men in the family beat the rice for this ahead of time. Other delicacies are prepared with great attention to detail. For example a half slice of orange, surrounded by strips of turnip previously soaked in sugar and vinegar, with spinach in the centre, was supposed to represent a flower. His three children were all avid stamp collectors: they were excited to receive stamps from parcels we received from England. I played tennis with the pastor on one occasion.

He had kindly, and with discernment, arranged a Japanese language teacher for me, a Mr Shibakawa (meaning Firewood River) and his brother, who, he assured me, were from a Christian family but belonged to what was known as the 'no-church' movement. They did not want payment for teaching but would appreciate English Bible study in return. The friendship and association with the family turned out to be long-lasting.

Language lessons

Pastor Sasaki introduced me to the Shibakawa family, with three sons at home specialising in literature, commerce and science, and two of them would teach me Japanese. Rinya – the second of the brothers, who was a student at the Commercial College of Otaru became my teacher during his vacations. The family was going to mean much to us in our years in Japan. We gradually found out more about this remarkable family.

Mr Shibakawa senior had in fact been baptized in the early days of the church when laymen performed the baptism. He refused to be baptized again by an officially ordained pastor who took charge of the church so he was expelled from that church, but he remained a committed Christian outside the church with his family. He owned lands and a mountain near the suburb of Kitami city, had prospered in the production of peppermint but had to change his business to forestry and wood production because natural peppermint had been replaced with a synthesised one during the Second World War. He built up the wood-manufacturing firm: exports included oak to England. His eldest son became seriously ill with TB but with a radiant Christian testimony. All his siblings were drawn to Christ through seeing the serenity of their brother, until his death. The second son, Masayoshi, took over the responsibility of carrying on the business. By arrangement of the families their sister became engaged to the second son of a Shinto priest (the eldest son would follow his father as priest) but the Shibakawas realised that she should marry a Christian. What could they do about it at this late stage? The answer was simple, 'pray', which they did. Before the marriage their sister's future husband had become a Christian. Arranged marriages are still very much the norm. Mr Shibakawa senior had not met his wife before their wedding. Masayoshi asked me whether Doug and I had chosen each other. 'I don't know how you do it,' he commented. 'I am so glad that my parents will choose for me.' It is usually a very successful system.

Masayoshi wished for English Bible study after the Japanese lessons. He needed English for the firm's export trade. They grilled me about life in Cambridge. To them so many women studying was a novelty, 'usually men obtained the highest marks,' I informed them – nods and smiles all round. I continued, 'usually men obtain the lowest marks'. No smiles.

I was invited to listen to their gramophone records of classical music. The recording of Beethoven's 5th Symphony was below standard technically but the conductor was Sir Thomas Beecham. I was able to explain Handel's *Messiah* to them; they had not realised there was so much repetition. The records sounded better on my portable gramophone – but that was 1953.

At New Year they came excitedly with camera, tripod and all, to take our photographs. Later they returned with the prints – two had come out well, but they asked me to explain why the other two had not. I think this was their joke as, afterwards, they admitted that they had not wound the film on.

On one occasion the church was holding a bazaar on the Sunday. I felt I should stay away. Margrit feared it would offend the church, nor did she share my convictions. I shared my thoughts with the young men. 'Was it possible,' they wondered, 'to take a lone stand on principle?' They watched me. The impression on them was profound when they discovered I had stayed away.

Their house was up a hill. I looked forward to my visits up the hill in the snow-covered road in the winter. Children would be playing on skates, skis or sledges. There was a very sad ending to the day when Masayoshi warned children of the danger of sledging down the hill to the major road at the bottom. Traffic was sparse. Ignoring the words of the adult, one lively school boy lost his life that day. Unbelief can be dangerous.

Rinya was an exceptional teacher. He was able to push me to the limit, but not beyond. I did not have to push myself. One day, having a meal with the family, I asked the meaning of a phrase; Rinya answered, 'You should know that. I taught you that yesterday.' When he was returning to college I said to him, 'Mind you study as hard as you expect me to do.'

'Impossible,' he replied, 'I would become ill.'

Tract distribution

Miss Kambara, the diminutive eldest daughter of a church elder, herself a Christian of five years' standing, came with me, distributing tracts round the neighbouring houses. We used a series, so visited the same houses every fortnight. She was puzzled when I asked her if she needed snow to distribute tracts. I had said *yuki* (snow) instead of *yuuki* (courage).

Some folks were at first afraid, because the tracts reminded them of charmed papers they received at the Shinto shrines, for which they had to pay. Only one household categorically refused the tracts. At one other house, although the tracts were received well, I had an overwhelming sense of evil. When some months later the Bible Society colporteur visited Kitami, he found that in the area we had tracted the sales of Gospels or Gospel portions was significantly higher than average, but in the area around that one house he sold nothing.

Miss Kambara was especially helpful to me in my lack of language. The local blacksmith expressed appreciation of the tracts. One day, as there was no horse at the entrance of his house, we knew that he was not too busy so accepted his wife's invitation to enter. They really appreciated the work we were doing, acknowledging the supreme importance of religion, and, 'After all,' they said, 'aren't Christianity and Buddhism really the same?' No matter what point of difference one mentions there is sure to be some sect in post-war Japan that has adopted a thought from Christianity. The wife was so eager to talk that the husband could do so only if he spoke at the same time. With this two-way traffic I had to give up, despite Miss Kambara's plea on my behalf. 'Please do not use polite language as she doesn't understand it.' She nobly answered questions, but afterwards told me that she would need a ministerial training to tackle the situation.

One small grey-haired gentleman had always encouraged us by his gracious manner and cheery smile. One day he had a request: the tracts were in series but two were missing. He disappeared into an inner room and returned with a neat pile of a dozen tracts. 'Numbers 44 and 45 are missing, please would you let me have them if you have any left.' The missionary who took my place later led this gentleman to faith in Christ and he became her language teacher.

Mrs Yamamoto received the tracts eagerly but was leaving the district. She asked if the tracts could be forwarded to her promising to send her address – but we have heard no more.

A tradesman eagerly received the first tracts and had passed them on to his brother. He asked for more teaching but was too busy over the New Year, and we have heard no more.

A barber, who had become a Christian through the Salvation Army ten years ago, now a backslider, was moved on receiving the tracts to return to the church. He came one night, repented and has come no more.

Entering a wood factory we met a worker who told us that he had been baptized in the south of Japan and wanted to come to church – we have seen him no more.

So often we find an initial interest, then nothing further.

(This was 1954. Miss Kambara was puzzled: she asked me why English school girls were forbidden to wear slacks as reported in her newspaper. The normal dress of the Japanese young women was slacks.)

A new home help

The Japanese lady we had helping us in the house was not satisfactory, frequently did not turn up. I don't think she wanted to work for us. Dr Togasa found us a new help, Miss Kudoo, who was excellent. Many things that Margrit and I had done, we found were done for us, relieving the pressure. We can guarantee that she will come unless seriously ill. Dr Togasa's concerns for us were interesting: he was ashamed that we might think all Japanese women were like our previous helper. When Miss Kudoo came we noticed the change. Dr Togasa commented, 'That's a real Japanese woman.'

Mr Street (our OMF leader) used to take the six-hour train journey from Sapporo to visit us, help us if we had any problems, consider our progress and check our quarterly accounts. Margrit used to do them in dollars and yen, and could not account for 6 yen (6p?) Mr Street was not content with the discrepancy and was determined to find the cause. At last the mystery was solved. Margrit, being Swiss, would naturally write one as 1 and seven a 7 but she deliberately followed the English pattern 1 and 7. Only once had she used 7 instead of 1 − a 6 yen difference.

I boasted to Mr Street about our new helper and he teased me about it. After he left we went round to Dr Togasa's house for our Monday bath. Margrit said to Miss Kudoo, 'Mr Street always says when he visits us that the cat needs a bath too.' Returning from our bath we found the cat in a somewhat sorry condition, with definitely wet fur, but a dirty face. The following day Miss Kudoo told us that the cat had protested and brought out her claws.

But Miss Kudoo was an excellent helper and responsive to the Christian message. She brought friends along to a small group of ladies in our home. Mrs Tamiya, a very needy lady, responded to the message, her husband was in hospital so she was moonlighting to make ends meet. Although she professed to believe in Jesus she was unwilling to change her questionable lifestyle.

One young lady from the church gave a very meaningful talk. She was Mrs Tokuno, a young, attractive, Christian wife in a Buddhist family. In such a household the Buddhist altar would enshrine the spirits of dead family members, rice would be offered to them and prayers chanted. If this was neglected, would the spirit be unhappy or even return to trouble the family?

Mrs Tokuno struggled, and, with an open Bible, sought to discover what the dead really wanted. She told us that she had prayed and written, prayed and written as she prepared.

She spoke from Luke 16 vv 19–31. She said,

> This is not called a parable. It could have been a real situation. The rich man lived in luxury, Lazarus begged at his gate. They both died: the rich man was buried with great pomp but went to Hades; Lazarus was simply taken by angels to heaven (Abraham's side). The rich man in torment beseeched Abraham to send Lazarus to relieve his thirst. He was reminded of his behaviour while on earth, and told that there was an impossible chasm between Heaven and Hades. 'Then please send Lazarus to warn my five brothers so that they won't come here,' he said. Abraham replied, 'They have the Bible.' 'But' said the rich man, 'if someone came back from the dead, they would repent.' Abraham replied. 'If they don't listen to the Bible, they won't be convinced, even if someone rises from the dead.'

Mrs Tokuno concluded, 'The wish of the departed spirit is for the remaining family members to repent, and trust in Jesus who did rise from the dead, and then enjoy the comfort of Heaven.'

Mrs Tokuno was a real friend and helper, a positive, witnessing Christian. She took us one day to her tea-ceremony teacher,. We witnessed the strict rules observed in this ritual, with the gracefulness of movement of the kimono-clad ladies.

A miracle

It is the Wednesday night prayer meeting. I am sitting listening and understanding. The Pastor is expounding the parable of the Pharisee and the Publican.

'The Pharisee's prayer was perfect. He knew exactly how to stand, he knew how to address God, his language was perfect, his grammar was perfect, it was a perfect prayer and absolutely useless. The Publican did not know how to stand, did not know how to address God, his language was pretty hopeless, he did not get the right words, the prayer was effective.'

I sat there and listened. Language no good, grammar no good, how to address God no good; it fitted me absolutely. I had to pray in Japanese that night. I don't know if anyone else understood what I prayed. I don't know if I understood much myself but that was my first prayer in that new tongue.

During the week Mrs Tamiya approached us in distress. Despite our requests to visit her husband in hospital, she had steadfastly refused. 'Wait till he is a little better.' This time she pleaded with us to visit him. 'We've just had an awful row. He is in a foul mood. There are only three beds in his room. One has been empty for some time. The man in the other bed has just died. He was expected to live. My husband was expected to die. Please help.'

She took us to the city hospital where he had been languishing with tuberculosis for two and a half years. We entered a small, miserable three-bed ward with dingy pink walls. An empty bed was across the window, another along the wall from which the body had been removed that morning and an emaciated invalid in the third bed along the other wall. Mr Tamiya lay there, the oxygen tank by the bed, pain in his side, breathing laboured and speech one syllable at a time. My heart went out to him. I said to Margrit, 'Somebody has to pray for him'. Margrit didn't feel she could. Had I not prayed in Japanese in public the previous Wednesday, I could not have prayed that day. I put my hand on his side and let the Lord's compassion pray through me, 'Lord, if it is to Your glory and purpose, please let Your healing power flow through him'.

We left the hospital and shortly afterwards I was designated to another town not knowing what had transpired. Two and a half years later, I returned to the city with my husband and little baby girl. Margrit said to me, 'You must go and see Mr Tamiya'. He had been visited by the Christians, given a New Testament★ which he had propped up above his head to read and been baptized. He was radiant. He spoke rapidly and clearly. I learnt that the pain in his side had ceased when I had prayed for him. Now he told me, 'I have been in this hospital' – he paused to think – 'for five years. Folks are sorry for me but I am sorry for them. Their bodies may be OK but their souls are sick.' His transformation in the hospital had resulted in his doctor coming into faith and others wanting to know why. With his broad smile and joy of the Lord, there was no way I could pray for further healing. He was a strong witness where he was and I could only praise the Lord for what He had done in his life

The typhoon

26 September 1954

The following was published in the local newspaper in NE England.

Anxiety is felt by the friends of Miss Olga Rutherford of Earsdon, Whitley Bay, for her safety in Japan, where she went as a missionary.

She was travelling in the district recently devastated by a typhoon, with the loss of thousands of lives, and no news has been received of her since.

Miss Rutherford distinguished herself as a schoolgirl at Whitley Bay Grammar School and won a scholarship to Oxford, studying at Girton College and becoming captain of the hockey team.

Coming down she took employment under the Northumberland Education Authority and taught at Bedlington, Blyth and Wallsend. Then she answered a religious call, joined the China Inland Mission, and went out in its service to Japan as Chinese territory had been closed to it.

Japan's need

In letters home Miss Rutherford spoke of the great need for such work in Japan and her satisfaction in it. Recently she became engaged to a fellow missionary and they were planning to be married in December.

It appeared because news of the loss of life in Hokkaido through a typhoon had reached England. The reporter contacted my mother while she was

---

★It was our house-help, Miss Kudoo, who gave him the New Testament. She had received a mid-year bonus from us, did not feel it was really hers, so bought New Testaments to give away.

teaching in a local elementary school. She was not prepared to talk or give him any information: so he had to make up the story including some facts.

In Kitami we were aware of strong gale force winds. I was certainly not travelling in the district, nor was I missing. I did not win a scholarship to Oxford, and Girton College is in Cambridge. I had been engaged to Doug for four years.

The southern islands of Japan are often in the path of typhoons and subject to earthquakes but Hokkaido is relatively free. This typhoon struck the SW of Hokkaido including Kutchan. Doug recorded his experiences.

Dave and I want to praise the Lord for His preservation during the night of 26 September last. It was a Sunday and wind had been violent and rain heavy all day, and by evening it was a full typhoon. After having a time of hymn-singing and prayer by the light of a candle, the two of us ventured out about 8.30 p.m. to have a look around. Outside the ground began to heave under my feet, but I discovered that it was only a tree being blown over. Just a little up the road a group of men were struggling to keep a partly built warehouse on the ground and every now and then a sheet of metal from the roof would rip off into the darkness. We gave him a hand, but the racket was deafening. I remembered the lines of the hymn, 'cover my defenceless head 'neath the shadow of thy wing'. Just a bit later the entire roof of our former house ripped off and crashed into the street. We had to batten our wall down on the windward side and then rescue our kit and the other people from their house and bring it into our two rooms. There we waited for the morning with rain dripping through in a dozen places, and the house rattling and shaking in the wind.

We were much more fortunate than those at Iwanai where over two thousand houses were burnt out. We went to see the people, they had been packed into two large school buildings which had escaped the blaze and they were taking it all with great calmness. The Japanese have an immense capacity for suffering. Calamities are frequent in Japan and the Government is well able to cope with these situations. One longs that the very uncertainty of life in Japan might cause them to think on eternal issues but such is not the case. Our landlord's relatives were amongst those who lost their houses so, of course, they moved into the two rooms in town which had just been renovated, praise God.

These were the rooms our landlord had prepared for us!

There was a further tragic accident. The ferry from Hakodate to the mainland was blown onto the rocks. It was delayed in leaving so an unusually large number were aboard (about 1,000) and there were only about 200 survivors. One of Dr Togasa's friends lost his life. We were told that the delay in leaving was because of the captain's reluctance to set out in the storm. A large group of important businessmen were anxious to continue. The ferry started out; because of the intensity of the gale the captain decided to return to the harbour, moorings broke causing overweight on one side and the ship collapsed on the rocks. The ferry tragedy was the first of its kind in the history of Japan. Previous sinkings were through bombings. One American soldier lived to tell the tale. Amid the jeering of his fellow soldiers he decided he was not going to risk the voyage and disembarked.

Interlude

Autumn and winter

18 October 1953

D R TOGOSA CAME ROUND FOR the whole afternoon and then took us out to a salmon 'hatchery' on the river near here. The river is dammed and there is just one spot where the salmon can get up. The experts catch them easily in nets and take the eggs for hatching. They caught two for us to see and then threw them back. We also saw the salmon trying to jump the waterfalls, but the wooden slats prevented their success.

With us were an American army captain and his family which added to our enjoyment. The children like to play at being the British royal family: their mother heartily approves of this because they feel that they should match their behaviour with their status. The eldest girl was really excited to meet and hear me. She said on the side to her mother, 'She talks just like Queen Elizabeth.' (Where's my Geordie accent?) The Japanese also have an interest in British royalty wondering how the monarchy and democracy can function side by side. They do not want war again.

I had sad news from England concerning a serious car crash. Kathleen (in the form below me at school) was in the back seat with her baby girl. Her brother was driving, her husband in the passenger seat when they had a head-on crash. Her husband died in hospital, the baby completely untouched, and Kathleen badly injured, requiring a six-month recuperation in hospital, her face built up again. In reply to my letter of sympathy to her, she wrote that she could not have got through without the Lord's help.

(Footnote: we are meeting in church again, both aged 80).

To my mother, 8 November 1953

On 3 November we got our first snowfall. It will be another fortnight before it lies and heralds our six months of winter. I've woken up to a white world, a covering of about two ins. of snow on the roofs, and now a steady patter of water as it thaws. The snow has already made the weather feel warmer. Kitami this morning was like a Christmas card picture with the hills in the background. Most of the houses are single storied, so that from my upstairs room I get a grand view. There is not enough traffic to turn the snow into dirty slush. During rainy weather or the thaw the roads are just mud. About six ft of snow is expected here. Kutchan about twelve ft.

24 February 1954

In February, returning from a language exam in Tokyo, I saw Doug for six minutes when my train stopped at Kutchan. The journey from Sappora to Kitami (six hours) had a strange beauty: there was a carpet of snow, sometimes over flat stretching plains, sometimes over hillsides with streams managing to trickle through, sometimes with dark green pine trees giving a contrast in colour against a clear blue sky, making a Christmas card scene. The snow picked up the different shades of the sun as night approached.

The snow and the dry cold gave us much pleasure. Sometimes we saw horse-drawn sledges and once a man in a small sledge drawn by a dog. Ladies choose to shop on skates – I wouldn't carry eggs that way.

Christmas was a happy time, much celebration in the church. Pastor Sasaki's sermons have increased meaning (to the congregation, not to me) and ten baptisms. At home, we celebrated Christmas Swiss fashion on Christmas Eve. This was more than acceptable to me as it is my birthday.

The New Year is important for the Japanese. On our return from the watchnight service in the church we saw many people on the streets. They were visiting the Shinto shrine with wishes for the year.

I have had some communication from Graham. Quote, 'I hope you have received this letter, if not let me know and I will write again.' What did come as a pleasant surprise was a Christmas cake he had made, wrapped and sent to me. Very tasty, and in time for Christmas. Also the vests our friends have knitted and sent to me are great for below freezing temperatures.

In reply to a letter from my mother, 'Don't worry about the cold for me. Houses are warm and comfortable: I am well wrapped up for outside, and enjoying the variety, new and interesting things all the time. I like the people of Kitami: the Pastor and the Doctor are frequent visitors, concerned for our well-being, and my teachers' family a delight.'

1. *Cambridge University Women's Hockey team (1946). Author (captain), centre, goal keeper, Helen Roseveare on the right (see page 18)*

2. My father, Thomas Dixon Rutherford, M.A. 1863–1943

3. My mother, Elizabeth Daisy Rutherford 1890–1978

4. My brother, Thomas Graham Rutherford, about 18 before call up, 1921–1996

5. Author, b. 1925, a schoolgirl standing in the garden in front of the Anderson air raid shelter

6. Olga and Doug, with their children and spouses, with seven grandchildren

7. Mr Ega, an Ainu (aboriginal) in his traditional dress (see page 83)

8. Author and husband, centre front, with Japanese Christians at the farewell gathering at Shizunai (see page 119)

9. Doug and Olga with baby Grace in the cabin on the ship leaving Japan (see page 120)

10. Dr Roslyn Hayman with Pastor Haga and David Hayman

11. *Meal with the Shibakawa family at their retreat near Kitami (see page 187)*

12. *Doug standing beside a statue of sumo yokozuna wrestler Taihō (in his village on our tour with the Shibakawa family (see page 185)*

13. *Author, photographed at their request with two* Ainu *gentlemen in their traditional aboriginal dress and the bear (see page 185)*

14. *Mr Shibakawa in the foyer at the Sapporo Grand Hotel with Doug and author (see page 265)*

Akan National Park

Three times a year the missionaries of different societies and nationalities get together for the Hokkaido Missionary Conference, at varying locations, to exchange experiences and be spiritually refreshed. This October 1954, the plan was to meet at a hotel in Akan National Park, not far from Kitami. Mr and Mrs Street took the six-hour train ride to Kitami with Doug on the Saturday and we set off together the following Tuesday. The bus that took us there stopped at various beauty spots for us to see the view. I was reminded a little of the Lake District. At the first lake where we stopped we could dig a short distance into the sand to reach water too hot to touch. We stayed at a hotel at Kawayuu Spa (*Kawa* – river, *yuu* – hot water). From the hotel we could see the steam and burning sulphur gushing out of the hillside. We climbed up and heard the eerie sound of the effusion of steam through small holes.

The hot water is run into the bath. The bath is like a small bathing pool, water about eighteen inches deep, surrounded by semi-frosted glass. Normally in a spa men and women would bathe together but as we were a large party of foreigners and had the hotel to ourselves we arranged our own times. The sulphur fumes get quite powerful after a time bringing on headaches.

The curio shops were well stocked and nearly all had tame bears tied up outside. The bears are a feature of Akan: the people themselves carve wooden bears of varying sizes, often with a salmon in the mouth. They have a great sale and are famous all over Hokkaido.

(Once when I was leaving Japan the customs officer asked what I was carrying. I replied in Japanese, 'a bear'. He was taken aback. I had used the word for a live bear. I should have used the word for a carving. When I said 'Hokkaido bear' he glanced at the box and laughed.)

(Another friend, back in England, being invited out to dinner was asked, 'Do you carve? 'Oh, no,' he replied, thinking in terms of Hokkaido bears, rather than Sunday roast!)

Some shops have the double attraction of aboriginal ownership. The *Ainu* (pronounced Inoo) men are most easily distinguished from the Japanese by their beards: they are much more open featured and smaller, more Caucasian in appearance. The older women used to have tattooed upper lips, but this we rarely saw: they would cover the lips with their hands if they were in public.

We had already had frost in Kitami, and snow while in Kawayuu, so the leaves of the trees had obtained their autumnal beauty. The whole area is richly forested with a variety of trees including the maple, adding a deep red to the riot of colour on the mountainside.

We left Kawayuu for Lake Akan. The four-hour bus journey from Kawayuu to Lake Akan afforded us continual breathtaking views. The road had been cut out of the mountain side – the cliff rose perpendicular on one side; the other side was a sheer drop into the ravine. The back of the bus hung precariously over the drop as we turned a corner; from the back seat I was scared.

During the most dangerous-looking part of the trip, the conductress kept up a continuous stream of talk, explaining the area, interspersed with *Ainu* songs over the loud speaker. The drivers know their job; the Pastor assured us that there had never been an accident on that route. We were relieved to arrive safely and had appreciated the feast of colour and mountain scenery.

Lake Akan was spectacular. The lake is warm. In it grows an unusual plant, the marimo, green and round, six to nine inches in diameter, floating in the water at different depths according to the temperature. The Emperor has made a particular study of this protected species.

The mountain rises steeply from the lake. In the autumn it is like a painting, dark green, greens, yellows, oranges, reds covering the hillside and the whole reflected in the still waters of the lake. To this day, I regard it as the most magnificent National Park in the land, unspoilt by the Shinto shrines littering other parks, for this is very much *Ainu* territory. The *Ainu* do not worship the traditional gods of Japan. I was due to leave Kitami for Shizunai the following Tuesday: it was like a wonderful farewell celebration.

A surprise move

Towards the end of September, I received a letter from Mr Street asking me to move in the middle of October from Kitami to Shizunai on the south coast of Hokkaido. Doug and I would be there after our marriage. The girl there at present was returning to Australia at the end of October. I had to be introduced to the different people there.

This brings me to thoughts of the mission rules and my time in Kitami.

Engaged couples were required to live in the country for two years and achieve a certain language standard before marriage. No-one was to do specialised ministry, e.g. student, literature, children, etc. until he/she had experience in general church planting. Marriage to a national was not allowed. New missionaries had to be under thirty.

The rule re over thirties was relaxed for those who had been waiting, trained for China in 1951, and delayed in sailing. This was why Doug was thirty-one on arrival here, others who had applied to go to China too old were turned down. It was a reasonable rule: the younger folk can acquire the language more easily. We were expected to start language study amongst the people, not in the homelands. Occasionally a missionary came out already speaking Japanese, but not aware of the customs. The Japanese are much more forgiving of behavioural and language mistakes when we are just beginning.

The two-year rule – before marriage – on the whole is sensible. It gives the woman a chance to get the language, experience the culture and missionary life, become acclimatised before the arrival of a family. Doug and I found it hard to take, at my designation to Shizunai. We had been engaged over four years; Doug was thirty-three, I had been ready to sail with Doug but, on the grounds that no more single ladies were being accepted for Japan at the time, I was delayed six months. Now I was being asked to run a mission station on my own, but not allowed to get married because I had not been in the country for two years. Mr Street appreciated the situation, pleaded in vain with HQ to waive the remaining two months. He also felt that October would be a much better time to move than during the cold December winter. I think it highlighted a problem the Japan missionaries continued to face, that Singapore HQ in the heat of the equator was not in touch with Japanese workers battling with the snow and cold of Hokkaido.

I had been especially privileged in having a year with a cordial senior missionary, excellent help from Dr Togasa, effective language teachers, experience in a Japanese church with a friendly pastor. I loved Kitami and would have liked to continue in the neighbouring town of Bihoro. Another two months in Kitami would have been good for my language study.

The weeks before I left Kitami were blessed and encouraging. Especially encouraging was the development of the Tuesday meeting in our home: record attendance sixteen. A law court clerk received the Lord and continued in church. Mr Maekawa and Mrs Tokuno continued to serve and witness; two men contacted through tracting attended. Different church members speak each week. A chemistry teacher (his life was preserved because he was trapped in a building in the Hiroshima bombing) has been preaching in the open air with Mr Maekawa (a former charismatic pastor). The Kitami Christians had become more eager to tell others about our Lord Jesus Christ, crucified and risen for them, because of our presence and limited language. We had come a long way to reach souls for Jesus, studied to learn and speak Japanese. But they had the language: why should they not also spread the good news – this was their comment not ours.

CHAPTER 3

Early married life in Shizunai (1954–1957)

Shizunai

I REACHED SHIZUNAI IN MID OCTOBER to learn all I could in three weeks from Dorothy, before she left for home assignment in Australia. The situation was a complete contrast to what I had experienced in Kitami. There was no established church, no influential helper like Dr Togasa, no guiding friendly Pastor, no established friends. The town was smaller, less sophisticated, population 15,000, with a largely farming, timber and fishing community. It was in a valley, mountains on both sides, stretching from the sea in the south, to mountains in the north.

I was pleased to be beside the sea, but disappointed to discover that no-one went swimming after leaving school, the children swam in the river not the sea. The mile of beach was grey sand, probably due to volcanic ash. If I was determined to swim (which I wasn't), I would have to go at night or early morning.

Our missionaries first came here, with very limited language just under two years ago. One had been invalided back to the States, the other about to leave. There was no church here except for a group of zealous Seventh Day Adventists. Two Christians in the town met together regularly on Sunday evenings in their homes. Mr K had been a Christian for six years, was hard of hearing and deformed. Mr Ega, elderly, with training as a preacher, a deep love for the Lord, is an *Ainu* (one of the aboriginals of Japan). He was small, Caucasian features, typical of his race. He felt that he had compromised during the war, working in a town office. He was expected to bow to the Emperor's photograph each morning before work, but nobody noticed he had not bowed because he was so small. In 1915, an Anglican missionary had reduced the *Ainu* language to writing, preached, and many became Christians. *Ainu* communities remain in Hokkaido only, and are often a tourist attraction. The Japanese subdued them through drink and inter-marriage. There are few pure blooded *Ainu* left.

Two others became Christians: Miss Matsuura, our house-help, clear about her own salvation but feels limited in knowledge and ability. She is lonely, living with her sister, parents no longer alive, and the rest of the family scattered. I was sitting beside the stove with the rug my mother had sent me round me – a lovely Otterburn rug, green, the colours I love. Miss Matsuura, who knew my mother had sent me the rug, was saying almost under her breath, rather wistfully, 'a good mother, a good mother;' – I agree.

Miss Mizuno is our language teacher, but has recently started office work to earn enough money to go to Bible School. She is the able Sunday School teacher for the twenty children. These four are the foundation members of the recently started Sunday morning service. A high school Bible Class meets on a Saturday with only one Christian.

I was trying to take all this in, while making further preparations for our wedding on 2 December and Doug joining me here.

Roslyn had been to Tokyo and bought me a length of white silk for a wedding dress. An exceptionally capable American missionary offered to make it for me. There were good dressmakers in Shizunai but they were not accustomed to fitting a foreign figure – the Japanese ladies are so dainty and petite. I remember Mrs Adams working on the dress while I watched. Her little daughter asked, 'Why doesn't the lady help you?' Mrs Adams then realised my nervousness so I was able to sew up the hem.

From 29 November I stayed with the Streets in Sapporo – then the wedding, next chapter.

The wedding day

I stayed with the Streets in Sapporo from 29 November to finish all my preparation. Roslyn was permanently living with them. This morning I have been kept in bed for breakfast, so I am contented and not rushed. Roslyn gave me a sleeping pill last night to make sure excitement didn't keep me awake. She also advised me (among other things) not to change my hairstyle – a kind of bun at the back – as that was how Doug knew me. Everyone was overwhelmingly kind.

We were married in the Hokkaido Christian Training Centre. The rooms were decorated by Roslyn and two Japanese young ladies, who arranged flowers Japanese style. It was a cloudy day, but the temperature was 20° above the average of the previous weeks. I was wearing the beautiful silk wedding dress Mrs Adams had skilfully made. An American missionary in Sapporo was a professional florist. 'Please may I make the bouquets,' he had requested. I carried pink roses, my veil secured with roses; Mary my bridesmaid wore a light blue velvet robe with chrysanthe-mum buds in her hair. Mr Street escorted me into the 'church' while Mrs Brownlee (American Lutheran) played the wedding march on a portable harmonium. Doug, with the support of David Hayman his bestman, stood at the front waiting for me, with Bill Pape conducting the service, and fifty guests from eight nationalities. During the service a mixed quartet sang beautifully 'The Lord's my Shepherd'. Bill, a gifted and unusual preacher, spoke from 'Song of Songs' Ch 2 v 2 'Like a lily among thorns is my darling among the maidens.'

Mrs Street with Ruth Young's help had arranged a wedding breakfast in full British style. It was a delicious feast, to the horror of some American guests who were used to a drink and cake only. Speeches had to be short because we had to catch the express train to Tokyo for the consular wedding. I was especially pleased that Pastor Sasaki from Kitami spoke.

Ruth had made a three-tier wedding cake (we were able to send the top layer to my mother in England to distribute to friends and relatives). Mr Kennedy took many photographs: Mr Adams recorded the procedure.

We arrived at the station in good time to catch our train but inadvertently stood in the queue for the slow train. As our train was about to pull out, two Japanese young men, with great presence of mind, ran up to us, 'You are booked on the express, aren't you? It's about to leave.' They rushed us through the barrier. We managed to board the moving train in a rather undignified fashion, received our luggage thrown in afterwards amidst cries from the station porters, *Abunai! Abunai!* (dangerous).

Dorothy Pape and Gladys Muir met us in Tokyo where we stayed one night (3 December), half married; then they came with us to the British Consulate in Yokohama to be our witnesses at the legal wedding. The table was spread with a Union Jack, pictures of the Queen and Winston Churchill looked down on us. The consul asked if the details he had recorded were correct. Doug answered no concerning his age – not thirty-three but thirty-four because today was his birthday.

Then to the honeymoon.

The honeymoon

We had not planned in advance for a honeymoon. It had been a lean quarter financially and we had no money. But folk had been extra generous to us, so we walked from the British Consulate to the Japan Travel Bureau and booked into two hotels, one night at a Japanese style hotel, one night at a Western style. They were in the Hakone National Park area dominated by Mt Fuji. The accommodation was interesting, the food excellent, chicken and asparagus, etc.

We continued on to Karuizawa for several nights. Mr Kennedy had arranged for us to stay in Dr Eitel's summer bungalow. (It was Dr Eitel who had operated on Doug's knee.) The house was chilly, the bed hard, but the Karuizawa missionary community exceedingly kind. They invited us out for meals so that we wouldn't have to do our own cooking. Mr Kennedy presented us with sets of our wedding photos and the negatives. He had also added an introduction to the tape recording.

We left Karuizawa for a restful four day stay with American friends in the village of Odamura on the Tokyo plain. Their two little children, two and a half and three and a half gave us constant entertainment, especially in their speech (we were reminded of Harry Hemsley, 'What did he say Winnie?' BBC 1940s). The village was unlike the Hokkaido villages, bordering on subtropical climate. We were eating pickled figs picked from their own tree. We were also able to have several games of table tennis which Doug managed with little pain in his knee. From there we had the long haul through the length of Honshu to Aomori, then the four and a half hour ferry crossing to Hakodate, then the express train to the city of Tomakomai, where we had a two minute change to catch the 'puffer train' to take us slowly along the coast to Shizunai.

We were looking forward now to working for the Lord together, and we had been designated to Shizunai. It was new to Doug. I had had a few weeks there. We got off the express train at Tomakomai, alighting from the comfortable express onto a cold crowded platform. There opposite us was a little train, snorting with impatience. It looked solid enough on the outside, perhaps a little dirty and a little old. It reminded me of the drawings that Emmett used to do in *Punch,* those ridiculous looking wobbly engines which pulled equally queer passengers to their destinations. We rushed across the platform with the throng and pushed our way toward the carriage door, clambering into the already-crowded train with our cases and parcels to add to the confusion. I don't think we have ever seen an empty train in Japan, unless it was at a siding. This one was no exception.

The atmosphere in the train was friendly. Tradesmen and women were returning home, their day's work accomplished, and a feeling of well being prevailed. Women in long baggy trousers rested their legs on their large empty packs. Men were sprawled out over the seats. The aisles were littered with packs and people. We picked our way through them to two empty seats. Opposite us was a coal-burning stove with its chimney going through the window of the train. A weary traveller snored contentedly with feet outstretched on the stove. The guard edged slowly along the compartment. We were ready with our tickets. He stopped opposite us, shovel in one hand and coal scuttle in the other; he stoked up the fire. The stove door clanged shut and on he trundled to the next stove. Strange smells cut the air. Even empty packs betrayed the trade of the fishmongers. Some of the passengers were enjoying chewing dried cuttle fish. The air was thick with tobacco smoke. Suddenly we got a new rich smell and a startled growl from the gentleman with his feet on the stove – the refuelled stove was a little warmer than the comfortable footstool he had used before falling asleep! Undaunted, he produced from a large coloured handkerchief an old piece of fish and placed it on the stove. When it was sizzling hot he ate it. Hungry as we were, the combination of fried fish oil and baked woollen stocking completely robbed us of any appetite that we had.

The train continued to snake out along the coast. The sand is grey with volcanic ash, and the greyness of sea on our right reflects the greyness of the sky. On the left the country is flat right away inland: mostly grassland, the grass bending in the stiff breeze, a horse or two looking over a fence, scattered farm houses and silos. After a bit the terrain changes and we find ourselves running along a narrow ledge, the sea within a few feet of us on the right and a steep cliff on the left. Here the coastline improves and autumn reds, greens and yellows stand out vividly against the clear blue of sea and sky.

The atmosphere was getting a little thick. We were weary and our heads ached. We had stopped at innumerable small stations during the last two hours. At last we jerked to a standstill at our station. 'Shizunai! Shizunai!' bawled over the loudspeakers was music in our ears. The trades folk with their huge packs got out first, and at last we reached the door. A breath of cold air shocked us into life again.

We looked around the platform. Many hurrying figures sped on their homeward journey, but there was no one to greet us. Strange. We had sent a telegram to Miss Matsuura, the house-help, so surely she would be there. Were we dreaming? We watched the dark brown begrimed little train pull out of the station and wondered what had happened.

We struggled with the luggage to the house to be greeted by an embarrassed Miss Matsuura. Yes, she had received the telegram saying we would be on the 4 p.m. train. She had searched the time-table. Problems can arise through the mistake of one minute. To her the 3.59 p.m. arrival was the 3 p.m. train, there was no 4 p.m. train. (Not an auspicious beginning.)

We still had to look at our wedding presents and write many letters. I fear that some may have been overlooked.

Dr Togasa had been unable to get to the wedding but had composed a Japanese poem, the 5–7–5 syllable 'haiku', and drawn and framed it for us. It read: *Ro n do n no ki ri ha na re ru to ba ra ni ri n.* When the London fog clears, behold two roses. (He was delighted to receive my bouquet, brought back to Kitami by Margrit and Pastor Sasaki.)

We had received three clocks, one a cuckoo clock, another with Westminster chimes, all excellent clocks, but noisy together. As there was no clock in our headquarters in Aomori we offered it for use there. Unfortunately, the superintendent at the time thought it was a personal gift and took it back with him to Australia.

The single ladies had clubbed together to get us a beautiful hanging scroll with bamboo and birds. Their good wishes concluded with 'from the thorns' – with reference to Bill Pape's sermon.

Bill himself had given us his services free as a present. Margrit had given us a complete dinner and tea set of Noritake china – the top make in Japan.

Our teachers from Karuizawa had sent an engraved tray, typical of local craftsmanship. Pyrex from my mother proved invaluable.

Doug gave me an extremely useful present, a pressure cooker. He had seen Dorothy Pape wield one usefully and skilfully when we were on holiday together.

Our new home

Wearily we had left the station, turned up a slight slope between wooden houses, to enter our first home somewhat bewildered. We slid open the front door, stepped into the *genkan* (porch) and called out to announce our arrival. Miss Matsuura slid open the room door, greeted us on her knees, very embarrassed. She knew we would have expected her at the station but she had searched the time table in vain for the four o'clock train.

Leaving our shoes and coats in the *genkan*, we stepped up into the eight-mat room (twelve ft square) on to the plywood floor. Doug made no attempt to carry me over the threshold. He was conscious of the swaying of the floor as he walked across. I was glad the plywood had been put down, as I had seen the original floor underneath. It was of solid planks of wood with gaps between. Probably the wood had dried out after the floor was laid.

There was a wood-burning stove in the centre of the room. Doug for some reason always liked to have a full kettle boiling on the stove. He tells me the fad dates from his time in the guardroom in the army at night. There were two rooms further in, both of six tatami mats (each mat two yds × one yd), and a built-in cupboard where the bedding was stored during the day and brought out each night. There was also an alcove for decoration and a smaller cupboard meant to house the 'godshelf'. We stored our boxes covered with cloth in it, the wireless on top, and a curtain screening the whole. Our landlord desperately wanted to know what precious object was concealed. Curiosity one day got the better of him: he sneaked across the room, peeped behind the curtain and was puzzled. He had expected to see at least a cross. At eighty-one years of age, he was free from all normal social restrictions: the preschool children and the elderly were permitted to behave any way they wished.

Our first night was disastrous. We sat down to eat the meal Miss Matsuura had prepared for us before she returned home as the snow began. A storm was brewing up. We couldn't get warm no matter how many blankets we piled on top of us. The electric lights failed. In the morning we discovered the wainscoting round the top of the walls hid a gap of about six inches right the way round. We later stuffed newspapers into the gap and hung thick curtains right round.

The house was a typical Japanese dwelling, sparsely furnished. We were supplied with a desk and chair each, wicker arm chairs, wardrobe. *Zabutons* – thick square cushions – were for guests. We would all sit on the floor on these cushions, talking round a low table. There were no beds. In those days there were no washing machines, fridges, running water, vacuum cleaners, etc.

Water had to be pumped up from our well underground for all purposes. It was hard work to fill the *ofuro* (bath tub) before lighting the boiler to heat it. At first there was no drainage, the water would seep away through the soil and into the well. We noticed the change in quality of the water after the landlord arranged for drainage pipes. (We always boiled our drinking water.) Our well must have been relatively deep: on one occasion in a dry summer, neighbours were coming into our kitchen for water as their wells had dried up.

We used our wood-burning stoves for cooking also. Doug had bought me a pressure cooker as a wedding present. We used it on the stove, and it would hiss every time we walked across the plywood floor. The rest of the cooking was done over charcoal in the *shitsurin* a kind of fire-clay pot in which charcoal is placed and lit (with difficulty). A kind of tin box oven was placed on top.

The toilet was the usual primitive kind – reminiscent of the old English earth closet, let into the floor, with a lid. It was emptied from outside the house with a long ladle. Early one morning we were awakened by the noise of a lady emptying it. Our landlord had assured her that she could have the contents – fertiliser for her crops.

An old paraffin tin hung outside our front door for kitchen scraps, collected regularly by a man to feed his pigs. Anything else that could be burned went into the stove. There was no rubbish collection.

When we had unpacked and sorted our luggage we were fairly well settled, with our portable gramophone, wireless, violin and mouth organ. The sewing machine, bought cheaply from a reliable fellow missionary, had been damaged in transport. The local repairer asked us, 'Where did you get it? It has been made from old parts.' It never worked well but I did succeed in making curtains, largely for warmth. We hung a white calico curtain, with a text printed boldly in black, on the glass of the front door. The words could be read easily from the outside when the light from inside shone through.

This was our house. It took us some time to adjust to living together. Doug was the lark, I was the owl. He found it difficult at first to have regular prayer with me. I was longing for it. We had no one to advise us: we just had to find our own pattern. Doug could no longer cycle because of his painful knee: we had previously enjoyed cycling together. Sitting on the floor, cross-legged for any length of time was painful for him. We were both struggling a little with the language. But the one thing we both wanted was to see Japanese trusting the Lord, and God's name honoured.

It was already 20 December when we had arrived. Preparations for Christmas and the New Year gave us little time for further adjustment.

First fruits

Shizunai climate is similar to England's, unpredictable, but relatively mild: not as cold as Kitami, not as much snow as Kutchan. We felt warmer when the snow fell: children came to ski down the slope from the cemetery at the back of our house.

We celebrated Christmas Day with a meeting for the High School Bible Class followed by party games. Two of the girls had believed in Jesus: one with an invalid Christian mother was not likely to face opposition from her atheistic father; the other faced difficulties in her Buddhist home, where offerings were made daily on behalf of her dead mother. Another girl who had been a Christian for some time, had started a Sunday School with fifty children in her own village.

With Mr Ega, the *Ainu* believer, and three Japanese young ladies we celebrated the Christmas Service the next day. Mr Ega would always give a hearty 'Amen' and 'Hallelujah'. All was on a very informal basis. Mr Ega might well reproduce the sermon in his prayers.

Mr Katō, very hard of hearing, later joined us Sunday by Sunday. He and Mr Ega had previously met together to praise and worship God. He was very poor, living with his wife and eight children in a shack. At the birth of his eighth child we gave him a present with the strict instructions that we did not want anything in return, according to our custom. Sure enough he did bring a return present with the explanation that this was Japanese custom.

Miss Matsuura, with a clear faith, was sure to attend. Gentle, philosophical Miss Fukuhara, the second oldest teacher at twenty-six in her primary school, was regular. Girls were expected to marry and not continue working. She helped to support her father who had fallen into a hole when drunk and broken his leg. He told us that if he had to choose between heaven and no drink and hell with alcohol, he would choose hell.

Doug and I prayed over how we should try to tell people about Christ, apart from regular tract distribution. We planned first a seven-day series on the 'I am's' in John's Gospel. We had 300 bills printed and distributed them locally. This involved sliding open the front doors, calling out, 'Excuse me' and giving the invitation to the meeting in our house, the church. The response appeared to be positive – 'yes we will come.'

We were prepared to start at 7 p.m. Doug had succumbed to bronchitis, so the series was left to me. At last at 7.45, Miss Fukuhara arrived, alone. Our first outreach was not crowned with success.

Our next attempt was to arrange a Bible Study group on a Tuesday evening. This time we again had bills printed advertising the studies, indicating time and place. We followed a local procedure which was to ask the newsagent to insert the bills in the daily newspaper: when the paper was delivered, the bill was also with it, covering the whole town. Tuesday came. Would there be a better response this time? Would anyone come? We were ready, my violin tuned, about eight young men arrived. Two men turned up a little late. One, smartly dressed, intelligent, the other, despite the cold, wearing a thin pink T-shirt, plimsolls in the snow, head shaven. The two had come together, but the poorly-clad visitor stared blankly ahead apparently understanding nothing, while his well dressed pal showed a wide knowledge of scripture. Doug had chosen to explain the book of Romans – quite an undertaking with limited language. Nor was it easy to understand, let alone answer questions. We felt the lack of Japanese Christian help. Yet, as the last of the group left, we praised the Lord for those He had sent along, and asked for His blessing on the word that had been given.

So began the answer to Doug's specific prayer. He had felt the lack of knowledge and practice of spoken Japanese. Book knowledge was one thing: speaking and listening to the language required someone to talk to. He asked the Lord for opportunities to use the spoken language. His other prayer was for the conversion of someone well-known in the community. This poorly clad, apparently senseless young man, was the answer to both these prayers.

The next morning the front door slid open and there stood the one visitor of the previous evening who appeared to understand nothing. I invited him in. Doug was in the next room: his response to me was,

'What's the point? He can't take anything in?'

'Look,' I answered, 'I'm trying to cook here. Please invite him in and talk to him.'

We had little faith. He and Doug sat on *zabutons*, facing each other, Doug straining to catch his meaning. Doug has written a full account of Mr Nakagawa, the boxer. I would just add that this was the answer to Doug's prayers. The boxer, rough, a drunkard, without hope was transformed by the power of the crucified and risen Lord. After his return home from years as a boxer and gang life in the south of Japan, a friend of the family had told him he needed a religion, any religion. He first went to a Seventh Day Adventist meeting, heard the Ten Commandments and remarked 'that club was no good for me. I've already broken all the rules.' Doug said two things to him as they faced each other that first morning. Firstly he got him to read the story of the prodigal son. It fitted like a glove.

Then Doug said, 'Christ died for sinners.' But Nakagawa heard 'Christ died for criminals.' (The word for sinner and criminal is the same in Japanese.) He was a criminal and a prodigal. He was amazed that Doug should know all about him. He was indeed transformed through Christ, and the whole town knew it. He went on to become a Pastor. The townspeople knew he had changed; but instead of coming to Christ themselves they said 'We'll see if it lasts.' This was the outstanding conversion Doug had prayed for (recorded in Doug's book, *Man and Missionary*).

Not only that but Mr Nakagawa wanted to know more about his new found Lord, learned to read. to study the Bible and Christian books; he would keep on until Doug had understood his question and answered it. He was round at our house talking to Doug for four to eight hours every day. Doug had received the answer to his prayer for practice in Japanese conversation. (The full story requires a book, which I wrote about fifty years ago, but it was not published.)

January to June 1955

Mr Nakagawa's new life in Christ set the tone for the next few months. He asked to come to the Sunday School: we were surprised that he wanted to teach so soon. He didn't. He wanted to sit and learn with the children. I helped two of the teachers with the class. The children watched open-mouthed as our cuckoo clock announced the end of the lessions at 3 p.m.

Miss Fukuhara was a real friend. She brought round gramophone records of classical music, and I played some of ours also. She was especially fascinated by the finale of Gounod's *Faust*, and asked to borrow it. I had always been moved by the apparently triumphant cry, 'Perdue,' she's lost, of Mephistopheles, countered by the reply of the angels 'Sauveé,' – she's saved. Miss Fukuhara herself had already become a Christian, knowing salvation.

One day she brought us a gift of a branch of cherry blossom. She offered to arrange it for us. Cutting it here and chipping it there, she finally realised that her efforts had resulted in failure. I would never attempt to arrange flowers Japanese fashion: the Japanese regard the English arrangements as no arrangement at all. We think in terms of colour and pattern. The Japanese *ikebana* concentrates on the individual blossom. The heavy metal rose supporting the stem ensures stability. I used to be afraid that the whole would topple over. In answer to my query concerning learning flower arranging, Pastor Sasaki of Kitami, advised me, 'If it is something that really interests you, then do it. But do not take it up simply to get friendly with Japanese ladies.' I never did.

Mr and Mrs Kuga, both English teachers at the high school, were also good friends, and helpful. They belonged to the Seventh Day Adventists but had questions about the teaching. They ran a Bible class in the school. They invited Doug to help with English conversation in their classes. This resulted in getting to know the pupils, and also gave him the privilege of buying some of the produce of the school farm, especially butter and milk, of a quality not obtainable elsewhere. The butter was so good that I refused to spoil the flavour by adding marmalade. We boiled the milk: when it cooled we could scoop off the layer of cream from the top.

I made marmalade from 'summer oranges' a cross between a grapefruit and an orange, available in the winter. Neighbours asked Miss Matsuura what the foreigners did with so many oranges. We realised that we were constantly watched. We could buy liver or kidney very cheaply if we got to the butchers before it had been thrown away. Chicken and pork were plentiful, and fish. When the local fishermen had a bumper catch they had a celebration with drunkenness, and soon spent their money. If it were a poor catch, they bemoaned their poverty. The philosophy was very much, spend what you have.

Returning to the Kugas – Mrs Kuga introduced me to the procedure at the public bathhouse, as our boiler had broken down. Doug had been before, so advised me, 'Go in the afternoon when it is not crowded. You just need a small hand towel.' But this, I discovered, was from a man's point of view. The women go in the afternoon, and it is crowded; the men in the evening – and the ladies use large towels.

Mr and Mrs Kuga called on us one day with a gift of fresh spinach, with the assurance, 'it's home grown. You need not worry: the manure is from our own toilet.' Generally, 'night soil' is used to fertilise the crops. Tokyo missionaries often would eat vegetables treated by chemical fertilisers only. We would have starved had we followed that pattern. We knew we would have to use readily available worm medicine.

I hoped to visit Sapporo, take another language exam, and consult my doctor, Roslyn. Sustained language study was difficult, as visitors were frequent, and Doug and I took turns preaching on the Sunday, taking the whole week to prepare a sermon in Japanese and have it corrected. I was tired.

Roslyn confirmed that a baby was on the way, due in October. She recommended elastic stockings, vitamin and iron tablets and sleep (the latter has never been a problem). I was glad to be able to sleep while Doug had long sessions with Mr Nakagawa. I had a craving for hard-boiled eggs, easy to obtain, but sometimes with a fishy flavour according to the hen's feed. Roslyn told me later that my body was telling me exactly what it needed. I continued with the high school Bible class. There was a convenient break when end of year exams took place in March.

Plans were started to have tent meetings along the coast in June. OMF supplied the tent. Doug with David Hayman reckoned they could keep going for about fifteen to twenty minutes each. A Chinese evangelist, who spoke good Japanese, was recommended to us to help. Mr Nakagawa still had no work and was enthusiastic to reach souls in this way.

So we went ahead.

Tent campaign – a washout

Mombetsu, about one hour by train along the coast to the west, was a town of about 3,000 to 4,000 inhabitants. Lady missionaries had been living there for about two years. It was there that we decided for our first tent campaign. (We use the term tent, but marquee would give a better picture.) There was a delay in starting because of the late arrival of the tent. Doug and David left Shizunai to put it up. Mr Ega had painted a large sign on calico, 'Christian Tent Campaign' and other posters. No-one in the town could fail to know about the meetings. Mr Ega and Mr Katoo felt we should be praying daily before the campaign as well as during it and arranged for prayer daily at 6 a.m. He emphasised that we were in a battle against the devil and his host. In fact, our companions all over the world were asking God to show his power and grace at this time – Australian friends of Dave, American friends of Lucille, our English friends, as well as many Japanese colleagues. Mr Lee arrived in time for the start.

Miss Sasaki, language teacher to our Mombetsu friends Lucille and Eileen, gifted with children, told about 150–200 children most evenings, about Jesus and His love. She was an enthusiastic young Christian, who had been greatly moved by concern shown to her by a young foreign Christian writing to her when unwell herself. (She later was thrown out of her comfortable home because of refusal to marry a non-Christian, and is now wife of a pastor.)

About fifty to seventy adults attended each evening. I received an urgent message from Doug. 'Mr Lee only preaches when he feels led, and so far has not felt led. Please pray.' Through personal contact he (Mr Lee) brought a young fishmonger, Mr O to assurance of faith in Christ. Mr O spoke of his faith at the following Shizunai campaign.

The Shizunai campaign was much more turbulent. It started with a fire, ended with a flood, and David a reluctant guest with mumps.

The site was ideal, centrally placed, but we feared interference from the local cinema that had no sound proofing. The week before at 11 p.m. fire broke out destroying the cinema, but not spreading to nearby buildings, and with no loss of life. Many of the townspeople were glad. Previous protest concerning the noise had been ignored.

The relative quietness was welcome. Some Christians told us that Shizunai and the neighbouring town of Niikappu were the Sodom and Gomorrah of the area. Shizunai had unusually high alcohol consumption per head and drunkenness was rife. Doug was aware of the prevalent evil in the cafés. We asked our friends to recommend a good restaurant. 'Sorry,' they replied, after thought. 'We do not know of one.' Mr Lee constantly chose to proclaim over the loud speaker, Romans 1 vv 26–31 – 'they have become filled with every kind of wickedness, evil, greed and depravity.'

The plan was to reach the town with the Good News.

Three meetings were arranged – for High Schoolers, children and adults.

The high school meeting was small but encouraging. Two school girls, Miss Mikado, and Miss Kitajima had, since October, become Christians under Mr Kuga's teaching. They not only attended regularly but also brought friends along, came to the morning prayer meeting, gave out tracts and invitations to the evening meetings. They had increased opportunity to tell other High Schoolers about Jesus.

The children's meeting was packed each night: some parents also heard the message. Mr Nakagawa and other local Christians were a great help. We heard the children singing the hymns all over the town.

About eighty adults attended each evening; a few stayed to talk afterwards. We were aware of the hardness of the atmosphere.

Doug and Dave were finding it difficult to sustain preaching. I took a turn one evening: Mr Lee decided to leave on Saturday. Mr Ega gave the message. He spoke on the need for repentance as in the days of Noah, and the destruction that followed the flood, and on Sodom.

On Sunday night it began to rain so Doug borrowed David's mac with a promise to bring it down to the tent in the morning if it was still raining. (Dave was sleeping in the tent but wanted to catch an early train back to Sapporo.) It rained heavily during the night so Doug went down about 5.30 a.m. with the mac and David left us on the 6.30 train.

At 8 a.m. Doug resisted the temptation to go to sleep and decided to go and have a look at the tent. Water was already covering over two thirds of the tent and to a depth of about six inches at one end. Some of the bedding was floating, and the benches and organ were in the water. Two boys who had had a interest in the Gospel through the campaign arrived with a kind of wheelbarrow and brought everything to the house in three trips, leaving the tent empty.

Meanwhile, David returned: the railway was blocked about two stations away and the trains could not get through. David himself had been much moved by the scene at Seppu, water two or three feet up the houses and people standing in the rain covered with blankets, but obviously homeless. After the things had been brought back from the tent, Doug and David decided to make up lost sleep. About a quarter of an hour later, Eileen and I set off to have a look round. We could not reach the main road from the house; people were already wading through two feet of water frantically bringing bedding and furniture piece by piece into our little area. We could hardly believe the sight of the road turned into a river, especially as we were on higher ground. This state of affairs continued for several hours before the water began to subside. The river at the far side of the town had burst its banks about two miles from the sea and had flooded almost the whole town. About 95 per cent of the town must have been under water to a depth of six ft; our area of about twenty houses, and about fifty near the beach and the out-lying area only having escaped.

The majority of Japanese houses are one-storey wooden shacks, so the people could only flee to two storied houses, our area or public buildings. After the water subsided, there was a real mess to be cleared up as you could imagine. Everything was covered with mud, and the famous Japanese tatami matting ruined. Concrete buildings and two storied houses escaped a lot of the damage but needed much cleaning up. The town's loudspeaker sent out warnings about not eating raw food. The overflow of all the town's toilets also did not add to the general hygiene, and the fear now was of disease. Town officials went from house to house with pills to be taken by everybody to prevent disease.

Just in case it may be imagined that we were rushing around doing relief work I may mention that this is the most difficult thing to attempt in this land. We offered the use of the house to any who were in need but shyness and lack of desire of anyone to be under an obligation resulted in no-one taking up the offer, except for two newspaper men who did not belong to Shizunai and who left after they had found a drier hotel than the one they had had to leave previously. They brought some homeless women who stayed for about half an hour and then left.

Doug was able to give a hand in clearing mud from the houses of three of our Christian friends. The wife of one of these friends gave birth to a child the morning after they had been flooded out of their home. That particular area was still very wet; it was a kind of basin and the water does not drain away. The house where our first missionaries here used to live was completely flooded. The lady in the house behind the tent said that the water rose so rapidly that she had only about ten minutes to collect a few things and leave the house. A mother and child lost their lives here and another person was not traced, but in the neighbouring town of Niikappu, the death role was up to twenty-six, several of these being patients of a hospital Doug had visited. Some people on rooftops were rescued by helicopter but it was too late for others.

The railway was blocked in both directions so we have had David and Eileen with us. Eileen was able to get back again the next day but David was held up still because of his illness. No post came in or out, but the following day postal services were back to normal. Trains were running and fresh food available. The Japanese have amazing adaptability in getting things put straight again but Doug reckoned that there was more damage here than in Kutchan at the time of the typhoon, and that it would take longer to repair. Fortunately, since the rain stopped we had fine warm days. Japanese working for business firms were not too badly hit but those who had their own private work had little security against disaster. When the mess was cleared up there were feasts to celebrate.

After the flood

Immediately after the flood there was much clearing up to do. The weather was fine the following days, and communications opened two days later. David was a gracious, if unwilling, guest. He was in pain with mumps, yet very concerned for me, fearing that his infection might affect my unborn child. Food was initially unobtainable, so it was fortunate that Mr Lee had decided to leave earlier: he was a large man with an enormous appetite. Before he left he had given us a Bible talk on John 21 – the disciples had returned to fishing, had toiled all night and caught nothing. The risen Lord, on the shore, ordered them to throw the net on the right side of the boat. They caught 153 large fish. The message was prophetic. Despite all our efforts and prayers, no one had clearly believed. Mr Lee pointed out that there were two miracles in this story. The catch of 153 fish was obviously miraculous. But for experienced fishermen to catch nothing was also a miracle.

Some Christians reckoned that the flood was God's judgment on the town for its great wickedness and refusal to receive the message.

I took the train to Samani a few miles east where we had planned the next campaign. Don and Winnie Morris greeted me at Samani, with, 'Why has the tent not arrived?' They had not known about the flood. Samani had been enjoying clear skies and not one drop of rain had fallen. The flooding had been local.

The tent was still wet and further, David was immobilised through mumps. There was no alternative but to postpone the campaign.

I brought back to Shizunai a chicken and other food supplies. In the train, I overheard a conversation. 'Did you know about Mr Ega's words in the tent last week? He spoke about the flood. Now we have experienced it.' Another comment to me was, 'You must have a great God. Only the church and houses around it escaped the flooding.' We ourselves had not realised that we were on a slight slope.

In the days that followed, our hopes were further dashed. Children stopped coming to Sunday School. Although we were prepared and gave announcements over the loud speaker, attendance at the Sunday morning meeting dropped. Miss Matsuura, our helper, had formerly shown genuine spiritual life. She had been unable to resist the pressures of family and friends, to renounce the 'foreign religion'. The last straw came through a dream. Her deceased father appeared to her, saying he was lonely. Could she not at least bring some flowers to his shrine? She did, and lost her Christian faith.

To add insult to injury a Buddhist temple and a Shinto shrine were brought near us. The Buddhist temple was moved to a point on the hill where it overlooked our back door. Within sight of our front door construction was started on a Shinto shrine. I felt that Satan was thumbing his nose at us. I cried to God in anger against the shrine. 'Lord, whether the people believe in You or not, may they know that You are God, and may Your name be honoured.' Years later we learned that the priest had died before the completion of the building. This discredited the whole: the shrine was never finished.

We had a lovely respite in July. We rented accommodation in a chalet in Takayama (see page 55), where we had been two years previously in a farmhouse. The first night we tried to analyse our feelings: then we realised they were due to the quietness of the place. Shizunai literally means 'in the quietness', certainly a misnomer. Noise from the two cinemas and announcements from the speakers on the telegraph poles subjected us all to perpetual strain. The quietness of Takayama revealed how much strain we had been suffering. Temperatures were in the 90s (33°C). We were refreshed swimming in the cool waters of the Pacific. We had the sea almost to ourselves at first. I had been afraid of being too obviously large – six months pregnant – to appear in public, although easily out of sight once in the water. Our doctor, Roslyn, was also on holiday here. Missionaries from the Tokyo area come to escape the heat. Frequently we learned much about Japanese culture from them.

One American lady told us of the experience her little girl had in her Japanese primary school. The mother was impressed by the teaching staff (herself a qualified teacher) and their dedication. Her daughter's teacher had the girl well summed up, but was puzzled by low marks on one paper. The questions were simple. Pictures side by side showed one child doing the right thing, the other the wrong thing. The American girl had given wrong answers. So they asked her,

'Look, here is a child hanging a toothbrush on a nail, and another with the toothbrush on the floor. What would you do?'

The child replied disdainfully, 'I'd hang my toothbrush on the nail, of course.'

'Then why did you give the wrong answer on your paper?' the teacher asked.

She replied, 'I wasn't going to have the boys always doing the right thing.'

She had noticed that that was how the questions had been presented – the boys always doing the right thing, the girls the wrong, in accordance with Japanese philosophy.

We returned refreshed to Shizunai for three weeks before our annual conference of missionaries in September. There was little activity to cheer us. On 24 August Doug was looking at the scripture verses in Daily Light. He read out to me, 'Preach the word, be instant in season, out of season occupy till I come,' etc.

'You'd better go then,' I answered.

He set off alone to preach in the open air, in the evening. He walked along the high street to the noise over the loud speakers and the cinemas. How could he preach against that noise. He sent up an arrow prayer. 'Lord, if You make it quiet I'll preach.'

The noise suddenly stopped. There had been a power failure – just at that time. He pinned up a poster.

'The wages of sin is death but the free gift of God is eternal life,' and proclaimed the message to all who came around and listened. As the sun went down he returned home.

We set off for OMF Japan missionaries' conference near Aomori, the northern town of the main island. Our plan was that Doug would afterwards return to Shizunai and further tent campaigns in Samani, while, to avoid extra travelling, I would go further south with Roslyn, to the clinic she was running, for the birth of the baby. Doug would join me to bring the three of us home – and so to the story of the arrival of our first child.

The first baby

Our annual conference was held in a Japanese hotel in Aomori. It was good to meet folks we had not seen for months. I especially enjoyed hearing from Margrit a full report of Kitami. Because there were so many of us in a Japanese style hotel, most of us had to sit on the tatami mats on the floor. Everyone seemed sorry for me with this 'ordeal'. In fact, I've always been more comfortable sitting on the floor rather than on wooden benches or hard chairs.

We heard sad news of the death of a young American missionary lady through sleeping-sickness, caused by mosquitoes. There were 700 cases in the year in Tokyo. Doctors have no way of treating it. Those who do recover are often left with limited mental or physical ability.

There are signs in mid-September of autumn: the fleas are making the most of the time left to them.

Doug is returning to Shizunai after the conference. He is involved in tent campaigns. He is also trying to seal the cracks in the house before winter sets in. Miss Matsuura is impressed by his hard work. The Japanese have been surprised by the poor condition of the walls as the landlord built the house for himself.

I am not returning immediately so that I can avoid the extra travel. Our Japan Headquarters is now in Aomori city, no longer Sapporo. Mr and Mrs Street have left and Mr and Mrs Searle are now responsible for leading the OMF work in Japan. His name is somewhat unfortunate when put into Japanese. It should be *Sa-a-ru*, but if shortened to *Sa-ru*, it means monkey.

I am spending two weeks with them. I can enjoy listening to the chimes of the clock, our wedding present, which we gave to Mr Searle for our Headquarters.

I travel down to Kitakami (not to be confused with Kitami), a five-hour direct train journey south. I shall be with Dr Roslyn three weeks before the baby is due. Roslyn is glad to have me there in good time. There are four beds in the clinic. I have the choice of rooms as the first patient. Roslyn tells me it is a beautiful spot. I will be staying with Mr and Mrs Holcek, an American couple married ten years, with one adopted child. Mrs Holcek has longed even to experience pregnancy. They are missionaries of the same society as the doctor who founded the clinic. Mr Holcek speaks Japanese fluently. When he was able to read the newspaper the cordial relationship with Japanese men ceased; they realised they could no longer hide the news from him. Nor was he inferior to them in being unable to read. Two American nurses have continued to work at the clinic after the departure of the founding doctor.

In a letter to my mother, 1 October, I wrote 'I am sitting on the floor of my room overlooking the river. It is dusk, and the sky with its pink clouds, and the quietness of the river after the wind of the typhoon last night, is really peaceful. I am reminded of Rothbury. (Rothbury in Northumberland is where we often had family holidays when I was little).

'We had fresh salmon for dinner today, whether from this river or not I couldn't say. But it tasted good especially at the equivalent of 1/- (5p) each. Mr and Mrs Holcek are overwhelmingly kind to me.'

I had received lots of baby clothes, a supply of American diapers from the single girls, a carrycot on the way, a baby basket, letters and books. My Auntie Vi had sent a monetary gift for Mam to forward to me but I asked Mam to turn it into baby soap. I was quite chuffed at the gift unexpectedly from Auntie Vi because it was her excellent violin we bought when arthritis had prevented her playing. I sent the message, 'let her know that the violin is well used, even if not well played.' She had played professionally in a string quartet.

Doug came down earlier than originally planned, in order to be present at the birth.

Roslyn and I discussed many things including the promises of God to Noah in the rainbow, and our personal rainbows. Sunshine and rain or both are necessary for a rainbow. My room had a lovely outlook across fields to the river and mountains beyond.

Everything seemed quite straightforward until shortly before the birth. Roslyn was a little concerned that there was more than normal fluid protecting the baby. Five days before the birth she could no longer hear the heartbeat. I thought the weather had turned cold. She knew it hadn't. She was worried. She took an X-ray, revealing a low placenta and a dead baby. She told Doug that his unborn baby was dead. Doug was devastated. He came upstairs to tell me. I sobbed. Then Roslyn called to Doug 'Tell Olga to look out of the window.' There across the river was a complete magnificent rainbow and a secondary one below. (The sign given to me by God just then has remained with me over decades: every time I see a rainbow I am blessed and whenever there is sunshine and showers together I search for the rainbow.)

The next day Roslyn decided it was necessary to induce the baby at the clinic. I was oblivious of the danger. Roslyn knew that a placenta-praevia usually resulted in a haemorrhage. She had found that the blood group of the nurses and her own matched mine. She also drugged me quite heavily knowing that extra painkillers would not affect an already dead baby. The delivery turned out to be relatively straightforward, the enema being sufficient to start the labour. I found myself unusually witty. I knew what I was saying but couldn't stop it. Roslyn told me it was quite a help in a tense situation for doctor and nurses to be laughing. After about eleven hours a tiny 3 lb little girl arrived with, miraculously, no haemorrhage. I was told she had black curly hair and looked like Doug. Roslyn had anxiously watched, expecting bleeding at some point. She could only conclude that the placenta had come away gradually through the pregnancy, showing no bleeding, but producing a starved embryo – baby Roslyn (for we named her after the doctor) was full term yet only 3 lbs.

Roslyn was more than a doctor. She was a good friend and a deeply compassionate Christian. She said she would write to my mother, giving her full details. My mother kept the letter. I have it fifty years on. I have been deeply moved by Roslyn's love and concern, finding her letter after so many years.

God bathed me in His presence. I was filled with peace and joy in sadness. I knew that my little girl, with a nine-month life span, was happy and safe with Jesus who loves children. Visitors coming to comfort me found it was not necessary. The peace and joy of the Lord was visible to them all.

The nurses carefully and prayerfully selected tapes of hymns they hoped would be a blessing to me. They were. Especially,

> There is a place of quiet rest
> Close to the heart of God

reached to the depth of my being.

Scripture verses I had been sent came to life,

> While you were in the womb, I knew you.
> Come unto me . . . I will give you rest.

While I was basking in the Lord's presence, with doctor and nurses looking after me, Doug was having a hard time protesting to God over the loss of the baby. That night in his quiet time, reading the Bible through habit rather than desire, his portion from Isaiah Ch 49 v 20 (AV) jumped out of the page. 'The children which thou shalt have after thou hast lost the other, shall say again in your ears, "The place is too strait for me: give place to me that I may dwell".'

We worshipped the God who gave such a promise at such a time. With the loss of the baby I clung to Doug, with an irrational fear of losing him also. The promise God had given him dispelled the fear and was very precious to me.

Physically and spiritually I healed quickly. Emotionally I took longer.

Afterwards

Leaving Kitakami we travelled south to Tokyo. We planned to visit Joy and Arthur Reynolds, have a few days with Bill and Dorothy Pape, have a few nights at our 'honeymoon' hotel by Mt Fuji and to see the dentist. Roslyn had packed up the baby things for us, with instructions to keep them for the next baby. She herself had given me a present of a pair of nylon stockings. She had previously prayed about it, thinking it strange not to give baby clothes, but felt sure the Lord would have her give me something personal. She would have advised us to stay longer in Kitakami had I not been so well, and planning a holiday before returning to Shizunai.

We met again David and Timothy Reynolds whom Doug had watched anxiously during the typhoon on the boat coming to Japan while their parents were helpless with seasickness. Timothy prayed, 'Please Lord Jesus, give Aunty Olga another baby.' A fortnight later he asked his mother, Joy, 'Has the Lord Jesus given Aunty Olga another baby?' I reminded him of this when he met our thirty-eight-year-old daughter, Grace, at our Ruby Wedding Celebration.

He now had a baby brother, Martin. Joy handed Martin to me with his bottle to feed him. I was a little nervous, yet amazed at how comforting and therapeutic was nursing and feeding the little one.

Dorothy and Bill put us up in their small apartment. Bill was teaching in a Bible School, Dorothy teaching her two girls. Doug took another language exam.

We travelled back to Shizunai in stages. From the train we sent a telegram to the Brownlees in Tomakomai asking if we could stay overnight. We received the reply on the train. Mrs Brownlee had been the organist at our wedding. She had offered to come to Shinzunai to help me with my first baby.

Back in Shizunai, the folks were very sympathetic. Doug had written to Mr Ega, so the Christians knew of the loss.

Miss Fukuhara had not informed her father: He came round to see the baby. He had always been full of questions. He must have asked the price of everything in the house. Doug chuckled to himself replying, 'that was a present,' or 'this belongs to the Mission, not to us personally'.

This time he was wanting to know details about the birth. His questions would have embarrassed us if a Western man had asked them. We never knew exactly what the Japanese concluded about a stillborn baby.

Our loneliness and sense of disappointment was slowly alleviated by the steady growth of the church and the Christians.

Mr and Mrs Kuga decided to put in their weight with us. He had heard Doug preaching in the open air in August. He had not had time to stop, but the Lord had spoken to him then. 'You should be with that man.'

The high school group was meeting regularly. The two high-school girls, Miss Mikado and Miss Kitajima, were coming with a third. Numbers were increasing again at the Sunday School. There was hardly a day without a visitor.

One unexpected visitor arrived bringing a valuable gift. He was Rinya Shibakawa, my excellent language teacher from Kitami. Sliding open the front door, he stepped into the porch calling out, 'Excuse me'. (His father and brother had attended our wedding and given us the cuckoo clock that has adorned our various living rooms for fifty years.) Leaving his winter coat and shoes at the entrance, he stepped up into the house, at our invitation, expressed his sympathy for our loss, and presented us with a large mysterious parcel.

'Please open it,' he urged us. Normally one does not unwrap a present in Japan until the giver has left – but we did as he asked. There in a bamboo cage was a canary.

It proved to be an exceptionally welcome gift. Doug was frequently away; the canary was a living companion in my loneliness and required little care. It would fly around the room and was particularly fond of our coffee.

It was winter time. A wood burning iron stove warmed our room. One day, as I knelt on the floor to put a log of wood into the stove the canary jumped on to the log and into the fire. 'It's gone!' I cried out to Doug. There was a flutter of ash and out he popped barely hurt. We had to name him Shadrach after one of the three friends of Daniel who survived the fiery furnace of King Nebuchadnezzar.

We enjoyed him for several months. Summer was coming and our second child due in September. As usual we slept on futons on the tatami floor, 'cardboard' sliding doors separating us from the next room where Shadrach's cage stood on the window-sill. As usual we slept soundly through the night. One morning, to our horror we saw that Shadrach had been attacked by a rat. It had gnawed through a bar of the bamboo cage, bitten Shadrach who must have been petrified – we had heard nothing.

Shadrach lived another thirty-six hours but never recovered. Sad as we were to lose him, the warning to us was clear and fearful. Our baby arrived safely the following month. We had been alerted to the danger of letting her sleep alone in the next room. We shuddered at the thought of the possibility of our little girl being attacked by rats. We were grateful for the life and death of Shadrach.

Christmas was coming. Doug felt an urge to arrange a public lecture in the town hall on 'the significance of Christmas'. To increase interest, especially amongst High Schoolers, Doug would speak in English and Mr Kuga interpret. The church agreed to hire the hall. We advertised through bills in the newspapers and posters on the hoardings. Two days before the meeting the weather was atrocious, with high winds and driving snow, even to defacing some of the posters. There was no way to go out for street preaching. Even on the Friday morning of the meeting the storm continued. It looked disastrous. As Doug prayed, the words, 'Even the winds and waves obey Him,' came to mind. A number of us prayed together between four and five in the afternoon. The wind dropped and the snow ceased.

Doug and Mr Kuga spent time together going over the message to ensure correct interpretation. About 100 people, including twenty children braved the cold to come to the meeting. We had hoped for more but felt encouraged by the united effort of the Christians, who came and who helped in the preparations.

Lionel Thomson joined us for his Christmas holiday from language study in Aomori. While in Australia he had learned about Shizunai from Dorothy who had worked here before us.

We had a very happy Christmas – a joyful Christmas Day Service, and parties with the High Schoolers and with the Christians. It was a joy to watch some of the older Christians convulsed with laughter as they played party games such as 'Squeak Piggy Squeak'. They were impressed that they could have such enjoyment without 'sake' or other alcoholic drinks. Mr Nakagawa commented that it was the first Christmas he had not been drunk.

Next we were planning for the New Year.

January 1956

New Year is a time of festivity in Japan. By the end of the year debts are paid, borrowed goods returned, homes cleaned, and rice pounded to make rice cakes. Thousands see the New Year in by visiting the Shinto temples, clapping their hands in prayer, making a wish and placing money in the offering box. New Year postcards issued by the post office are kept for delivery in the New Year. The first of January is especially the day for the family to celebrate together, eating glutinous rice balls in red bean soup; 2 January, relatives visit one another; 3 January, friends bring their greetings, 'Congratulations on the New Year.' In most families honour is given at the household shrines to the departed ancestors.

It can be difficult for Christians who now worship only the one true God as opposed to the millions of gods of Japan. The family cannot understand the 'disrespect' shown to a deceased father.

At our Conference in Aomori in September, we had agreed to arrange a conference in the new year for Japanese Christians. The group in Sapporo, mostly university and high school students, took over the responsibility for arrangements. It ran from midday Wednesday, 4 January, to midday Saturday, 7 January. There were three speakers: Mr Takahashi, KGK (Japanese IVF) staff worker from Tokyo, our own David Hayman and Mr Noguchi, an independent pastor from Sapporo. He had been impressed some years ago in reading the life of Hudson Taylor, founder of our mission. There were about forty-five present, all having come from small groups, and they were thrilled to meet up with so many believers. No longer did they feel they were isolated nonentities, but were part of a family. I was not present at the Sapporo conference but saw the joy and radiance of the four who had gone from Shizunai – Mr Nakagawa, the boxer, and the three high school girls, Misses Mikado, Kitajima and Sugimoto. Miss Sugimoto professed to having become a Christian just before the conference. They could not keep their faith to themselves. They have since helped in tract distribution in neighbouring villages, told of their faith publicly and tried to win others for Christ.

The high school Bible class restarted through the enthusiasm of the three girls and now included members from all three years. The academic year finishes in March, and they will all be seeking employment. Miss Kitajimia will be going to Sapporo to study. She faces the most opposition from the family, not least because of her refusal to pay homage to her dead father. The family think she has gone out of her mind. Miss Sugimoto, daughter of the East Shizunai primary school headmaster is working in another town. She is able to get to church every other Sunday. She is fearless in her witness and getting friends to distribute tracts over the whole of her village.

Miss Mikado has been accepted to work in the local telephone exchange. She didn't want the job but her parents insisted she should apply. Her hearing was not good so she expected to fail the entrance test. She was asked to point in the direction of a certain sound, vaguely waved her hand in the direction and was right The verse the Lord had given her as she prayed for guidance was Proverbs 19 v 21. 'There are many devices in a man's heart: nevertheless the counsel of the Lord, that shall stand.' Later I noticed that verses in her Bible were underlined in red or blue.

'Do they have any special meaning?' I asked her.

'Yes,' she answered. 'The red ones I like: the blue ones I don't like.'

What colour have you used to underline Proverbs 19 v 21?' I asked.
'Blue,' she confessed.

The telephone exchange became a hive of Christian activity. Christians who worked there had no difficulty in having Sundays off. Pay was double on a Sunday, so others were very happy to exchange their working times. I think of Misses Mikado, Kitajima and Sugimoto as 'The Three Little Maids from School.' Now they were young working women.

We learned of the destruction of two god-shelves. Tradition dies hard. If a member of the family who does not have family responsibilities becomes a Christian, the most he can do is to refuse to worship at the shrine. Most families have a Shinto god-shelf usually on a high shelf, often in the kitchen; many families have an ornate cupboard, enshrining the recently deceased, in an inner room. Mr Nakagawa managed to persuade his father that the Shinto god-shelf was useful only as a dust collector and would be better destroyed. His father agreed, but his mother was frightened. 'The hands that destroy that god will be paralysed in the morning,' she warned. He assured her that if the image he had thrown into the stove was a god, she would be right. The family was amazed at the dust and rat holes it had harboured. In the morning, he opened the stove to find a solidified mass of molten metal that had been the outward shell of the image stuffed with sand. His mother still clings to her Buddhist family alter.

The second god-shelf belonged to the head of the house. He was a repairer of saws and had come to us through the recommendation of his older brother in another town, who had recently become a Christian. His name, 'Utsunomiya' is hard to remember, so I will call him Mr U. He came along to the Bible study in our home (the church) and in a short time understood his own sin before the one true living God, and the need of a Saviour. He described himself as having a pain, but not the kind a doctor can treat. He trusted in Christ and then wanted to follow the Lord wholly, and his wife also believed. He faced the problem of what to do with his god-shelf, not wanting to upset his wife. After discussing the matter with her they agreed it should come down. She was glad to see it go: she was spared the twenty minutes it took her every morning to prepare the rice and offer it to the ancestors, and recite the required prayers. Bibles were displayed where the altar used to stand. Visitors were amazed and asked for an explanation. His friends were opposed, not because of the 'gods' but because he refused to come out and drink with them. or to smoke. Living in the house were Mr and Mrs U, their three little boys, Mrs U's sister and a twenty-year-old apprentice. The apprentice was not opposed to the change but his father advised him to enjoy life and taste its pleasures. The father was a drunkard with five wives and twenty children. Polygamy is illegal in Japan but only the wives can take legal action.

The year 1956 turned out to be a wonderful year for us in Shizunai when we saw many people turning to Christ and telling others. This was happening all over Japan, God working in hearts. Doug has written many details in his book.

We were busy, continuing to study the language three hours a day, except when interrupted by visitors, yet often inexplicably depressed, despite a sense of progress and Japanese friends.

The new believers enthusiastically spread the Gospel, rather like the Christians in the early church in Acts. We would go out together up and down the villages along the coast, taking tracts to houses, occasionally holding impromptu meetings in the open air for children who gathered round curious to see the white foreigners. One village had been known as a Christian community but the evidence had disappeared as the children did not follow their parents' faith.

On Easter Sunday the church celebrated a sunrise service. Before breakfast we climbed a hill overlooking the town and sang hymns rejoicing in the resurrection of Christ. I found myself in Doug's arms wondering what had happened. I had fainted. It was no joke, even though it was 1 April. I had fallen flat on my face, due no doubt to an early morning climb without food, and being three months pregnant.

The Sunday Services, in the church, our eight-mat room, were regularly attended by ten or more believers. Doug usually preached, but Mr Ega, Mr Kuga and I took turns. The service was always informal, partly because of our language limitations. The Christians took the Bible readings. Mr Ega always prayed at the end, usually giving a summary of the sermon.

A new attender asked for 'the hymn to the Japanese tune'. Doug was quick on the uptake – the tune was Auld Lang Syne. When a ferry leaves a harbour this tune is always played.

Miss Sugimoto arrived one Sunday morning with six young ladies in tow, swelling the congregation to twenty. Doug had prepared a sermon on James 3, opening with 'If many of you do not become teachers it will be a good thing.' The six were all from the teacher training college.

Miss Sugimoto was the lone Christian in her village of East Shizunai, a pretty seaside village of about 500 houses, twenty minutes by train from

Shizunai. Her headmaster-father and family were mildly interested in the Gospel because of her zeal – she was uninhibited by the Japanese reluctance to teach older people, or those on a higher social level. She was gaining experience teaching Sunday School and hoping to start one in her own village.

She was especially keen to have a tent campaign there. Her friend, Miss Kanda, wanted to help. Her father was the village postmaster, interested and helpful. He arranged for us to pitch the tent in the centre of the village, next to the post office.

The two evangelists, Mr Yamaguchi and Mr Shinada, were theology students from Tokyo. Mr Yamaguchi, who already had oversight of a church in Yokohama, later became principal of a Women's Bible College, but had previously attempted suicide. He informed us that it was very hard to take one's own life and God had rescued him, transformed him, and given him joy. Mr Shinada was amongst the first fruits of OMF evangelism in Hokkaido. He had come to the missionaries, full of arguments. Eva understood something of what he said but limitation of language prevented a full reply. So, instead, she pointed him to the Bible and said, 'read this' on many occasions. He became a Christian and went off to Bible College. These two men were delighted to come and help us, having much more freedom to preach than they would have had with a Japanese pastor. They commented to us, 'Here in Hokkaido the Japanese tell you what they think. In Tokyo we tell the foreigner what we think he wants to hear.'

The weather was not too good for the campaign, but numbers of people attended and sat on the mats on the ground. I supplied the music on my violin. We stayed at night in the village hall. I remember Mr Yamaguchi's illustration of the one true living God as opposed to idols. He spoke of the hundred gold images of the sun goddess in the temple in Kyoto. In the temple 'They stood there, silently, not moving. There was no sound . . . Suddenly there was a scuffling . . . a mouse had walked across a foot.' (Only a Japanese could have given this kind of illustration. We would have been seen as mocking their culture.)

The last night of the campaign was remembered for its heavy downpour of rain. As we sat on the straw mats on the ground inside the tent talking to numbers of enquirers, the water seeped in covering the floor; finally we had to retreat and by morning the tent was down. We were able to dry it out and pack it off to Shizunai. Five adults including Mr Kanda, his daughter and Miss Sugimoto's sister professed to believe. After this, Miss

Sugimoto began her Sunday School with sixty children the first week. This eighteen-year-old young woman, just nine months a Christian, with a strong desire to let others in her village know of her Lord, and a real joy to us. She later studied in the Bible School where Mr Yamaguchi was Principal.

The church group had met together to discuss the possibility of a tent campaign in Shizunai. 'You know what happened last year,' Doug explained. 'The results were disastrous. Not only did we finish up with a flood, but also there were no clear decisions to follow Christ or to learn more.'

'True,' replied Mr Ega, 'but the responsibility for decisions to believe in Him is God's. Our responsibility is to obey Him and to preach the Good News so that every one hears. We should definitely have a campaign.'

So we planned to invite Mr Noguchi who had been one of the speakers at the Christian Conference in Sapporo. Mr and Mrs Kuga offered to provide the accommodation. The Shizunai Christians advertised the meetings, invited their friends and prayed.

Mr Noguchi first conducted a campaign in Tomikawa where our friends Lucille and Eileen were missionaries. Christians from Shizunai helped also even though they themselves had only recently believed. They were prepared to stand up in the tent and tell how they had come to trust in Jesus and what He meant to them. Mr Nakagawa, the boxer, was disappointed not to be able to join the team because he now had a full-time job, but the fact that he was in work spoke more to those in Shizunai who had known his past, demonstrating the genuineness of his changed life through Christ. Mr Okuda, the independent fishmonger from Mombetsu, took two weeks off work to help in Tomikawa and Shizunai. He had become a Christian a year before in the tent in Mombetsu. Several men and women who had had no previous contact with church or missionary listened to the message in the tent and professed to becoming Christians.

The Tomikawa campaign gave us an encouraging foretaste for Shizunai. Mr Noguchi arrived the night before we were due to start. He met with about a dozen Christians in our house for a special time of prayer. After a short message, the group began to pray for souls, for God's mighty working in the hearts of the needy people of Shizunai. One girl from the telephone exchange, broke down in desperation, saying that she knew in her head the facts of the Gospel, that Christ had died for her sins and had risen again, but she wanted these truths to be real in her heart. Mr Ega said quietly to Doug, 'Go and lay your hands on her'. Hesitatingly, Doug got up, laid his hand on her head, and recited John 3:16, the one verse of the Bible he knew with confidence in Japanese. Miss Oohara relaxed and burst out full of joy, praising the Lord.

I heard the voices of praise and prayer from the adjoining room to where I had retreated on account of an itchy rash on my legs. An American army doctor had diagnosed it as 'nerval dermatitis' due to my anxiety through the loss of the first baby showing in my bodily reaction in my second pregnancy, even though I was not conscious of feeling anxious. Wet cloths round my legs relieved the discomfort.

When I played my violin for the songs in the tent I sat at the front with a small screen in front of my legs and wet cloths round them. Doug did his best to conduct the singing. The hymns were written in black letters on white calico and hung at the front of the tent.

After the preliminary singing, Doug handed over to Mr Noguchi. He preached simply, clearly and powerfully, finally giving an invitation to any who wanted to know more, or who wanted to become Christians, to remain behind. Dotted across the tent we saw the Christians, with open Bibles, sitting on the benches beside those who wished to know more, explaining the Christian message to seekers. We returned home about 10 p.m., tired and hungry, cooked a snack of bacon and egg, thanking God for His presence with us, before collapsing into bed. (When Elijah was exhausted, God gave him rest and food, as recorded in I Kings Ch. 19 v 8, 9. We felt we were following this example!) By the end of the week, when forty-seven people had professed to becoming Christians, we were full of joy.

Autumn 1956

Lionel Thomson had joined us, from language study in Aomori, from the beginning of the tent campaign in Shizunai. He was a large Australian, with a large heart and a large appetite. We found a room for him in the home of the truck driver who lived opposite us but he had his meals with us. I reckoned that if there was nothing left over at the end of the meal I had not cooked enough. Lionel had been in the language school set up where any food left over needed to be eaten up. I kept cooking more and more; Lionel kept eating more and more, until we discovered what was happening. Then I reduced the amount of rice cooked. He had worked on a farm in Australia where meat was in abundance, while I had been in England with continued rationing. The OMF allowance for food was

$1/person/day, flexible, but we tried to budget accordingly. How could I cater for the large, though reasonable appetite of this energetic young man? The answer came in the form of half a sheep. Mrs U called one day to tell me that a friend of her husband regularly went into the mountains and returned with half a sheep. 'Could I use it?' She explained that they did not like the smell or taste of hot mutton. We arranged for me to cook her share also in my pressure cooker. She was delighted with the cold meat and I regularly received my portion.

Lionel was a great asset. He struggled with language study and failed the prescribed course. He received with indignation and strong disagreement the suggestion that he would be sent back to Australia if the language results did not improve. He had been called by God to bring the message of eternal life in Christ to the Japanese people. Nothing would divert him from this path. We observed that he had the gift of an evangelist: with the minimum of language he was able to lead a Japanese to trust in Christ and have a changed life.

He led the singing for the Sunday service with such enthusiasm that the shaking of the plywood floor caused the music on my violin stand to jump around, sometimes off the stand.

All our meetings built up – the Sunday school, High School Bible class, midweek meeting, the outreach to surrounding villages, with the Christians growing in their knowledge of God. The telephone exchange buzzed with spiritual activity. Several from the exchange came regularly to the Sunday services: they had no difficulty in exchanging duties with others, as pay was double on the Sunday. Miss Mikado showed her love and concern for the children as she ably taught in the Sunday School longing that they would received Jesus into their hearts. I remember her young brother who normally had no problem reciting the memory verses, being stuck with 'I am the good shepherd. The good shepherd lays down his life for the sheep.' He would say, 'I am the good shepherd. The good shepherd died for my sins.' He had understood not only the words, but also the spiritual meaning.

One of our favourite choruses for the children was *Makoto no kamisama* – the true God. The six verses with repetition were easy to remember and taught many basic truths. Translated –

The true God – only one,
  Everyone quickly let us believe.
The true God – the creator

Everyone quickly let us believe
  – the living God
  – the righteous God
  – the Saviour
  – the God of love.

The children were brought up with the concept of many gods, of idols of stone, etc. They were able to understand 'God' more easily than their parents. One mother approached me saying, 'my boy has been singing there is only one true God. But there are thousands aren't there?' Most parents were quite happy for the children to come and hear about Jesus. Some told us how pleased they were at the improved behaviour of their children. Conflict could arise when a son or daughter asked to be baptized, or in a refusal to worship the deceased family member.

My next venture was a journey to Aomori city, to stay with Mr and Mrs Searle until the birth of our next baby.

The births of two babies

Roslyn was still my doctor, but now living in Aomori with our missionary midwife, Daphne, another Australian. I was to live with Mr and Mrs Searle at our mission Japan HQ until the birth of the baby. The garden shed had been set up as a clinic. Mr Searle had an older daughter, but had lost his first wife in China. He and Ruth had a seven-year-old boy, and she was expecting again after several miscarriages. We wondered which baby would arrive first.

I had spent early days in Karuizawa with Ruth catering and was aware of her small appetite. How was I going to manage with my increased appetite in the final days of pregnancy? I bought a packet of processed cheese; then in my evening Bible reading was the story of the feeding of the 5,000. God spoke to me, 'If I can feed 5,000, don't you think I can feed you?'

Because Ruth's ankles began to swell, Dr Roslyn prescribed bed rest. The housekeeping responsibilities fell to Mr Searle's secretary and myself. The meals were adequate; God has a variety of means to provide for our needs!

My baby, Grace, arrived safely in the night of 29 September. I had been too tense to relax; Doug came across from the house to see us. He was thrilled but overwhelmed at the sight of his healthy little daughter. I had to ask Roslyn for a cup of tea for him.

Ruth went into labour the following day. The cord was round the baby's neck. Ruth, herself a nurse, was aware of the seriousness of the situation. Roslyn fought for the life of that little one, having an oxygen supply delivered on time. Daphne commented that she had never seen a doctor fight to determinedly to save a life. After six hours the little boy returned to his maker. Ruth declared 'The Lord has given, the Lord has taken away. Blessed be the name of the Lord' (Job 1v21). Then she said 'I am so glad that this has happened to me and not to Olga'.

I marvelled – and still do – that a mother of a new born baby watching her child die could have such concern for me because I had lost my first baby the previous year.

Roslyn was sad and disappointed, but her reactions were positive. She observed, 'In Australia, in the maternity ward if a mother loses a baby we can do nothing but put a screen round her and let her howl, but with Ruth's and Olga's losses I can see the presence and comfort of the Lord Jesus himself. It confirms my faith.'

Far from having any jealousy, Mr Searle looked upon Grace with an affection as though she were his own child.

For Ruth's sake, Roslyn and Daphne moved me with Grace into their house. There they gave me postnatal care, much advice and help, assisted me in nursing Grace and looked after her through the night so that I would not be disturbed, and Grace would not need to be fed in the night. They commented, 'If we have two weeks of disturbed nights, it will save you two years of disturbed nights.'

Doug was helping with an English Bible study group of ladies meeting in the house. I was lying relaxed in one room and could hear Doug clearly through the cardboard doors. He solemnly pronounced, 'Man made God in his own image. I repeat, Man made God in his own image.' Then he interpreted it into Japanese and got it right this time.

We set off with Grace to return to Shizunai. First the four-and-a-half hour ferry crossing took us to Hakodate, then the express train to Tomakomai, and then the crowded slow train along the coast to Shizunai. On the train the white foreign baby interested the other passengers. The usual questions, even from men, were, 'Are you breast-feeding her?' 'Have you enough milk?' In time I got used to these questions but at first I was shocked.

The Japanese knew that American babies were usually bottle-fed. I appeared to be American, hence the question. Concern that the mother had sufficient milk to feed the baby was usual: and the baby crying usually resulted in the comment, 'She's hungry.' I had to be sure to use the right word for milk. The word I would normally use for milk meant cow's milk. There was no embarrassment nursing Grace on the train.

And so back home . . .

Final days

Back home in Shizunai, the three of us received a welcome, with Grace the centre of attention. Lionel was there to tell us what had been happening during our absence. The number of meetings had doubled, a small church committee had been formed, there was renewed power in the meetings and a sense of expectancy amongst the Christians. Weekly meetings included Sunday School for the children, middle and high school Bible classes, a church Bible study and prayer meeting, early morning prayer meeting, a cottage meeting in the town of Atsuga thirty minutes away by train, Sunday school and evening meeting in East Shizunai, fifteen minutes away and Doug had meetings in a mountain village of about 3,000, three hours by bus from the coast.

My life style changed through having to look after a baby. She was a lovely little girl and rarely woke up at night, thanks to the care and advice I had received. I found myself prone to worry over the smallest thing that seemed to go wrong. One visit back to Aomori to discover the cause of her diarrhoea showed that she was taking twice as much milk as she needed. Miss Matsuura would carry her on her back while we had our meals. This was a comfortable and soothing experience for Grace.

In the winter I would go out Japanese style with her strapped securely to my back with a coat over us both. Once, as I walked along the street like this, I saw a cyclist approaching and was about to greet him when he went straight past me without recognition – it was my own husband! Bystanders smiled at the situation.

We planned a Christmas outreach, again hiring the town hall. The Christians took tracts and invitations to every home in the district. The Sunday school, middle school, high school and Christians practised carols; open air advertisements with carol singing from place to place made known the meeting and the spirit of Christmas.

We arrived at the hall in good time. I had wondered how I was going to manage to play my violin for the singing and to look after Grace. Miss

Matsuura offered to take her on her back. We were especially pleased because it brought Miss Matsuura to the meeting for the first time for a year and a half. The choir made an imposing picture on the stage, but it was the children who made a significant contribution. Twelve of them displayed and announced a verse of scripture, each related to Christmas, six from the Old Testament and six from the New. These verses spoke to one gentleman whom I call Katoo, the hunter. He had been out hunting in the hills round Shizunai, old soldier that he was, with his gun cocked ready to shoot, as he scrambled up a hill. The trigger caught in a twig, wounding his own leg. In hospital in Shizunai, he contemplated what would have happened had the bullet gone through his heart, and what of the afterlife? Buddhism and Shintoism would have been no help. He had previously had contact with Roman Catholics and read the classical Japanese New Testament several times without understanding. He came from the hospital on crutches to our Christmas meeting, listened and observed the quotations from the Old Testament. 'Perhaps,' he thought, 'I need the OT also.'

He bought a Bible from us. Inside was a card addressed to us for anyone wanting further information. He posted it. Christians visited him and he broke down in tears when Mr Kuga told him the story of the Cross. He returned to his village, a lone witness for the Lord, expecting opposition on pulling down his god-shelves but hoping to lead his wife and three children to the Lord. Later, Doug and Lionel visited his village.

In the New Year, fifteen of us joined the seventy to eighty believers from different parts of Hokkaido for the conference in Sapporo. Of the four from Shizunai who had not believed, three came to know the Lord and His joy; the fourth returned hardened in heart. Mr Noguchi was again one of the main speakers.

After the Conference, Doug and I with Grace, paid a brief visit to Kitami. I was thrilled to meet Mr Tamiya, in hospital still, but radiant (see Kitami, p. 73). We stayed at the Station Hotel. The staff almost ignored us as they carried off the three-month old baby, treated her like a princess and made sure that she had the best futon available. They expected that Doug and I would appreciate privacy in the *ofuro* (bath) and led us along the corridors to the hotel bathroom. We left our clothes in the baskets in the chilly changing room, entered the bathroom through the sliding doors and enjoyed soaking up to the neck uninterrupted in the hot water. To our horror, when we tried to get back to the changing room, we found ourselves trapped in the bathroom, unable to open the doors.

Steam had condensed against the glass doors, the water had run down into the runnels and frozen there, sealing the doors. There seemed to be no-one to help. I dived back into the bath while Doug managed to attract the attention of one of the hotel staff who chiselled the ice out of the runnels.

I was overjoyed to meet up with so many of my former friends in Kitami (including Pastor Sasaki who was due for transfer from the Kitami church) although the visit was so brief.

Back in Shizunai, in preparation for furlough I bought a kimono with the help of the ladies – choice of colour, how to wear it, underskirt, matching lining, etc., how to tie the obi, etc. While I was out on this important shopping expedition, Doug realised that Grace would be needing a bath and that he should learn how to bath her. He made the preparations, hot water in the tub on the desk, towels, etc., ready. As he lifted her into the tub he heard a faint tittering. Looking round he realised that he was in a goldfish bowl, the neighbouring ladies having gathered outside the windows of the room to observe this ceremony.

Our remaining months in Shizunai were happy and busy. We were due for furlough in April. Seventy Christians came to our house to say goodbye to us in our farewell meeting. We all posed for a photograph. Doug and I were asked to come to the front – and as we did the floor caved in. Lionel was to take over from us so simply said that the repair of the floor would be his first job in charge of the church.

Interlude

Voyage to England

WE HAD BEEN GRANTED FURLOUGH from April 1957, expecting to travel from Yokohama on the P&O liner, *Chusan*, on which Doug had first sailed to Japan. To our delight Margrit was travelling with us. She and I reminisced over the precious memories of our time together in Kitami. Arrangements had to be altered because of war over the Suez Canal, resulting in routes via the Cape of Good Hope. We had a frantic rush to get packed and leave Shizunai earlier than anticipated. We had to catch a ship from Yokohama to Hong Kong in order to tranship to the *Chusan*, which was making up time by docking in Hong Kong. From Yokohama our ship called in at Kyoto and Kobe so, having left the shores of Japan, we came back to a few hours in Kyoto: seeing the city of idols, including the motionless hundred goddesses of mercy that Mr Yamaguchi had preached about in East Shizunai. At Kobe we visited friends at the JEB (Japan Evangelistic Band) headquarters.

We had a delightful three weeks in Hong Kong, hearing the noise of the mahjong tiles as men played in the evening, enjoying Chinese food, and seeing some of the delights of the colony – the beautiful harbour, vendors of oil-paintings on Nathan Road – and also the problems of water shortage. The supply was available over limited hours. We also began the process of returning to British culture instead of Japanese, learning that 'yes' meant 'I'll do as you ask' and not, 'I have understood what you ask.' And that 'aren't you going?' did not require the answer 'yes, I'm not going.'

We boarded the ship in relatively familiar surroundings. Our cabin steward was the same Goanese as I had had on the *Corfu*. The nursery stewardess came from Tyneside, my home; also, she was particularly helpful, bringing suitable baby food for Grace, who until then had breast milk only, at seven months. The stewardess reckoned that for her sake and mine she needed extra. I had been reluctant to expose her to anything requiring water on the ship. We stupidly washed out the nappies and hung them round the cabin instead of taking advantage of the ship's laundry service.

120

Margrit and Grace got on well. Margrit gave her the Swiss diminutive 'Gracely' which I liked and have used it since. Some passengers thought that Margrit was 'Miss Abrahams', not attributing the title to a seven-month old.

The ship was crowded, especially with servicemen returning from Malaya. One of them I recognised as a school friend and fellow-member of the cricket team with Graham (my brother). I recalled the sadness in his family when his younger brother, disabled from polio but a strong swimmer who enjoyed the sea, dived off the raft used by the bathers in Whitley Bay and was drowned. We never knew whether he had hit his head against the bottom of the raft or had simply been swept away by an underwater current.

We still enjoyed visiting friends and fellow missionaries at every port. Having our names called out over the loud speaker each time made us feel important.

One visit to Colombo was sad. Rachel welcomed us, but explained that her husband's family had rejected her, partly because she had brought no wealth into the family and partly because she was not compliant enough to sit and do nothing while her mother-in-law took charge of everything, including the children. She was now separated from her husband, living in the gate house while he was in the main house. Although she officially had custody of the children, they were free to go from one house to the other and it was the father who had the means to give them presents. Rachel had been a French teacher but French was no longer required in Ceylon. She was finally given custody of the children provided she did not leave the country. Simply she had married, not one person, but into a culture different from her own.

The voyage round the Cape was long: faster than usual, with no leisurely docking in ports. We were welcomed at our South African Mission headquarters. Up the east coast of Africa we stopped at Lagos, the only port on the whole journey where we knew nobody.

And so to Tilbury and England.

A year in England, 1957

Every five years we were expected to return to Britain for a year, for readjustment to life in England, physical and spiritual refreshment, to meet up with family and friends, and particularly to report back to those who had helped us through their prayers on all God had been doing through us, and life in Japan.

When we went to Japan we expected to take time to adjust to life in a new culture. We had not envisaged the greater difficulty of readjusting to British society. Society had changed and we had changed in five years. The Japanese have a story of Urajima Taroo, a fisherman lured by the Princess of the Ocean to live in her luxurious underwater palace. After years of delight he returned to his own village to find it completely changed and he knew no-one. I wondered if this tale was for the comfort of families who had lost husbands or sons at sea. The occupation of the many Japanese fishermen is hazardous. Our own story of Rip van Winkle is similar, and in a small measure appropriate to our own experience.

Whatever, we were delighted to meet Doug's family and especially his brother, Ron, and his wife. We spent some time at our London headquarters at Newington Green before being launched into a deputation programme. For the year we lived with Doug's parents in Tottenham or my mother in Earsdon.

We had the use of two bedrooms in Doug's home – the one Doug and his two brothers had occupied as youngsters, with the gas bracket still on the wall, and a second room with Grace's cot in it. I detected a smell of gas in her room – no-one else had. The gas company tested everything, pulled up the floor boards downstairs and found no source of a leak. At last they discovered the source several doors down the terrace. The gas had travelled under the houses as far as our corner house and then found its way up into her room.

My mother's house was in the north of England, where coal fires were never shut down for the summer, but lit whenever the weather turned cold. In August the fire burned brightly, yellow flames shooting up and red coals underneath. Grace was mesmerised. She was seeing an open fire for the first time, with its fascinating attractiveness.

Language was a problem, not that we had forgotten English, but Japanese words kept asserting themselves and we had to interpret them. 'Yes' sometimes meaning 'No' or 'I've heard what you said.' 'Oisii' meaning yummy. *Yooji ga aru* (I have something to do) an excuse for absence without giving the reason. *Shikataga nai* a fatalistic, it can't be helped, and *tadaima* I'm back with the response. *Okaerinasai* welcome home, regularly on returning home. Some words just had no English equivalent.

Both families were eager to share news. This turned out to be a sad catalogue of deaths of friends and relatives.

Doug decided we needed our own transport for all the travelling we would be doing. He bought a 1936 Morris 8. The journey up the A1 through all the towns on the way, sometimes facing traffic jams, took time. There were no motorways in 1957 but we were young.

Because we were the first back from the 'new fields' (the countries OMF had gone to after expulsion from China) we were very much in demand to speak at conferences, in churches and small prayer groups. We were both involved in speaking, reflecting how OMF regarded both husband and wife equally as missionaries. On one occasion we had both been scheduled to speak when the conference centre told the OMF organisers that children were not admitted. My mother volunteered to look after Grace. She was in fact looking forward to it but, unfortunately, got phlebitis and had to stay in bed. Doug looked after her and Grace, as I was required at the conference.

I had two interesting meetings in my home town. My mother was an active member of the Women's Institute. They were eager to hear from me. I gave a demonstration of the kimono to a packed audience of 100 ladies. They were amazed to watch me put on layer after layer – fourteen pieces in all – including the long obi (sash) which went round me twice, tied at the back in a butterfly bow. (My mother had nobly offered to tie it. She was having trouble, unbeknown to me, because she had cut her finger and didn't want to risk blood on the sash). The combination of colours, matching to the Japanese, clashing to the English, purples and pinks, surprised the ladies.

My father had worked for the W.E.A. (Worker's Educational Association) and my mother continued as secretary of the local branch. She met a teacher from Bedlinton Grammar School who had known me on the staff. She approached my mother at a W.E.A. rally.

'Mrs Rutherford,' she said, 'I hear that Olga is home from Japan. Do you think she would be willing to give us a term's lectures on Japan? We have been offered new premises but have no course or tutor.'

I was delighted with this opportunity. W.E.A. lectures require one hour of lecture, followed by one hour of discussion. Language, written and spoken, customs, the kimono, Shinto and ancestor worship, gave ample scope for in-depth presentation.

Gordon Welsh, a large jovial man, had been a teacher at the school for missionary children in China. The Japanese advanced through China, and interned the whole school with Mr Welsh and family. At the end of the war he returned to England and became deputation secretary for the CIM in Newington Green. He organised our deputation programme efficiently.

How can I describe our year:

A time in Bristol, where Grace at last enjoyed drinking milk – full cream, fresh. It was there she took her first steps.

In Wolverhampton, the Vicar being a former CIM missionary. They did their best to warm up the bed in the cold vicarage for Grace: car windows were frozen up, and a future OMF missionary drove us to the station. In between we watched Wolves football team, with interjections from bystanders. 'Sorry, vicar', as they felt their language had been inappropriate.

Hearing about the other 'new fields' from friends who had trained together with us in Newington Green. Isaac and Eileen from Thailand, Jean from the Akha tribe of North Thailand, Margaret from Malaysia, June from Hong Kong, Margaret from Taiwan, Leah from Indonesia.

The final meeting with the Christian Union of my old College, Girton, Cambridge, when we stayed with Denis and June Lane at his vicarage. Doug helped June in her women's meeting. Another friendship forged.

And packing up all our belongings to return to Japan on a restful voyage.

Voyage back to Japan, 1958

Once more we said goodbye to friends and family and boarded the familiar RMS *Chusan*. Grace was excited when we came on board, and soon was enjoying the nursery with lots of toys and other children to play with. The ship's doctor was formerly a Harley Street gynaecologist, so I could have expert advice as my baby was due in June after our arrival in Japan. Our cabin was spacious: the first couple of days were a little worrying in that our cabin luggage, packed with clothes for the voyage, was missing. Other passengers had the same problem so a search was made and ours turned up in someone else's cabin.

The ports of call were similar to those on our first voyage. We had a short stop in Gibraltar this time and watched a hockey match played on a solid earth, grassless pitch.

Port Said seemed to be quieter, sadder than on our previous visit. There were few tradespeople with little boats, and no-one diving for coins. We were delayed at Port Said because the last northern bound boat in the convoy had grounded in the canal. We went through Suez at night.

Graham was in Beirut and sent a message that he would not be able to come to the boat. He commented that Beirut was a wonderful place to live, just as Baghdad had been a bad one.

Before we reached Bombay an announcement over the loud speaker informed us that we were passing SS *Corfu*. It was a perfect day, the Indian Ocean like a lake, the sun shining: it was quite a majestic sight as the ships passed. The *Corfu* passengers had also been informed so there was much waving from ship to ship. We saw the salute of the dipping of the flag. (The *Chusan* was the flagship of the P&O fleet. The captain, now Commodore, had been the longest in the service. The crew were really proud of him and thought highly of this captain.) As the ships passed they sounded their hooters. I was surprised at the expression produced by ships' hooters, obviously a sisterly greeting.

Bombay was hot, and we had to be vaccinated again because the certificates had not been correctly stamped. This could result in delays in entering Japan. We stayed on the boat, admiring the attractive view of the harbour, and watching the porpoises playing around the boat. When they were chasing fish, the lazy revolutions suddenly changed to a sudden dart for some distance, the gulls following trying to snatch the same fish.

At Bombay we received a note from our friend, Ray, in Colombo. She was looking forward to our visit and her daughter Ayoma wanted to see Grace again. Ray herself was teaching in the mornings so we would have to make our own way to her flat.

On arrival in Colombo we hired a taxi. The driver tried to get Doug to collaborate with him in getting customers for his car tours. His attitude changed to respect when he saw the name 'Canekeratne' for our destination. Nihal, Ray's husband, must have been of some importance in the city.

Grace enjoyed playing with Ayoma and her toys, but Ayoma was a little young to understand what was happening. Ray kept saying, 'Grace isn't a doll.' Perhaps her colouring was strange to Ayoma. Ray had arranged with a friend, a 'Proctor', an educated woman connected with the law courts, to put a car and chauffeur at our disposal. In the afternoon we visited the zoo, of which the local people are justifiably proud. The cages are in a natural setting. Huge trees with brilliant coloured flowers are a feature of the island. The birds would be well camouflaged amongst them with bright reds, blues, yellows, greens. One of the heron family obligingly spread its wings for us, at least a two yard wing span. In all this Grace liked the ducks best.

There were five performing elephants on show. They walked around with the trunk of one entwined in the tail of the next, the leading elephant playing a mouth organ.

Ray's friend took us out in the evening to a delicious Chinese meal. Grace slept.

And back on board, it had been a memorable visit to a beautiful island.

In Singapore we were met off the boat and had a pleasant three days at our OMF International Headquarters. I was glad of the change of food and cool rooms but we did need mosquito nets. Grace was badly bitten. A ship can get very hot when anchored in harbour.

I received an unexpected message. 'Audrey Grobecker is looking forward to seeing you.' I had not known she was in Singapore. We had been fellow students in Cambridge, first at Girton (my atheist days) then at Cambridge Training College (teacher training, in my early Christian days). Audrey and Geoff, whom she married, were leaders in the Colleges' Christian Union. Now Geoff was Army Chaplain living very near our HQ.

Mike and Valerie Griffiths, with one-month old baby John, had been delayed in leaving Singapore with the rest of their group. They were new workers for Japan and joined us on the *Chusan*. They read books while playing Scrabble. The slowness of their game almost put us off ever playing.

So to a short time on shore again in Hong Kong and on to Yokohama, where we were met by Miss Sugimoto, now a Bible School student, and the Principal of the Bible School who had helped us in Shizunai.

We travelled up to Aomori, a fourteen-hour train journey from Tokyo. We were to stay there until our baby was born. We shared a house with Joy and Arthur Reynolds and their children, Christine (four) and Martin (two). There were four American boys next door, so Grace had plenty of playmates. Joy looked after us very well, giving me a restful time. We also had an excellent language teacher.

We were a little distance from our doctor, Dr Monica. The ship's doctor had given me a letter to pass on to her. When she read it (before she knew his qualifications), she said, 'This man seems to know something about the subject.' He was a Harley Street gynaecologist.

It was peaceful and quiet except for the continuous chatter of frogs from dusk onwards, and the barking of dogs in celebration of the full moon. The chatter of the frogs was a strange low-pitched sound causing no great disturbance. The dogs could not be ignored.

The Reynolds moved to Sapporo before we moved over to the medical house. This had been the home of American Southern Baptist missionaries, rented to OMF in the absence of the Southern Baptists. It was very comfortable.

Doug was busy clearing up the house where we had been staying, paying a quick visit to Shizunai to collect things we had left there, and searching with Mr Street for four days for accommodation in Hakodate.

Michael arrived safely, 11.30 p.m. on 6 June. Grace 'held' him and thought it wonderful. She was indignant if he cried and no-one took any notice.

Doug took her for a tour of the Aomori department store and especially the toy section. She was fascinated and chose an amphibious boat, a little car and an inflatable (toy) elephant. Japanese toys are cheap and novel.

We had been asked to go to Hakodate to start new OMF work in the city. So our next journey, when I was strong enough was, the four-hour ferry crossing from Aomori to Hakodate.

CHAPTER 4

A lovely city – but a struggle (1958–1963)

Hakodate city

I LOVED HAKODATE – THE CLIMATE, the scenery, fresh fish and vegetables, the mountain to the east, a view of the volcano to the west, steeped in history, a beautiful harbour and sea all around.

The mountain in the east is on a peninsular linked to the mainland by a narrow strip of land. The view from the top of the mountain is magnificent, from the volcanic peak in the north-west to the harbour dotted with boats, comparable with Hong Kong harbour. Small fishing boats go out for squid or salmon. Lights fitted with hooks attract the squid, so at night the sea is dotted with the lights from these innumerable boats.

Hakodate used to be an important port. It was linked to the main island of Japan by ferry to Aomori, and was one of the first ports opened to foreign trade in 1858. Fishing and farming as well as shipping are amongst its industries. The city is known for its Trappist Convent, lilies of the valley, the spectacular building of the Russian Orthodox Church, all tourist attractions.

Siberian winds crossing the ocean deposit heavy snow in Aomori, but there are no mountains in the path of the winds in Hakodate, so there is little snow. Frozen streets are rare, the summer is pleasantly warm. It remains my favourite city in all Japan.

We had been asked by the Japan committee to open up OMF work in Hakodate. We have always tended to go along with what we were asked to do. At that time, Mr Street felt it generally unwise for anyone to return to his first station, where he had probably made mistakes. With hindsight we think we should possibly have returned to Shizunai, as the Japanese welcome back old friends.

Mr Street and Doug had spent four days searching for suitable accommodation. Finally, they found a large house at the foot of the mountain, originally designed by the owner for presenting 'Noh' plays.

It was L-shaped, one section with two × twelve mat tatami rooms that could be made into one, a wide veranda a four and a half mat wooden floor

128

room, a large kitchen and bathroom; the other section comprised three rooms with independent front door. There were large gardens back and front.

Early beginnings

Michael was just a baby and Grace twenty-one months old when we moved in, knowing no-one. It was summer time, but with two children in nappies we sometimes had to iron them dry – the nappies not the children! I was unable to get out to buy necessary kitchen equipment until David and Dorothy Highwood visited us during their holidays. Most of my cooking had been frying meat from the local butcher: I think the excess of fat caused stomach problems for Doug, requiring help from the local doctor.

With school holidays, the neighbourhood children came round, curious to see the foreigners, especially toddler Grace.

The constant chorus 'Grace chan, Grace chan' became so irritating that we decided to invite the children in and start a Sunday school. Most were from primary school (ages six to eleven) but there were four middle school girls, a year older than the rest. After two years I asked these girls to become Sunday school teachers. I taught them the lesson on Friday night. On Sunday I divided the children into two groups, each to be taught by the older girls.

I also had a middle and high school English Bible class successfully using the English-Japanese New Testament.

Mike and Valerie Griffiths join us

Mike and Valerie Griffiths joined us after their initial period of language study. Their son, John, was slightly older than Michael. We enjoyed their company. The local Japanese folk observed us, noting that we did not have much variety of clothing. There is no word in Japanese meaning simply 'sister', so they referred to Valerie as my older sister. She is seven years my junior but in Japanese society more status is given to the older sister.

On one occasion, Valerie had ordered strawberries (cheap, delicious in season) from the local greengrocer. The following day I called in at the greengrocer's.

'How were the strawberries?' he asked me.

'Excellent, as far as I know,' I replied 'but they were for Mrs Griffiths, not me.' He apologised for mistaking us. But the next day, when I called in he was full of apologies. 'I am so sorry,' he said, 'the other day I mistook you for Mrs Abrahams!' I didn't divulge my identity.

Our first efforts of evangelism were unsuccessful. Mr Shinada, who had helped us in Shizunai had again come from Bible School to support us. There was a suitable shop front available in what seemed to be a busy area of the town. We arranged to borrow it but one after another of possible helpers became ill, and it turned out to be an area busy by day but deserted by night when we planned our meetings.

The Presbyterian Church

I had always wanted to work with a local church if possible. The nearest church to where we were living was Presbyterian and I had been associated in Kitami, before marriage, with the Presbyterian church there. The Pastor of the Hakodate church invited me to take their young people's group, John's Gospel, thirty minutes in English and thirty minutes in Japanese. I was delighted. I affirmed that there were signs in John which were teaching but also actually happened. I spoke on the words of the Baptist, 'Behold the Lamb of God that takes away the sin of the world.' I think it was on the third occasion that the Pastor attended and mentioned that the church was the resurrected body of Christ. I politely contradicted him. 'Yes,' I said. That is a good example. Christ actually rose from the dead and the church is His body.' I was asked not to come the following week because they were studying something else. Mistakenly I thought that meant the next week so I turned up two weeks later, much to the consternation of the Pastor. I had been dismissed I found later because I believed in the resurrection of Christ.

I also discovered much later that one girl had come to the Lord that first week. My message was new to her. The Pastor was friendly and visited us to discuss a problem. 'I have a girl in my church. She wants to go to Bible School but our Bible School is no use for her kind of faith. Can you recommend a Bible School? My deacons do not all share our views.' We were able to recommend an excellent Women's Bible College (Mr Yamaguchi, the Principal), where she graduated, worked for the Word of Life Press, then married a Pastor from the Free Methodist Church.

A dying man healed

I can't remember how we first met Mr Uchiyama, a sad young man, with thick glasses. He was interested in learning and speaking English but was far from well, suffering from TB and with an interest in the Gospel. Mike spent hours talking to him. One day he was lying in his room when he had a frightening haemorrhage. He called to his mother for help. She was in the garden, deaf from a cold, yet rushed upstairs having 'heard' the calls for help. He felt God had spared his life for a purpose. Later, he spent much time in hospital, but had, in the meantime, attended a believer's conference in Sapporo, where he had understood what it meant to follow Christ and was very happy. Then his condition deteriorated. Again in hospital, with no hope of recovery, he asked Doug for baptism. 'I know my salvation depends on faith in Christ alone but I would like to have obeyed Him through baptism before I meet Him.' Doug baptized him in his hospital bed. This was the turning point health-wise – his recovery started from that time. He reckoned it took three years.

He married a girl from across the straits. The engagement was conducted through correspondence, each especially checking on the other's doctrine! His story continues. We met him again in 2002.

The hairdresser, the journalist, the professor

Mrs Sakino was a great asset. She had been helped four years previously by a missionary from Shizunai, and her crumbling life was restored. She was in charge of a hairdressing business, and offered to perm my hair herself. She had not reckoned with the difference between my hair and the dark thick oriental hair. She was distressed when she realised that my hair was as straight as ever after treatment. (Others have faced the same problem with my hair.)

Mrs Sakino introduced us to an abacus teacher who was willing to let us use his room, at the other end of town from our house, for Christian services each Sunday. Her friend brought two excellent language teachers for Mike and Valerie. It was Mrs Sakino who took us to the delightful apple orchards of Nanae where later our OMF children's school was built.

Valerie and I delivered Christian literature regularly to the same houses in the area. Doug and Mike also worked together. In the open air, Doug preached while Mike stood by in support. Only on one occasion the police asked them to move on; a crowd had spread across the road and was blocking the traffic.

One of our visitors was a young reporter determined to master the English language. He went to every showing of American films seeing the same film seven times. He became fluent in gangster-type American. On one occasion, in his interpreting for a British Naval Officer, phrases such as, 'Don't give me that stuff', were not appreciated. Doug and I spoke in Japanese to each other in the presence of Japanese visitors. Our reporter commented that our language was OK but too formal for man and wife.

With the visit of this Naval vessel, Doug approached the city dignitaries to suggest a welcome, giving the men a taste of Japanese culture, staying in Japanese homes, not just introducing them to the red-light district that could be found in any port. With much trepidation they agreed to the plan, opening up homes to the men. Years later, in Hong Kong, a Naval officer approached Doug and thanked him for what he had done for his crew in Hakodate.

Mr Uchiyama introduced us to the lady superintendent of an orphanage at the other end of town. Doug and I took turns in taking meetings regularly with the staff and older girls. The superintendent was receptive, saying, 'For years I have kept Jesus standing at the *genkan* (porch). Now at last I have opened the door for Him to come right in.'

The Teachers' Training College wanted the help of native English speakers. I had permission to use the English New Testament and flannelgraph illustrations. The authorities reckoned that the students should know something of the Christian foundation of England as well as the language. The course was for composition not conversation. A chauffeur-driven car took me to and from the College.

One of the lecturers, Mr S, asked to attend the classes along with the students. Each week I told a New Testament story illustrated with flannelgraph to help their understanding. The home assignment was to write out the story, but not in a way they could copy straight from the Bible. One week I gave them the story of Zacchaeus and asked them to retell it as though they were Zacchaeus himself. Mr S's account was so brilliant and discerning that I asked him if he was a Christian.

'No,' he replied, 'but I am interested in ideas and that is how I thought Zacchaeus would have felt.'

With increasing interest he came regularly to our house to study John's Gospel with Doug. He seemed to progress. But one day he brought us a large present. It signified that he was coming no more; the gift was as a thanks for the teaching and avoidance of any obligation to embrace it. He explained: 'In Buddhism (or literature) I can accept what I like and reject what I do not like in the teaching; but Christianity requires me to surrender my life to a Person. I am not prepared to do that.'

Just along the coast from Hakodate was the resort of Yuu no kawa where OMF sometimes held our annual conference. Doug and I had a pleasant four-day break in the hotel after the conference. The royal treatment we received included a special delicacy of raw sea-urchins. Doug quietly buried his; I felt it my duty to eat them, but subsequently my stomach rejected them. Michael also had trouble because he insisted on eating sand.

Doug did later have problems with other raw fish. He had got to know a student who invited him to join him on a fishing boat to catch squid. He became the fourth member of the crew, the 'captain' being the only regular fisherman. The catch was successful. The squid, attracted by the light, wrapped their tentacles around the hooks, squirting out 'ink'. The crew returned to shore for breakfast and enjoyed the freshly caught raw fish. Doug joined in but arrived home with black stains on his jacket and feeling extremely sick. I enjoy cooked squid but find the raw variety too tough.

We had needed help for our tent meetings in September but Mike had been asked to look after a visitor, John Pollock. We were able to borrow land to erect the tent a short distance from our home. Doug was preaching and invited questions. He was grilled by about half a dozen men: he had noticed them coming in and sitting towards the front – unusual for Japanese men. When challenged, they denied knowing one another. The questions were all attacks on Christ. Doug patiently answered their objections but again challenged them on being a group together. He returned home drained. But the sequel – the next morning a Mr H was at the door, saying he wanted to talk to Doug. The 'attackers' were the committee members of a militant Buddhist group, fiercely opposed to Christianity who had come deliberately to disturb the meeting.

Mr H explained, 'I had helped you to put up the tent, so felt I had earned the right to come to the meeting. I watched the aggression of the committee: it was disgraceful that they should treat a foreigner in that way; it did not recommend their religion. And I watched you, patiently trying to respond to their attacks, without anger. Please tell me more about your religion, Christianity.'

That evening, the last of the meetings we had decided to close early. We were busy taking down the tent walls when a group of young men arrived in force, frustrated at being too late to repeat their attacks. A very small Salvation Army Captain had also arrived. They surrounded him. He took them on – 'I know who you are, and I know your parents . . . you should be ashamed of your behaviour . . .' He knew them by name. And proclaimed the message of salvation through Jesus Christ to them. He confronted them with the falseness of their beliefs.

Severe asthma

Our first year in Hakodate was exhausting. Doug had been engaged in tent campaigns, evangelism in other towns and teaching in a Bible school. Michael still woke regularly in the night. We were meeting new people and teaching the Bible. One elderly gentleman came regularly to an evening Bible class. We discovered later that it was not for interest, but that he had been appointed to find out about us and what we were teaching. We were also still engaged in language study. Doug was getting more asthma. We needed a holiday. It was too early for the seaside holiday in Takayama, so we set off for our mission home in Tokyo, a large, Japanese style house in Seijoogakuenmae. It had been given to CIM by the Chinese owner, and was now occupied by our efficient business manager, Arthur Kennedy, his wife Bessie and young daughter, Gwendy. They received us with love and hospitality. Gwendy especially loved to look after Michael. There were many places of interest around – the 'Romance' car every hour along the railway track, later used by the famous express 'bullet' train, a park at Enoshima along the line, with displays of dolphins jumping for fish through hoops, the attractive Hakone National Park with Mt Fuji as background. Also, other visitors to the mission home came and went. We attended the local church. The elderly pastor told us how years ago he had had to walk miles to buy a Bible.

We returned to Hakodate much refreshed and Doug with little asthma.

After Mike and Valerie Griffiths left us to take up work with students in Tokyo, Karl and Delores Baker joined us from the States. Karl had come to the Lord simply when a friend asked him if he wanted to go to heaven. His wife also, responded very simply. They had one son, Stevie. Stevie was a little boy when he arrived in Japan and had the unfortunate belief that the Japanese were heathen so he had to throw stones at them!! Karl himself was a practical joker and did not take things too seriously. Twice I was troubled by his refusal to believe me. Once he was standing at the entrance of our house when a young thief had run through our back garden, finding no way of escape except through the house. I heard him in our washroom and looked in. He pressed his hands together pleading, 'Bad people chasing me, help!' Knowing there was no way out I closed the door, walked to our front door and said to Karl. 'There is a man in the house.' Karl just thought I was saying Doug is here, ignored my request and the little thief ran right past him into the front garden and street.

On another occasion, I was alone in our part of the house. The coal burning boiler was alight to heat the *ofuro* (bath) we shared. I looked in. The galvanised iron chimney reached almost to the wooden ceiling where it bent at 90° to the side exit. The iron had rusted and flames were visible from the cracks. I rushed to get Karl's help. He didn't believe me, so Delores came to confirm my fears and persuaded him to help.

But it was Karl who was helpful to us when Doug's asthma attacks became alarming. Doug was all right when away from home, but on return he could barely breathe. We tried to sort out the cause – the mattress? the blankets? I even wondered if it was my fault as he had no problems away from me! We discovered later that one of Doug's allergies was dog hair, and that a stray had produced her puppies under the house. At the time there seemed no alternative but for us to move, first to the OMF medical house in Aomori; that was a miserable interlude. Then we moved to Hachinohe with other missionaries. Simply, Doug's health was such that he had to be somewhere where no replacement would be needed if he could not last out.

Escape to Hachinohe, 1961–1962

We finally moved to Hachinohe on 19 December to help Lee and Louise Little and John and Judy Chisholm, but not to establish anything independently in case Doug's health failed. We spent the first two days with Lee and Louise. The dust that arose from the borrowed futon (mattress and covers) as they were thrown down in the house triggered a severe asthma attack. Fortunately, I had received one lesson in administering injections and managed to inject Doug which relieved him. On 24 December he decided to go back to the medical house for further treatment. In the train he was reading an amusing book; trying to stifle a laugh brought on an uncontrollable bout of asthma. He succeeded in reaching the door of the train and alighted shortly afterwards when it stopped at an unscheduled station, nearest to the medical house. He managed to convey to an anxious taxi driver where he wanted to go, was rushed to the medical house and collapsed into a chair. Dr Monica soon revived him with an injection. She reckoned the upset of moving had caused the attack. He returned to

Hachinohe on 29 December, not cured, but with instructions how to continue treatment, and medicine was ordered from England.

Meanwhile, I was trying to unpack and get settled in our new home. Lynne Little was a few months older than Grace, so they enjoyed playing together. I had the companionship of a girl on holiday from our language school. We put planks on top of wooden boxes to support a mattress, so that Doug would not be sleeping on the tatami floor. Lee was an expert carpenter and fixed cupboards for us. The house was comfortable despite the address, 'Village under the Swamp'. The villagers call the bus stop, 'Cherry Tree'. Despite this difficult beginning we were able to stay in Hachinohe until our next home assignment. This is what I wrote home after three months.

> We have now been in Hachinohe for three months and are better able to give you a picture of the town. It is a thriving seaport with an expanding population, at present 160,000. It is a long narrow town following the coast most of the way but wandering inland at our end, the north-east. Mr and Mrs Chisholm live amongst the fisher folk about twenty minutes from us by bus. Beyond them there are two churches but nothing at our end of town. The country around is farmland, paddy fields and apple orchards. Our house stands on land that was used for rice cultivation until recently and we look out into a valley of paddy fields. The stream beside our house, the main road and the mountains cut off a small area which is a community in itself. The people are very friendly. Mr and Mrs Little have worked here for some years. There are about a dozen believers. On Sunday morning we meet at the home of Mrs Hanawa, a blind old lady, who loves the Lord. She has been much helped by another older Christian. On one occasion, as this lady was declaring how she was content with food, clothing and shelter, not needing a perm, or hair dyed, etc., granny Hanawa challenged her with a toothless smile, 'But you do have false teeth don't you?' Mrs Hanawa's house is next to the Public Bath House which we use, and we have permission to put up posters there. I am sorry that 'Cleanliness is next to Godliness' is not in the Bible!
>
> An evening meeting is held in the home of Mrs Fukuda (Blessed Field) a convert from Roman Catholicism. Her teenage daughter is believing: the husband seems to have believed recently although is still fighting his love for drink. The three have a time together round the Word each evening.
>
> English is in demand here, too. High School teachers meet each week to study the English Bible, and there are classes, too, for senior and junior high schoolers.

The winter in Hachinohe is much shorter than in Hokkaido: many people get by with a *kotatsu*, a charcoal heater in the floor covered with a raised quilt. It is cosy for those sitting round it with their feet under the quilt, but cold in the rest of the house. We have stoves! But the shorter winter is enabling us to make use of the newly acquired Mission Gospel van, like many similar vans on the road, the van itself being used for advertising on the back doors. Red against the green background are painted the characters for 'God' and 'Love' and on the sides a map of west Japan superimposed on a red cross with a text. There is plenty of room to carry tape recorders, film strips, books, posters, hymn sheets, etc. It is built for a Japanese driver. Mr Little, being a tall man, finds difficulty in fitting his knees under his chin, but his experience in driving a truck on a Canadian farm has equipped him for the difficult task of driving through the narrow country roads around Hachinohe. The van is being used to reach small communities living on the outskirts of the city in farming villages and country houses. It is too cold for outdoor evangelism but it is a slack period for the farmers and an excellent time to reach them. The first step is to find a possible meeting place: normally the fire station is suitable, for even a small community dare not be without its fire engine in this land of matchwood houses. Once the hall has been agreed we then go ahead in duplicating bills advertising the meeting: the first afternoon is spent in going from house to house with these bills and tracts, inviting people to the meetings and giving a word of witness whenever possible. The evening meeting consists of a filmstrip and simple Gospel message. We aim at spending three days in each village and collecting the names of those who are interested. The villages are all within easy reach of Hachinohe and any Christian could easily come into a central meeting.

Our first attempt was frustrated because the hall we thought we could use proved to be unavailable. The second attempt was more successful. Mr Little carried on with the help of Mr Nakagawa, while Doug stayed in bed with 'flu! (Mr Nakagawa is the boxer from Shizunai who has been living near here but will be leaving us next month. He hopes to go to a Bible evangelism school further south, taking his wife and baby with him.) The third attempt had to be abandoned as Mr Nakagawa was unavailable, and it was Mr Little's turn for 'flu!

As I write, Douglas and Mr Little are out together in the fourth village. (Mr Nakagawa's turn for 'flu), Mrs Fukuda and her daughter having joined them with enthusiasm and readiness to help.

Lee and Louise moved to Sendai to take charge of the children's school there. We moved into their house, although I had come to love the friendly neighbours at the 'Village under the Swamp'.

We discovered that the electricity rate was higher in that house. This was because a special plug had been fitted to take the power needed for Louise's electric frying pan. I explained I didn't need it because 'I was poor'. Finally, the local electrician explained to the company that 'I was poor'. He knew, and I knew, that we were using a phrase on the tongue of every Japanese then, 'We Japanese are poor.'

The water was highly chlorinated. To change the water in the goldfish bowl, I had to leave a basin of water out overnight to reduce the chlorine. As I put the cold fresh water into the bowl the goldfish floated to the top and lay on its side (dead?). The kettle was standing on the stove. As I poured hot water into the bowl the goldfish twitched several times, then righted itself and swam happily around again. It was a picture of 'the resurrection'.

We had a glorious refreshing holiday in Takayama amongst the pine trees by the Pacific Ocean. Michael at three spoke his first complete sentence in English, 'I want 10 yen to buy ice-cream.' He was getting bigger but still a little timid. Grace was outgoing. On one occasion we saw her from our window in Hachinohe across the rice fields with a group of Japanese children.

She attended a Japanese kindergarten in a Methodist church. She travelled by herself to it on the bus. On the return the driver would stop for her at our bus stop. Once he forgot, took her on to the next stop, and wondered what to do for her.

'It's all right,' she assured him. 'I know where I am.'

She remembered the way to the house of our fellow missionaries, who then let us know she was safe.

We continued with our regular programme in Hachinohe, Doug often away teaching in a Bible school, or helping others with tent-meetings.

Our third child, Richard, was born on 28 January 1962, an easy birth. David Michell (author of *A Boy's War* – the story of his internment in China under the Japanese) helped Doug in looking after Grace and Michael in our home. We were due for furlough in May.

The story of Hachinohe continued on our return.

Interlude

An active year

WE SAILED ALONG THE ENGLISH CHANNEL with a calm sea and clear skies but had to dock in the Thames at Tilbury overnight. In the morning, Grace and Michael looked out through the porthole. 'Oh, England's gone,' said Grace. 'Nothing but dirty water,' remarked Michael.

We planned to spend most of the year with my mother. She had nobly agreed to accommodate the five of us, and use her sitting room as her bedroom. Doug no longer had a home as his father had died after being cared for by first his son, Ron, and then his daughter. It was difficult for Doug, as we were in my old home, with my mother's friends as well as mine. He had good chats with Win's father and Enid's father, as well as a welcome at Whitley Bay Baptist Church and an extensive deputation programme.

We were invited to an anniversary gathering of the Young Sowers in South Shields: Doug to speak, and me to wear my kimono. The leader's enthusiasm fired the young people packed into a large hall, and rewards were given to those who had learned a verse from every book of the Bible. The local press took photos.

The R.E. teacher of our local high school saw the newspaper and thought, 'Ah! a missionary in the district. I'll contact her and see if she can speak to the Christian group.' What he did not know was that he was inviting me back to my own old high school, where I had been well known for my atheistic/communist views. It was a delight to talk to the enthusiastic group of young Christians. One of them later came as a missionary to Japan. It was inevitable that I should tell of my own conversion and call to Japan.

The R.E. teacher was thrilled and arranged another meeting with the whole of the sixth form, cutting across the timetable. My reception was a little mixed. One question could not be answered then. 'You changed from atheism to Christianity. How do you know you won't change again?' (forty years on, I haven't.)

The same week I was asked to speak at the Willow Club. This was largely of ex-servicemen, not all Christian, many with deep hatred of the Japanese. I was exhausted at the end of that meeting. Speaking to a group opposed to the Japanese and unsympathetic to the message of Christ was not easy.

Doug was asked to go to South London to take meetings in different churches and conferences, staying with great OMF supporters, friends of Mr Welsh, our deputation secretary, Mr and Mrs Wooderson, an older couple. He was puzzled by their politeness to each other as man and wife. He had not been told that they were just married!

Grace started school in Earsdon. The premises were new but it was in fact my old elementary school.

Our welcome at Whitley Bay Baptist Church was very warm as usual. The monthly prayer group at Mr Crane's had supported us so faithfully. Mr Crane had kept us in touch by frequent letters, telling us of changes in the church.

Packed to return, medical questions

After the year we were ready to return to Japan to Hachinohe again, our berths booked, our luggage packed for the voyage, and staying at our Headquarters in Newington Green on the way. It was then that we were told that there were serious doubts about our return because of Doug's asthma. He had had treatment, including a special appointment with a homeopathy doctor who attended the Queen, and asthma sprays. Our berths had to be cancelled pending the medical decision.

We sent out an urgent prayer request from Newington Green to our closest prayer companions.

(1) Pray for medical clearance for Doug.

(2) Pray that we may have accommodation in the meantime.

Concerning the doctor's decision, Doug's asthma seemed to have disappeared. The doctor asked him what he had been doing, the extent of the deputation programme and distances covered; he passed him to return to Japan. The doctor said to me, 'He seems OK at the moment but it is never possible to say asthma is cured. Don't worry. It could occur again.'

Provision of accommodation

Concerning accommodation, a prayer partner, Mrs Lindfield near Bognor Regis, received the request and immediately set off for a friend's house.

She had talked to her the previous day because this lady, a widow of eighty, was going for the first time to visit mission stations in Africa for three months and had said she was not bothering to rent the house, just locking up and going.

Mrs Lindfield showed her our letter.

'Oh,' she said, 'OMF. My dear one used to pray regularly for Arthur Reynolds of OMF. Certainly they can use my house. I'm taking the car to my daughter's so they can use the garage. The lettuce and gooseberries in the garden are ready to eat and I've given my house-helper a retaining wage. They are welcome to have her services. No, I don't want anything for rent.'

Doug and I went down to see the house the day following his health check. It was ideal. I had worried a little that in Feltham it would be a large posh house with fitted carpets, not too suitable for three small children. It was large, but not 'posh', mats and rugs on a wooden floor, and a stone's throw from a private beach.

We returned immediately to Newington Green. Doug went across to his brother Ron's house to collect the children. Ron had a friendly Golden Retriever. Doug got back to Newington Green with a severe asthma attack. Oh dear! The doctor had warned me. But had those two days been reversed we would not have been allowed to return to Japan. To me it was a clear indication from God that He wanted us back in Japan but did not guarantee freedom from asthma.

We had a lovely restful month in Bognor Regis. The house was perfect for us, the sea warm and safe. We watched Michael venturing in slowly by the breakwater, not thrown in as before (on the ship). Grace went to the local school – no problem about getting in, it was compulsory. Richard and Michael enjoyed playing together.

We finally set sail, a month later than scheduled, to Hachinohe once more.

CHAPTER 5

Settled and moved again (1964–1968)

The children and the school

ALLAN AND SHIRLEY KNIGHT NOW LIVING in Hachinohe had looked for a suitable house for us, avoiding possible asthma risks. We finally moved into a two-storey house in the rice fields. We left Grace at school in Sendai on our way. Lee and warm-hearted Louise Little were now looking after the children in our small OMF English school for missionaries' children. We were told that Grace was happy in the school, and shared a room with her friend Lynne. We later realised she had bottled up her loneliness in missing us until she came home for the holidays and then wept for two weeks. Dr Monica discovered that Grace was dyslexic. (She had previously shown a preference for using her left hand but changed to the right with little persuasion.) She had been slow in reading, but a return to the older teaching method (c a t spells cat), and with a brilliant Canadian teacher, she soon caught up.

Michael and Richard were with us, Richard still a cute baby, talking little but conveying his meaning. 'Walk daddy' = either I've been or I'm going for a walk with daddy, or 'walk daddy no' – I'm not going.

Michael was not due for school until September when he would be six. I was concerned as to how he would be ready for the English 11 + exam if he was a class behind, so started teaching him myself. He was definitely left-handed. When he copied what I had written for him, he had no problem, but when he wrote by himself he produced perfect mirror writing. (Leonardo da Vinci wrote his science notes in mirror writing!) He enjoyed numbers. He had a toy clock with the minute blocks separate to place in the appropriate holes on the clock face. That was how he learned the five times table. He quickly learned, 2, 3, 5, 10, 11, 12 times, addition, subtraction, multiplication and division. After learning Psalm 23 he wanted more psalms to learn. He was quick in reading. If I was not available to teach him for an hour in the morning, awkward behaviour showed and his dissatisfaction for the rest of the day. I realised that, apart from any teaching he might gain, the hour when he had me completely to himself was the most important.

Doug also saw that having the children in the house with us did not mean that they had our attention. He stopped other activities at 4 p.m. From four to five was their playtime with him. This was invaluable and satisfying for us all. I took Michael with me to bring Grace from school for the Christmas holidays. He was excited but after a few days asked when she was going back, commenting that there was more room when she left. The children all came down in turn with chickenpox, Michael's the worst. We dabbed the spots with gentian violet. Michael, with his love of numbers, counted them – 650!

OMF was looking for a new and more central location for the children's school. Karl and Delores Baker who were still living in Hakodate discovered a suitable site in Nanae about twenty miles away, a place we ourselves had visited with Mrs Sakino, the hairdresser. David Highwood, who had left his architect's profession in order to tell the Japanese about Christ, once again found his qualifications useful. He designed the school.

Her Majesty's Consul

When the school was completed, the British Consul from Yokohama came to Nanae for the opening ceremony. This was our second meeting with him. One day we had received a letter shattering our obscurity. It bore the stamp of Her Majesty's Japan Consulate. Inside was a letter from the British Consul informing us that he was visiting us within a few days and would like to see the city, especially the harbour. Consternation! We, in all our travels, had never heard of a Britannic Majesty's Consul who had left the confines of Yokohama before.

Consternation increased when a large black shining car pulled up outside our humble dwelling. Out stepped the representative of the city Mayor, black suit and white gloves. We asked him in and he knelt down in the old formal Japanese style on our tatami floor. We also sank to the floor and bowed low. Without ado he asked 'Why is the British Consul coming to Hachinohe?'

I could see that he had all sorts of problems about protocol and whether he should invite the Consul to a geisha party. In our best possible polite speech we answered, 'He is coming to see us.'

'And why does he want to see our fishing fleet?' We didn't know.

Her Britannic Majesty's Consul seemed quite at home on the Japanese tatami of our bed-sitter. I call it a bed-sitter because the bed, a large futon, came out of the cupboard at nights and went back in the morning.

We had expected a public school accent and an Oxford background. He spoke with a pleasant northern accent. We wanted to know why he had come to our home, what star had guided him. With a conspiratorial smile he began . . .

In the thirties I was working as a junior in the Post Office. I had grown up in the thriving fishing port of Hull and loved it. The Post Office was part of the Civil Service as was the Foreign Office. The FO thought of the bright idea of having some of their staff put out in other branches of the Civil Service. One had come to our Post Office! I questioned my manager. If the FO was doing this couldn't I have a go in the FO? My manager put my name forward. For months I heard nothing then 'You wanted to go to the FO, off you go'. So I departed from my provincial Post Office to the grey walls and brown lino of Whitehall.

'I let it be known that I would like to go to China. One day my boss called me into his office. Off you go to China. By then China and Japan were at war, the capital had been moved from Peking to Chungking and I went in via Burma. Still very much a junior, one day I am called into the Consul's office. 'Our Vice-Consul in Kwunming has died suddenly and we have nobody, except you, to replace him.' Off to Kwunming I went as an acting Vice-Consul. I am now a Consul.

He smiled. He was delighted when he discovered that he had expatriates in Hachinohe and in the realm of his responsibility he could and did travel to the north-east to see us, and the fishing fleet.

In September, Grace and Michael went off together to school. Don and Winnie Morris, our companions from Shizunai days, were the house parents. Michael was troubled with asthma and we did not know that Don was often spending wakeful nights with him. Miss Taylor was the teacher, formerly the Latin teacher in Chefoo, China. Teaching sums to primary age children did not come naturally.

Towards the end of term, Michael seemed to withdraw within himself and become very hard of hearing. He became ill and had to be sent home. Dr Roslyn rescued us. We took Michael to her home in Aomori, before his ear operation in Tokyo. His temperature was high, his hearing minimal. Roslyn gave him a new penicillin drug she had obtained for her own son. She gave herself unstintingly to Michael, keeping him warm with the stove going all night. He was not eating.

'Go and buy him ice cream, anything he will eat,' she advised.

What did he want? Kidney! As the temperature abated, and I was taking him to Tokyo, she told me,

'If the ear is not cleared now, the wax could harden and could result in a serious condition later in life. The operation should be successful but the condition could recur. Do not be afraid to have it done again, if necessary, but do your best to avoid his catching cold.'

It was successful and did not have to be repeated.

Michael was indignant at the hospital because the nurse told him there would be only one injection and he was given a second. The deceit upset him.

At Christmas time, Mrs Eno, a fisherman's wife and a Christian, our house-help, brought presents for the children – a pretty purse for Grace, a money box in the shape of a small tin store house with door, key and slot for Michael, and a toy for Richard. The Christmas tree my mother had sent was duly erected and decorated. Excitement abounded when presents were opened. Grandma's gift of a teddy bear for Richard he greeted with 'Me, me,' so after that they called her Mimi. Michael named his Simeon. We weren't sure why. These teddies became comforting companions to the children during their school days of separation from us. Richard went to bed with three teddies.

Our summer holidays were usually spent at Takayama, among the pine trees by the Pacific Ocean. There was a beautiful sandy beach, a safe bathing area, a beach guard on duty for the children, waves for body surfing, quietness, companionship with a variety of missionary families, and communication in English. When Michael was smaller I had wondered why he was so afraid of the small breakers, until I bent down to his level – then they looked huge!

Reaching the city

The city was the largest (about 180,000) of the area. We were surprised that the main line railway from Tokyo to Aomori stopped at the nearest town, Sannohe, but did not go through Hachinohe. We heard the explanation. The railway was built at a time when the farmers and fisherman of Hachinohe were honest and did not want those 'thugs' from Tokyo coming to their city. They never locked their doors, neither did they wish for heavy taxation. But in the twentieth century it seemed incongruous for Hachinohe to be by-passed. The problem was solved (after we left); they changed the name of Sannohe station to Hachinohe.

I visited the local high school and was welcomed to teach elementary English. I couldn't teach the Bible in the classroom but I invited the girls to a Bible class, and also arranged for English penfriends. The letters were not censored. About fifteen girls wrote: one of the penfriends was from my old school in Whitley Bay who later came to Japan as a missionary.

At the home of Mrs Kawachi, a young lively housewife living in an apartment block, we held a Bible cooking class. Shirley demonstrated a Western cooking recipe, and while the dish cooked, or cooled, I gave a Bible story. 'Oh, taste and see that the Lord is good' was the basis of the first message. We sold simple ovens and Bibles.

Hachinohe is a long, narrow port, stretching along the Pacific coast of north Japan, with churches dotted along the town. We had come to know several of the ministers. We suggested to the Methodist and Church of Christ ministers that we might have a city-wide evangelistic outreach involving all the churches. They arranged a meeting of the pastors to discuss it.

However, on the day, Doug was called away and I had to take his place. I knew that a woman would be regarded as inferior in such a group, and I did not know how much I would understand or be understood. Before I left home I prayed, 'Lord, help me to understand all that I should understand, and not to understand anything I should not understand.' I don't recall any other occasion when I have asked for lack of understanding.

At the start of the discussion I apologised profusely for my presence and Doug's absence, asking them to excuse my poor command of Japanese. They graciously accepted my apology and listened attentively to catch my hesitant comments. I understood most of what was said. Only one minister was opposed to such a campaign. That I understood clearly, but not another word of what he said. Later I learned from the Church of Christ pastor the reasons for his opposition. Had I understood I could not have made my contribution to the discussion and the opportunity of supporting the plan for evangelism would have been lost. My views were directly opposed to his.

There appeared to be general agreement so we were disappointed to find that it was to be put off for a year. There is a Japanese phrase *ato de* which literally means 'afterwards', but can imply 'don't want to'. We continued with limited co-operation. The Church of Christ pastor came to us to tell us of a young lady who had clearly trusted Christ in the meetings at his church. 'But she really belongs to your group,' he generously explained. 'She has been to your church several times.'

She was Seiko Taniguchi, who had been spiritually helped in under-standing the Bible and befriended by Mrs F's daughter and Judy Chisholm. I recounted her story in a children's book entitled *The Spider's Thread* and, later, slightly revised as *Seiko*. She was glad to tell me of her life. This stockily built young woman seemed to relive her sad experiences – escape in a boat with her family from her Russian-occupied home to Hokkaido, poverty, illness, rejection, struggle. She had been terrified on seeing the story of the spider's thread with a school party to the cinema. This was the old Buddhist story called 'The Spider's Thread.'

> A man who had been a rogue all his life one day spared the life of a spider instead of treading on it. It was the only good thing he had ever done. Then he died and was suffering agonies in the flames of hell. Suddenly, above him, he saw a spider making a long thread. It came lower and lower until it was within his grasp. Would it hold his weight? It was his only chance; he clutched at it and found that he could climb up this slender thread, out into paradise at the top. Yes, it was bearing his weight. Then he looked down. Hundreds of other people were trying to cling to this thread to lift themselves out of torment. This was no good. The thread might break. Clinging on to it with his hands he kicked back with his feet to throw the other climbers off. As he did so he broke the thread and fell back right into the centre of the flames.

She remembered the incident:

> I listened terrified. I could see the man. I could see his selfishness. I knew I was like him. I wanted my own way, I did not care about anyone else, and I was a thief and a liar. Already I was in a hell of my own and did not know how to escape. I did not want to change but I was scared. What was happening to me and where would I go when I died? No one had ever told me about Jesus and His love. All I knew was fear.

As she continued telling me her own story, her morose mood suddenly burst into radiant joy in recalling her new life in Jesus Christ. She had truly trusted Christ and went off to study for three years as one of the first students at OMF's newly opened Hokkaido Bible Institute where Mr Shinada, our helper in Shizunai and Hakodate was Dean.

She was greatly concerned for her beloved dying grandfather; the doctor was surprised to see a slight improvement when she had prayed for him. He believed that Christ had died for him and forgiven his sins before he went to meet his Maker. Her father was furious at her unfilial behaviour in refusing to take part in Buddhist ceremonies at his funeral – and ordered her never to return home. But her mother did invite me to call.

We encountered difficulties at the special tent meetings we held near the

Kawachis' (cooking class) home. The rain was heavy, a light bulb needed for the projector, the van broke down in the centre of town on our way. The children and I bundled into a taxi, in time for the children's meeting. Doug and Allan arrived about half way through. The joy that crowned our efforts was Mr Kawachi's announcement that he wanted to be baptized as baptism in Japan indicates a clear commitment to Christ. A little later in August we set off for the sea to observe his baptism. Despite the cold and rain we watched from the shore, under our umbrellas, and shared in the joy that Mr Kawachi was experiencing. 'Oh Happy Day.' His grandfather, living in Kyushu was delighted and wrote to him with detailed questions concerning his (and our) faith. He seemed to be checking up. His pretty sister also spent some time with them.

Reaching the surrounding towns

The first venture to Gonohe was with the Methodist Pastor Nishido, whose church kindergarten Grace had attended. He had a branch church building in Gonohe, with one deacon looking after it, but no regular meetings. He arranged with Doug for three days' evangelism in the town, and asked the deacon to open up the room. On arrival they found the church still closed.

'I thought you agreed to open up the premises before our arrival,' Pastor Nishido remarked.

The deacon answered, 'I would not have been so rude as to say "I wouldn't do it".'

The three days went smoothly. The kindergarten teacher who had come with them became assured of her faith in the meetings. As a thank you present the Pastor received a box of chocolate liqueurs. On the way home in the car he was very happy. Doug suggested that the teetotal Methodist had had too many of the delicious chocolates.

Takko was a village thirty miles from Hachinohe. Roads were rough in Japan those days and the way to Takko was no exception. At our first meeting in the village hall all present indicated a desire to trust in Jesus except for one lady who said she wished to study more of the meaning of Christianity before deciding. Sometimes everyone at a meeting will raise their hands if they think that is what the speaker wants them to do, irrespective of the reason for the appeal. This lady became the leader of the group of Christians, as numbers grew. Most of the others who had raised their hands did not continue.

On one occasion, when Allan and Doug were visiting, the Christians asked them to call on an invalid up the hill. When they entered the shack they saw the lady lying on her futon on the floor: she had been bedridden for nine years. Doug read a little from John chapter 4, when she interrupted saying, 'If I had something to live for, I'd get better.' Doug closed the Bible, prayed, and then they left.

Six months later they returned to Takko. The lady was in the meeting. 'I can walk down,' she explained 'but I have to get a taxi back.' Another six months and she was working part-time.

Allan and Shirley were due for home assignment. About fifty friends and acquaintances crowded into the hall to say goodbye to them and wish them well. Folks we had not seen for some time appeared for this special occasion. Bill and Sheila Fearnhough came instead of Allan and Shirley, giving us a change of fellow workers.

Back in Hachinohe we had a surprise visitor.

The outer door of our *genkan* (porch) slid open and a voice called out *Gomenkudasai* (excuse me). I knelt down on the tatami matting in order to open the inner door to greet the visitor, a rough-looking burly man. He wanted to invite Doug to come to his home with some of the Takko believers and explain the message of Jesus to his family and friends. He had twice attended tent meetings in Takko, and then for three days at the yearly believers meeting near Aomori had been shown more clearly what it meant to be a Christian and been baptized in the river. He explained that he had felt shame watching his children at play imitating their drunken father. Now that Christ had entered his life the family wanted an explanation. Grandma had seen a changed grandson, his mother a sober son, his wife commented that he no longer knocked her about, and his children said, 'Daddy plays with us now.'

Doug went to his home to speak to the crowd in the old farmhouse. He reckoned that the great wooden beams of the roof re-echoed the hymns of praise that were sung.

Our next outreach was to Sannohe. Mr Nakagawa, the boxer, had lived here and married a local, slightly crippled, bright young Christian, but they had moved south. Previously we had held meetings in the town but we could no longer hire a hall so were unable to continue. But we were able to find a suitable place to put up the tent.

It was an apple growing area, in a town largely of farmers where there were no known Christians. Four-year-old Richard and I gave invitations out from house to house, leaving Doug with Bill to put up the marquee on the side of a hill. The Japanese, who love children, were fascinated by the pale-faced, large eyed foreign lad. At one house after another he received a big apple in exchange for the invitation. I quietly hoped that the exchange would establish a right to the giver to come to the meeting rather than no obligation to do so. When the bag of apples became too heavy for us we had to stop giving out the invitations and return to the tent site sooner than planned. To our astonishment there was the marquee, large and white, gleaming in the sunshine, walls flapping gently in the breeze, already triumphantly erected.

'How did you do it?' I asked Doug.

'Well,' he answered, 'as we were laying the equipment out, doing what we could Bill, a taciturn Yorkshire man, broke the silence and queried with concern. "You know after we have everything ready and in position we will need at least another three people to hold up the centre poles while we run round and fix the guy ropes and pegs".'

'Yes, I know,' I replied.

'We had everything in place on the ground when over the crest strode three young Japanese men looking like characters from a Western movie, hats, boots and all. They advanced without a word, each grasped a central pole and thrust it up to hold the canvas roof in position. Bill and I speedily knocked in the tent pegs and looped the guy ropes over them. The three men then continued on their journey without a word.' Maybe they were angels.

Another move

The American Airbase at Misawa was not far from Hachinohe. We sometimes saw American airmen in the town. Doug was surprised one day to see a small uniformed man distributing Christian tracts to Japanese shoppers in the town. He was the Methodist chaplain from Misawa. He invited us to his home on the base and friendship developed. On one occasion we stayed overnight, sleeping in their upstairs bedroom. It was so hot that we opened the window. In the morning they said to us, 'It was strange last night. Even though we increased the heating, it didn't seem to get warm.'

The work of a dedicated Christian chaplain with integrity is not easy. Bill never received promotion and finally left the air force and worked for

Disneyland in Florida. We were unable to accept their invitation to Orlando, but were delighted years later to entertain them in England and to take them to the place where he had been based.

We bought a dinner set at a Misawa shop. The assistant was surprised when we spoke in Japanese. Then she explained that 'Noritake' was the famous firm for exporting but the Japanese chose another make – which she sold to us.

I never have liked 'pop' music. We called in at a restaurant in Misawa for a meal. Seeing us as an 'American' couple, the proprietor immediately switched the background music to 'pop'. Wanting to enjoy my meal, I said to the waiter, 'I really prefer Beethoven.' The next we heard were the opening bars of Beethoven's 5th symphony. The Japanese are fond of Western, classical music.

We were constantly giving out tracts. 'This would probably interest you,' remarked a girl who passed one on to her sister. The sister was the girl-friend of our near neighbour, Mr X. She saw our address on the tract and came to ask questions. She was indeed receptive to the teaching from the Bible. She introduced us to Mr X. When Doug explained the Christian way to him, he responded rather sadly, 'You have chosen a good way. I am afraid mine is very different.' On another occasion Doug found an airman also in his house He had gambled away all his money the previous night, so he had stayed overnight with our neighbour. Mr X told Doug that he, Mr X, was going on a trip and would be away for about six months.

We were often asked to help with English. Doug's pupil, a judge, had been in Hiroshima as a baby when the bomb dropped. The house he was in had collapsed, trapping him, and protecting him from the radiation. He gave the reply, 'yes' to Doug's question, meaning he had understood the question, e.g. 'Is snow black?' 'Yes,' – pause, No, snow is not black – as he would have answered in Japanese. He asked Doug, 'Do you know who your neighbour is?' 'Yes', Doug replied, 'I have had several talks with him, but he told me he would be away on a trip for about six months.'

'I know,' responded the judge. 'I sent him on it.'

We were also being sent 'on a trip', but not for the same reasons. The overall strategy for the OMF in Japan was decided by an elected Field Council, headed by the Superintendent. The couple in charge of our Christian bookshop in Hirosaki were due for furlough in North America, and would need to be replaced, so we were asked to move to Hirosaki to take responsibility for the bookshop before Abe and Jackie left. We first had to look for a house to rent. Abe and Jackie contacted the estate agent who showed us a number of possible places. We returned to Hachinohe to pack up and prepare to move.

The removal van was ordered and our goods all packed, when a message came through, 'The house you agreed on is no longer available.' We had no address to give the removal men. 'Go to the bookshop opposite the university and we'll tell you where to go from there.' (Abraham went out not knowing where he was going. Hebrews 11 v 8!)

We all arrived safely in Hirosaki – but where next? The estate agent had noticed that I had shown interest in a very odd looking house. 'That one is available,' he told us. So that is where we went. The houses in that small section of the town had been converted from warehouse buildings, resulting in lower than usual ceilings. It had two storeys. Doug could reach to the landing while standing on the ground floor. There were alcoves in the downstairs room giving space for desks.

We had brought the bunk bed that Allan Knight had made for us in Hachinohe. There was only one space upstairs to put it, because of the low sloping roof. We had to go through the coal-house to the bath: a tree was growing through the roof of the shed next to the bathroom, a little pond outside was home to a toad. The house was near the park – I liked it.

Hirosaki

Hirosaki is a city of outstanding beauty and of historic interest. In the early twentieth century it was famous for horses, evangelists and apples. The apples were introduced into Aomori Prefecture by an American missionary who noticed that conditions for cultivation were similar to those of his own home area. The workers in the orchards cover the young apples with paper bags to protect them from insects. Red 'Delicious' apples are large and round; if misshapen they are not sent to market. Tasty squeezed apple juice is cheap in the area but not in Tokyo. The English proverb 'like carrying coals to Newcastle' would be in Japanese, 'like carrying apples to Aomori'.

The picturesque black and white castle was built in the seventeenth century as fortress-home of the Lord of Tsugaru, with three moats round the fort. It was approached by a street of thirty-three temples including a pagoda housing Buddha's tooth, so that invading soldiers would have to attack the temples before reaching the castle. The streets were also designed so that the enemy would advance up the road towards the castle only to find that the direction of the road had changed and they were riding out of the city. We suffered from the problem the invading army faced. We also got lost in the town.

The remains of the huge iron gates, arched bridges over the old moats, and the vast grounds have become an attractive public park, with 5,000 cherry trees, the largest selection of cherry in the country. The cherry trees produce their blossom before the leaves, so the bleak winter scene of bare branches is suddenly transformed into a massive show of white and pink blossom. The wind blows the petals on to the ground producing a pink carpet. The Japanese cherry does not bear fruit. A Japanese proverb expresses the sentiment: 'Life is like the cherry, three days of bloom, then gone.'

Mount Iwaki dominates the plain in May when the snow-capped peak is reflected in the sun and, with the cherry bursting into bloom, the scene is a white fairyland.

Winds from Siberia hit the mountains of Aomori bringing heavy snow to Hirosaki. 'Golden Week' at the beginning of May is a public holiday when thousands come to enjoy drunken parties under the cherry trees. The city authorities rush to clear and repair the roads that have been damaged by snow that has settled for months in time for the crowds.

This was the city where we had come to live. I was very pleased to have a house so near to the park. Five-year-old Richard reckoned he was worn out by walks round the park – 118 acres.

Abe and Jackie had established a Christian bookstore that served the whole of Aomori Prefecture. Mr Katagawa, was the Japanese manager, tall and thin, with slightly Jewish features. Someone suggested that the ten lost tribes of Israel settled in Japan. Bank clerks often have Jewish features, especially the long nose, and have business acumen. Parallels between the Shinto ceremonies and those associated with the Ark are pointed out. The Emperor visits the Ise Shrine once a year, and only he is allowed inside. It houses the mirror, necklace and sword associated with the Emperor's ancestress, the Sun-goddess. The Jewish high priest used to enter the holy of holies once a year. In the ark were the Ten Commandments, manna, Aaron's Rod. The suggested parallels were (1) the mirror would be of polished wood, like the tablets of the Ten Commandments, (2) the necklace broken up, the manna (3) the sword – Aaron's Rod. Further, when the palanquin was taken from local Shinto shrines, carried on the shoulders of the devotees it had to be taken over water twice – the Red Sea and the Jordan. A book with these thoughts was presented to His Imperial Majesty, with a comment, 'It is an interesting idea.'

To return to our bookstore manager, he was sometimes taken for a foreigner. When taking books to churches with Doug, he was sometimes commended for speaking good Japanese. I was with him on our bookstall on the approach into the park during the cherry blossom festival. Granted the questioner was a little drunk, but I don't know whether Mr Katagawa was more embarrassed by the question, was I his mother? Mr Katagawa had become a Christian while in hospital. As a patient with TB, he had been visited by Christian friends. He was not interested in Christianity, but when they went home, he was bored so started reading the literature they had left. He was moved to realise that his sins could be forgiven because Christ had died on the cross. He believed the message, and got better as well! The bookshop was opposite the entrance to the University; students searching the meaning of life often dropped in. Several became Christians and joined in the College's Christian Society.

Abe took Doug to different churches in the district and to the Word of Life Press in Tokyo. Introducing him to the Holiness Pastor in another city, both were surprised to see Doug's photograph in the church. It was there that Doug had held tent campaigns previously. At the Word of Life Press, a young lady greeted him with, 'Your wife led me to Jesus in Hakodate.' This was the young woman to whom we had recommended the Women's Bible College at the request of the Presbyterian Pastor.

When Abe and Jackie left for home assignment in Canada we moved into their house near the bookshop and University. I was sorry to leave our quaint house by the park.

An American family, Nina and Harvey Taylor and their four boys lived opposite. Harvey was an academic, Nina cheerful and hospitable. They had previously worked in Vietnam. They would have nothing to do with Hallowe'en celebrations, having experienced the reality of demons in Vietnam. Harvey was now teaching English in the University. Their children were good playmates for Richard although it did not help in his learning Japanese. I was particularly grateful for their friendship once when Doug was away. I lost control of my speech. What I said was not what I was trying to say. They looked after Richard, contacted a doctor and calmed me down. Dr Monica, from Singapore, assured me later that this could occur once or twice in a lifetime and had been brought on by the stress I had experienced over the previous years. I was surprised to find, as I was recovering, that I had no problem speaking fluently in Japanese before my English returned to normal.

One evening Richard disappeared. We scoured the neighbourhood, enquired from the American couple and returned home worried. Then we saw him. He had climbed into his bunk bed and was fast asleep!

We had been four and a half years back in Japan and were due to leave Hirosaki for the next home assignment and more surprises. Doug had asked that he could spend the year either as an assistant Pastor or as Pastor in a church that was temporarily without one. We waited to learn the outcome of this request.

Interlude

Our first flight

WE EMBARKED WITH OUR THREE children on a French boat not anticipating anything unusual on our voyage back to England. Doug had asked for a year as Assistant Pastor. Pat Goodland, a member of the OMF candidates committee, was needing an assistant, but his letter to us did not arrive before we left Japan, so – like Abraham, we went out not knowing where we were going.

On board I thought I would ask for our cabin key in French. It was No. 53. So I managed the fifty in French, but the three in Japanese, resulting in poor pronunciation of fifty-five. I did understand the purser's request.

'This vessel is Roman Catholic. We do not know anything about Protestant services,' he explained. I was not expecting his request. 'I see your husband is a reverend. Would he kindly conduct a Protestant service for us on Sunday.' What a pleasure!

One cool evening from the deck we saw a glorious display of colours, beams of light of blues, yellow, red streaked across the sky. It was breathtaking. Could we photograph it? We feared that, if we took time to go below deck for the camera, the display might have faded. It lasted half an hour and remains imprinted on our memories. The radiant sky over the ocean was more magnificent than any rainbow or sunset. We did not know what it was.

Michael got a pleasant surprise when a birthday cake was brought to him in the dining room for his ninth birthday, candles and all. It occurred during the week of the six-day war in the Middle East, June 1967, but we were oblivious of the conflict.

When we disembarked in Singapore we learned of the war, and that shipping to England was at a standstill. We were given the choice of waiting indefinitely in Singapore for a boat or continuing by air. Meanwhile our HQ staff looked after us well. A Chinese couple arranged to take us round the Tiger Balm Gardens on a public holiday. Tiger balm is a special Chinese ointment, popular and profitable. From the proceeds, the owner had built these 'gardens' in many sites in the Far East. They consisted of stone or concrete images of animals, fish, etc. with an occasional mound of shrubs or plants. We were all enjoying the outing when disaster struck. Michael and Richard ran up one of these mounds only to land on a hornet's nest. The hornets protested, viciously, stinging both boys and injecting their poison to produce continual pain. Our Chinese friends kindly got us to a military hospital, as the city hospitals were closed on this public holiday. The doctors were uncertain as to the species of the insect (we had omitted to pick up a specimen) but gave them medicine as an antidote to the toxin and told them just to rest for a time. (The stabs of pain continued intermittently for several hours.) It was a sad ending to an otherwise enjoyable day; we were very grateful to the Chinese couple who had taken so much trouble on our behalf.

We were booked to fly on an Indonesian airline to Amsterdam and on to London. Shortly after take-off the plane lost height and the oxygen masks above our seats came down. The cabin crew came round to make sure we were all wearing them, including the children. The announcement that there had been a failure of pressurisation in the cabin was given over the loud speakers, but in Indonesian. We did not know the cause until we stopped over at Karachi. Neither did we know that the need to use oxygen masks was unusual – it was our first flight.

We had to change planes at Amsterdam, and on to London. In London we realised that some of our luggage was missing, no doubt because we had originally booked it as far as Amsterdam, the terminus of the plane we had boarded in Singapore. The KLM (Dutch Airline) staff were very efficient in tracing it; it was delivered to our room in Newington Green HQ the next day.

Doug's brother, as always, was there to meet us at Heathrow. He had a message for us from Pat Goodland to go to Stanmore immediately and look over the house the church had for us. This again took us by surprise as we had not received Pat's letter – we did about two months later when it came back to England from Japan by surface mail.

The church had been praying for accommodation for us. Mr and Mrs Sanz were next door neighbours of Peter and Carol Hewitt, members of Stanmore Baptist Church. Mr Sanz was Spanish, his wife English. They explained, 'We are not sure whether we want to live in Spain permanently, but we would like to go for longer than a holiday to decide. We don't want to sell the house yet. Do you know of anyone who would be willing to rent the house for a time, but not permanently in case we wish to return?'

'Yes,' replied Carol. 'It is just what SBC is looking for.'

Mrs Sanz showed us round the house when we arrived. I was struck dumb, overwhelmed by such a wonderful provision. My outward reaction, mainly silent, caused Mrs Sanz to ask Carol the following day,

'Do you think it is not good enough for her?'

We lived in that house for nearly a year, developing a deep friendship with Peter and Carol. It was the start of a rich association with SBC.

A year with Stanmore Baptist Church

Pat Goodland, the energetic, big hearted minister of SBC had studied at All Nations Bible College shortly after Doug. When he had been a pastor in Poole, Doug had known Pat's parents and brother. Pat also had wanted to go to China with the CIM, but was not accepted on health grounds, however, he trained a number of candidates for the OMF. His wife, Beryl, daughter of CIM's deputation secretary, 'Pop' Welch, had been interned as a pupil with her school in China by the Japanese.

Pat and Beryl had built up the church from small beginnings, ably assisted by talented deacons, including Dr Guthrie, a New Testament scholar, Geoffrey Grogan, a Bible School Principal, and Ronald Inchley, promoter of Intervarsity Publications. The increase in the congregation resulted in the need for an assistant pastor. Pat had just lost one through ill health so Doug's request to act as assistant pastor met Pat's need also. We were welcomed into the warm, vibrant atmosphere of the Christian church. They took us to their hearts, and we took them to ours.

Doug was delighted and surprised that Pat invited him to preach his first Sunday back in England, and Pat refrained from mentioning that some of the congregation disapproved of the message.

Grace and Michael at boarding school

After a time with my mother and friends in Whitley Bay, we settled in Stanmore. Richard started school there at Stanburn, near SBC. He walked with a neighbour's lad the mile to school crossing a disused railway line. There was no need to escort him in those days.

Parents living and working abroad usually had to leave their children to be educated in boarding schools. My close friend, Win, whose husband was posted to British Embassies anywhere in the world also left her boys at Boarding Schools. Hostel accommodation for the holiday periods and house parents to care for them was provided by OMF. We knew that our children would have to continue their education at boarding schools. Michael had been accepted for Monkton Combe School, near Bath. The junior school asked for the boys to start at nine years of age. We took him to see the school, buy the uniform and meet the headmaster. It was overwhelmingly strange for him. We visited him three weeks after he started in September. Mrs Poley, a retired African Inland Missionary, attending SBC asked me,

'Do you have anywhere to stay in Monkton Combe?'

'No,' I answered. 'I thought of staying with friends in Bristol.'

'I have some good friends, Mr and Mrs Gammon, in Monkton,' she continued. 'They would be glad to put you up.'

'But I've never met them,' I expostulated.

'Don't worry,' she replied. 'I know them well. They would be delighted to give you hospitality.'

So it was arranged – an unexpected provision.

They were indeed a lovely family. The father was a round, jovial barber, the mother an excellent cook. We were completely at ease in their home, only a step away from the school. They invited Michael to come every Sunday for lunch in our absence. Later they wrote to us to say he wasn't coming so often because he was much more settled. When family circumstances made it difficult for them to have us, Peter and Christine Carrick who lived near opened their home to us. They had been members of SBC before moving to Monkton.

Grace was due to go to Clarendon School. I knew the school because I had taught for a few months at Clarendon in Malvern before they moved to more spacious premises in Abergele, N Wales. There was a drive of about a mile from the main road to the front door, sheep grazing on the fields at both sides of the drive. Miss Kobrak taught Grace German (see page 195).

We had the children home for the holidays and were able to meet the couples who would have responsibility for them after we returned to Japan. My mother stayed with us several weeks.

The time with SBC was indeed refreshing, just what we were needing. Doug was refreshed and re-invigorated through preaching to a congregation of 200 instead of ten; and able to speak of more than the first steps of Christianity.

Pat's secretary, Joan Sewell, had taken me out with Beryl to buy me a new coat, typical of their generosity. She asked me to address the Women's Fellowship in three monthly talks on 'Basic Christianity', based on C.S. Lewis' book of that title. But I told them what I taught to Japanese children, who started with no conception of one God, no knowledge of the Bible or Christ. Nothing could be more basic than one God, living creator, righteous, love and Saviour – sin and salvation. I also gave talks to the Sunday School teachers.

We had a meeting of ladies in our home. One regular member came hurriedly one morning asking if it was OK that she had come in slacks! In 1968 ladies usually came to meetings in skirts or dresses. My spontaneous, cheery reply may have reassured her. 'You can't very well take them off.'

A young people's group also met regularly in our home, enthusiastic for Bible study. A number of them paired off and were married later.

The most exciting gathering of the year was the Children's Mission in the summer holidays. It had become a regular event, welcomed by the Council. Helpers (mainly students) were recruited from all over the country, and given hospitality in members' homes. A large marquee was erected in the adjacent school's playing field. Over 1,000 children heard the good news of Jesus for two weeks in the summer holidays and some gave their hearts to Jesus.

At the same time, Peter Hewitt with John Cooper organised a 'Missionary Mart'. They had realised that furniture was being discarded and could be sold on, raising money for missions. They worked hard collecting it, bringing it to the field and selling it. These projects continued year after year in the field, until problems of crime increased, making guarding marquee and goods impossible.

Before we left SBC to return to Japan, the church asked us for a list of things we needed so that they could choose from the list what to give us. They gave us the lot. We remember particularly a pair of bright red nylon sheets, with matching pillowcases, that lasted us for years. Two personal presents were *The Complete Works of Shakespeare*, given to us by John and Jean Cooper, and a Visitor's Book from Peter and Carol. As we used it, we had a record of where we went and whom we met over the years.

SBC continued to pray for us on our return to Japan, communicated directly with us through a radio linkup at Christmas, and welcomed us back on subsequent furloughs.

Return to Japan, 1968

We set off again for Japan in June 1968, travelling by an unknown route, in new circumstances, although we did know where we were going this time.

Sadly we left Grace and Michael in boarding schools in England. Six-year-old Richard was returning with us to Sapporo, via Russia, by ferry, train, plane, another train and ship, taking ten days. The arrangements were with the Russian travel agents Intourist who required us to stay one night in Moscow.

We took a train from London to Harwich where we boarded the ship to ferry us to the Hook of Holland. My memory of it was of a ship designed to get us across the North Sea, but not for luxury. Snacks were obtainable on board; the hard seats did not afford the comfort of the upholstered ones on the Aomori-Hakodate ferry we knew so well. At the Hook we disembarked and caught the train bound for Moscow, crossing through Holland and Poland. We settled in our private three-berth compartment for the long stretch. There was a restaurant car only on the section of the journey through the vast expanse of Poland. We looked at the incomprehensible menu in Polish but with the help of our neighbouring passengers succeeded in ordering a reasonable meal. After that, we had to rely on the food we had with us.

In England in June we had been given a Christmas cake by a gentleman who regularly made about a dozen and sent them on to missionaries across the world. He had suggested we take it with us, rather than his sending it later. We didn't wait till Christmas but ate it on our journey – Christmas in the summer! It was ideal for the journey, rich, compact, satisfying. We had also brought fruit. As we crossed into Soviet territory, the large Russian inspectress came round to look at what we had with us. She pointed a commanding finger at our apples, and ordered, 'Eat it.' Fruit was not allowed across the frontier.

Arriving at the Moscow railway terminal we were met by the Intourist guides who took us and our luggage by bus to the Metropole Hotel. Russian women tend to be large blondes, or slim brunettes. Our dark receptionist told us that Richard was booked into a first-class room, but there was no booking for Doug and me! Doug went to find our necessary tickets, leaving me comfortably seated with Richard in the receptionist's office. She opened her desk drawer, brought out a small Intourist badge, and with a smile, gave it to Richard. He smiled back and said, 'thank you' in Russian. She was touched and asked, 'Where did you learn that?' From then on we could do no wrong. She went to a lot of trouble to sort out our accommodation, worked out the cheapest way we could get our meals. When we finally left she made sure our heavy luggage was carried for us on to the bus.

We had wondered what the Metropole would be like. Rumours gave a picture of intrigue, rooms possibly bugged. I vaguely recollect a broken washbasin, but we had a reasonable night's sleep. In the morning, we tried to get hot water from the vacuum flask but the lid wouldn't move. Doug took it along to the 'kitchen' where he had a tug of war with a large Russian lady, pulling each other from side to side as they both held on to the flask trying to open it.

The previous evening we had made our way to the Bolshoi Circus, which was entertaining, professional and well worth a visit – bears on motorbikes, etc. My neighbour from Czechoslovakia confided to me in German that he did not like Russians. On our return to the hotel by bus, a little uncertain of the way, we were helped by a couple of men who had probably been asked to keep an eye on us – was it for security reasons or to give assistance? We were able to read street names as the Russian alphabet has similarities to the Greek; this was useful in finding our way.

In the morning we went for a walk taking care to watch our route. We turned right into the street from the main entrance, and took successive right turns along the street round the tall brick buildings on our right. On the fifth turn we should have been back to the hotel but we were not. Doug approached a police traffic controller and asked in Russian, 'Do you speak English?' The answer was a clear, 'No' but contact had been made. Doug then said 'Metropole'. The policeman understood and pointed to a clump of trees which was hiding our view of the hotel. We were glad of the week's study of the Russian language we had had in England. Two words we found invaluable were *spasiba* and *poshalsta*, please and thank you. Thank you needs to be said for every favour done – to the waiter in the café, the lift-girl, the cleaner – to maintain mutual acceptance and not give the impression of superiority. I would have been wiser not to have asked 'how much' at a street stall, as I had no idea of the price when she replied in Russian.

The gold domes and crosses glistening on the church buildings were a reminder of the Christian heritage of the land. New large apartment blocks had been built to give the workers good housing but we learned that they had been unsatisfactory because of their uniformity, giving no sense of individuality to the occupants.

When the time came to leave, our receptionist made sure that someone loaded our luggage on to the bus. We said, thank you and goodbye to her as we boarded the bus to take us to Moscow airport for the next stage of our journey.

We flew across the USSR over the huge expanse of Siberia, to the city of Khabarovsk in Eastern Russia, on the China border. We disembarked into intense heat. My watch indicated about 8 a.m. – could it be so hot at that time in the morning? I had not considered the vast distances we had crossed, nor the time zones. I pointed to my watch to the ticket official; she understood, showed me hers – it was midday. We were ushered into a large waiting room with only one entrance and thick glass walls around, giving us a feeling of being prisoners, free to walk around, perhaps under observation.

Customs inspection took place at Khabarovsk. We were a little puzzled because there had been none when we entered Soviet territory, nor was there any when we left. Possibly the nearness to the China border, plus luggage being transferred from train to boat later, gave the town its importance. A small pleasant-looking customs official looked at our luggage and decided to pick out one little case: it happened to contain Richard's toys. The official zipped open the case, took out a colouring book and studied it fascinated. Suddenly he remembered his job, hastily closed the case and passed it back to us.

The last leg of the journey through Russia was relatively short, by train to a port near Vladivostok. We boarded a Russian ship to take us across the Japan Sea, through the Tsugaru Straits (between Hakodate and Aomori) and south to Yokohama. Japanese trains are proverbially on time, but we were delayed in Tokyo because one of the frequent earthquakes had been strong enough to twist the lines causing a disruption of the railway system. Finally, we set off on the familiar fourteen hours on the express train to Aomori, the four and a half hour across the Tsugaru Straits to Hakodate, and then express to Sapporo.

The ten-day journey had been not only interesting but also more refreshing than air travel with jet lag, and also introducing us to the culture and climate of another nation.

CHAPTER 6

Literature Work, and then another move (1968–1972)

BACK IN JAPAN WE LOOKED FORWARD to a settled period in Hirosaki, but first a language refresher course in Sapporo. We wanted to master the 1,800 characters to read Japanese books, but never succeeded. The summer was lonely with Grace and Michael on holiday in England, and even more lonely when Richard went to school in Nanae.

The new house

We moved to Hirosaki in November to a two-storey detached house in a new residential area west of the castle. It was better than any house in which we had previously lived in Japan. We had usually slept on futons on the tatami floor, but this tended to provoke Doug's asthma, so we had to search for a bed. The Japanese rarely had beds: the possible source of supply was the American airbase, near Hachinohe. We bought a second-hand one with iron frame and springs, and brought it back to the house, to face the problem of getting it upstairs. Finally, with the help of friends, we pushed it through the upstairs windows. We looked at each other, 'Why did you choose this one?' we both asked. 'Because I thought you liked it,' we both replied. Communication had been lacking; but after it was made up with attractive covers (and the red nylon sheets), it turned out to be the most comfortable bed we had ever slept in.

Next was the question of furniture. We had been used to sitting on cushions round a low table with Japanese guests. But now, as their style of living had changed, we discovered our guests wanted to sit on chairs. Our pastor advised us, 'old furniture would be acceptable in the manse but the foreign missionary would be expected to have chairs and settee in better condition.' So, for the first time in Japan we had a settee and armchairs.

There was a small plot of ground beside the house where we were able to grow flowers and herbs, with seedlings from our apple-growing owner. He frequently brought us 'Delicious' eating apples usually misshapen, as only perfectly formed round apples were suitable for sale.

Neighbours

The neighbours were friendly. Several joined our regular small English Bible class. I gave the members English names, partly to avoid the cultural use of surnames, except within the family. The high school girl I called Joyce became a Christian, but later, against her parents' wishes, married a young man from a militant Buddhist sect. Both expected to win the other over in no time. Both failed, with tragic results.

The midwife

Across the road from us, was a lively midwife married to a doctor. Her profession gave her many friends and she belonged to a club called 'The friends' Meeting' which had a veneer of Christianity. She welcomed me to talk to a group of ladies interested in the Bible. Yet she herself would constantly bring in red-herrings to any clear explanation of the scripture, claiming not to understand. On one occasion, the ladies expostulated with her. 'That is very clear. Surely you can understand what the teacher has said.' Some time later she privately and sadly explained her opposition and fear. 'If I became a Christian,' she told me, 'my husband would divorce me. I can't risk it.' (I have since wondered whether a person's lack of understanding of the simple Gospel message is caused by a blockage that arises from a fear of consequences.)

The dressmaker

A little further away lived a friendly lady, the dynamic and capable organiser of a dress-making school. She prepared delicious Japanese-style meals for us, and Richard enjoyed the toy cars and space to play in her house. She altered a coat for me making it into a jacket and skirt; then she brought in the local reporter, had my photograph taken in the suit, and asked me to tell him that I was a student in the school. She was surprised at my unwillingness to lie ('a lie is a convenience' is a Japanese proverb), but undaunted she told him herself, possibly suggesting I couldn't speak much Japanese. Whatever, he did not ask me anything.

She invited Jackie Friesan, Doug and me to the end of term tea-ceremony party she was arranging for her students. On arrival we discovered that we were the attraction, kneeling on cushions on the stage in a large hall (fortunately I was wearing a full skirt), to take part in the tea-ceremony, in full view of the TV cameras and orderly rows of students sitting on chairs. She wanted us to bow to the ceremonially arranged dolls: but we had already explained we could not bow down to idols. With quick thought she placed herself between us and the dolls, bowed to us, so we returned her bow. We had bowed to her, but it could appear that we had acknowledged the dolls representing the Emperor and his entourage. Fortunately, we had all had a little experience of the tea-ceremony: as I raised my cup I was aware of the cameras focused on me and, as I did not want to be photographed drinking the tea, I moved remarkably slowly, conveying thought and deliberation in the most acceptable way. Yes, our dressmaker friend was an interesting personality.

Middle school English class

Several middle school (thirteen to fifteen year olds) with the enthusiastic backing of their mothers wanted me to teach them English. The mothers made all the necessary arrangements, providing low benches for their books, while the children sat on the floor, ensuring that they had notebooks, etc. They expected a textbook but I preferred to use my own method, with no pressure of exams. I enjoyed the group, using pictures and flannelgraph, giving simple Bible stories in English. We played the game of twenty questions, animal, vegetable, mineral, abstract, boys against girls. The boys chose 'mineral' and with each wrong answer would laugh, 'he, he, he.' They had chosen the word 'sun', *he* in Japanese. It was a delight to teach those eager youngsters, week by week, seeing their enjoyment of speaking and understanding English. It was a wrench when we had to leave Hirosaki.

Pastor Nakano, the church building

Hirosaki church in 1969 had no building in which to meet. Until Pastor Nakano became minister the services were held in the spacious home of the OMF missionaries, near the Christian bookshop and university. After that we met in the Pastor's home, rented property. He had moved about a dozen times in less than a year. It was not easy for his family, and no use for establishing a church. The need for a church building was obvious.

The plot

The believers agreed. A small committee met with the Pastor to decide on the way forward. The committee included Mr Katagawa, the book shop manager, and a capable music teacher; no one of wealth. The two main issues were (a) location, somewhere that could be found easily and not too far from the university, (b) finance, what could be guaranteed, or expected from church members? A plot of ground was acquired, plans laid for building and manse, architect, builder, etc. The pastor received a substantial contribution from someone outside the church, but would never disclose the source. The next stage was a jumble sale, including goods donated to us by Christians on the American airbase. Apart from the raising of money, the sale brought together church members in enthusiasm and partnership.

Doug had not previously worked in a church with a Japanese pastor, as I had in Kitami. He felt it superfluous to go with the Pastor to a small house meeting, but Pastor Nakano explained that if he did not go with him the believers would think they had quarrelled. I was reminded of my time in Kitami when Margrit and I were expected to attend every meeting until a robbery in our absence made it necessary for one of us always to be at home.

The pastor announced that he was going on a trip to Tokyo for evangelism. Enquiries revealed that he was seeking husbands for three single Christians in Hirosaki. Doug questioned him as to how this could be called evangelism. 'That is simple and obvious,' he replied. 'If I find husbands for these girls, I will have appreciation from their families and a wide open door to preach the Gospel to them.'

The broken bed

As winter approached, snow fell frequently on Hirosaki. We looked forward to Richard coming home for the Christmas holidays. This was exciting for us, even though Grace and Michael were far away in England, sharing their holidays with other missionary children. We had bought what was known as a 'summer bed' for Richard. It was canvas, on a steel frame, and could be folded in three or one section raised to make a chair or all flat as a bed. Richard was quite excited to use it but, in the morning, a sorrowful little boy came to my bedside, confessing, 'Mummy, I've broken the bed.' He had pulled a section up a little, and couldn't push it back again, not knowing that it would have to go through the full 180° before it could be made flat again. I assured him that it was OK, the bed was not broken: but it gave me a deep spiritual lesson. I had always promised the children that, if they did something wrong and the only way I knew about it was by their own confession, I would not punish them. Richard had come to me immediately, thinking that he had done something wrong. If he had waited until the evening, wondering if I would discover the misdemeanour, what a miserable day he would have had. I was reminded that we also need to keep short accounts with God.

The broken leg

A year later, when Christmas came, Richard wanted a pair of skis. We bought him a special 'safety' pair. Back at school enjoying the snowy slopes, he fell and broke his leg. The hospital in Hirosaki agreed to treat him, so he came across the ferry from Hakodate, leg in splints. The doctors had expected him the previous night and had waited for his arrival. They straightened his leg quickly despite his screams, put it in a plaster cast and sent him home, but no crutches were available. He stayed at home for several weeks but the bone was very slow in healing and he spent quite a long time in making toy aeroplanes. At school, birthdays were celebrated by the staff making a cake to the design the child requested, e.g. boat, lighthouse, etc. Richard was coming up to his eighth birthday at the end of January and wanted his cake in the shape of an aeroplane. How could I manage it? I was no artist. I made a flat sponge cake on the oven tray, then cut out the shapes of the wings and body of the plane and stuck them together with blended margarine and sugar. Twisted orange peel made a realistic propeller; the markings were round 'Peter's' chocolates wrapped in blue foil, the centre pushed out and a red glacé cherry inserted.

Mr S, the German lecturer, called on us at this time. He had been in the Luftwaffe. He took one look at it and exclaimed, 'It's a Spitfire.' A surge of pride enveloped me. Not only was my effort seen to be an aeroplane but recognised as a Spitfire. Our friends, an older American missionary couple, encouraged us and joined in the birthday celebrations.

It was a difficult period; backwards and forwards to the hospital, paying for treatment.

Then a professor of medicine on the hospital staff heard what had happened. I had been helping to correct the English of some of his papers, so he reckoned that I qualified as a member of the hospital staff and treatment would be free. Correcting his papers was not easy because the medical terms used were unfamiliar. He later invited Doug and me for a meal in his home. Raw fish was standard fare and no rice served until the end of the meal. We would have found it easier to eat the fish with rice, but this was true hospitality. His second wife seemed to have the status of a servant. His first wife had died and she dominated the room from her enshrined place in the god-shelf. We could feel the heaviness and darkness of the atmosphere.

One day, during Richard's convalescence, our friends, Neil and Peggy Verwey, sent us a package of vitamins and minerals with the note, 'We have received these and wondered if you could use them.' Healing began for Richard from the time he started taking them.

The International Christian Broadcasters' Conference

My time was occupied in teaching Richard and looking after him, feeling more and more shut in on myself. It was then that I received an invitation to attend the International Christian Broadcasters' Conference in Tokyo, as I had been on the Aomori 'Light of the World' Broadcast committee. It gave me the break I was needing, meeting with the producers of Christian broadcasts, enjoying their discussions and enthusiasm, and also talking to our own OMF worker, David Huntley, and General Director, Oswald Sanders.

The village headman and Sunday School

Abe and Jackie Friesen had started a children's meeting in a neighbouring village. I loved children's work so was pleased to continue it when they moved on. Doug drove me out to the unheated barn where the children gathered. I wore about sixteen pieces of clothing in the winter. We had to stop the children jumping out of the upstairs windows on to the snow. While I shivered and enjoyed teaching the Bible stories, Doug sat in the warmth of the headman's house talking and listening to him. Mr H's ancestors had owned the farmland around for centuries. Each successive headman had rented plots of land to the farmers and had been concerned for their welfare.

But, with the surrender of Japan, General McArthur had decreed that the farmers must own the land they cultivated. Suddenly many farmers found they could sell the land they now owned, with devastating effects on their way of life. Having sold the land they no longer cultivated it, what was their livelihood? Mr H also told Doug how the village was divided by a stream: those on one side of the stream would have nothing to do with those on the other. This explained why the children at Sunday School came from one side only. Mrs H, his second wife, was a Christian, and was delighted if the conversation turned to things of the Lord. But Mr H felt it his duty to maintain his spiritual links with the ancestors, especially as headman of the village, and previous owner of the land. Outside his house was the 'treasure' house. This was usually locked and kept private.

But when Pat and Beryl Goodland (pastor of Stanmore Baptist Church at the time) visited us, we took them out to call on Mr H. (Pat's personality must have charmed him). He opened it up and showed Pat its contents. No-one else ever saw inside.

We made a further visit to Mr and Mrs H when we were moving from Hirosaki to Sapporo. Nick Carr, our UK Home Director, was staying with us: we offered him the choice of a hotel or a night in their country house. Nick had no doubts. I explained to Mrs H that we would have our sheets with us, so I could make up the beds. Not withstanding, she had already put down the futon, three side by side, and a mosquito net over the 'triple' bed. Nick also experienced the Japanese *ofuro* (bath). This in the country district was a wooden tub, room for one person to soak up to the neck in the hot water. Nick did not appreciate the companionship of a dead frog that could hardly have survived the heat.

The holiday at Takayama

We had not seen Grace and Michael for over a year: communication had been through letters and tapes. We prayed for funds to fly them to Japan for the summer holidays, 1969. It was a thrill to us when, at the initiative of Doug's home church, West Green Baptist (with Stanmore and Whitley Bay Baptist churches joining in) financed their flight with BOAC (BA). They were given first-rate attention on the plane, and were allowed to visit the cockpit at their request. Michael felt a little put down when they were announced as Miss Abrahams and child – Grace at twelve was charged adult fare, Michael at eleven a child's fare.

We were all overjoyed to be together again. Richard had missed his brother and sister, and was as excited as a little puppy looking forward to their summer holidays. Grace arrived in an extremely short skirt, the fashion of girls of her age in England, but not acceptable in Japan. I obtained a longer one for her to wear until we reached Takayama, our favourite holiday resort. We were borrowing Bill and Dorothy Pape's chalet. The blue Pacific, the beach, the pine trees, swimming daily in the warm sea, with our shoulders protected to avoid sunburn, tennis, many friends, an English service in the Chapel, all combined to give us refreshment and enjoyment. Grace found it difficult to accept that her North American friends had been able to stay in Japan attending the American school, while she and Michael were boarding far away in England. One friend said to her, 'Isn't your mother wonderful to let you wear such a short skirt?' Because our time with the children was relatively short, I frequently prayed for a 'holiday in depth'. It was as though the deep hunger of separation from our children was being satisfied.

What appeared to be a casual conversation on the beach turned out to have far-reaching consequences. David Hayman and Doug were standing together, enjoying the sunshine and looking out to sea.

'I go on furlough to Australia next year,' remarked David, 'and was wondering who I could ask to take my place as superintendent for the year. What do you think about "A" or "B"? (Doug gave no reply, not imagining either of the men mentioned as suitable.) 'You don't think you could do it, do you?' queried David.

'I think I could manage for a year,' Doug replied.

The six-week holiday came to an end all too soon. Grace and Michael flew back to England. Richard returned to school in Nanae. Doug and I went back to our comfortable home in Hirosaki.

New responsibilities in Sapporo

David Hayman reminded Doug, 'You said you could do my job for a year. Please come to Sapporo now to take my place as Deputy Superintendent.'

We had never been so settled and contented as we were in Hirosaki. The house was comfortable, neighbours friendly, the surroundings pleasant.

We were sad to be leaving a growing church with Pastor and Mrs Nakano in the new church building; Mr Katagawa, the book shop manager, continuing after damage had been caused by a fire; the Christian students, some of whom had spent Christmas Day with us, and especially their lively leader who told me regretfully, later, of his inability to lead a consistent Christian life in the business world; the young couple with two boys, in a nearby town of Kuroishi, who had struggled against evil spiritual forces; the children of the Sunday School in the barn in the country village; and especially the lively middle school group progressing in their use of

English. The mother of one of this group who had lived in Sapporo, would like to have visited again, but told me, 'I have so many friends and relations in Sapporo, that I could not go there, as I couldn't afford the presents I would be obliged to take.' Presents are expected when visiting former friends.

We packed up everything and sent off the luggage, including our iron bed. A train took us north through the apple-growing countryside to Aomori where there were many crates of apples for sale. There we boarded the ferry for Hakodate where we sighted the majestic mountain, then on by train to Sapporo.

Sapporo was a modern city of about a million people, with wide straight streets mostly paved and geometrically designed. The headquarters of OMF in the NE of the city consisted of a new office block with living accommodation for the superintendent and secretaries. We were in the rooms above the offices, with a wooden floor kitchen and dining room, and three tatami floor rooms, including a guest room with bed.

It took time to adjust to the new situation. Doug became pastor and leader to the Japan missionaries. There had been a change in the administration, resulting in the appointment of a director as well as a superintendent. David Michell had been elected as superintendent but was due for home assignment, so we were regarded as temporary residents. But when Doug entered his office and started to record on the dictaphone, he felt sure he would be there for a long time – it turned out to be for twelve years. Instead of being back in a year, because of David's wife Joan's ill health, they did not return to Japan.

Richard was at school in Nanae, near Hakodate. Among other things the children loved, was the lively dog that caused great excitement when it produced its litter. Richard proudly returned home for his holidays with one of the pups as his own possession, a female he had chosen. Doug pointed out the problem if she produced her own litter – it was what DD (the name Grace had given him as a baby) had hoped for. 'I know,' replied Richard, 'that's why I chose her.' She was brown and white so we gave her the name Rocha. In Japanese *shiro* is white, *chairo* brown, so I put the words together, *shi (ro cha) iro* gave us Rocha.

The Japanese never kept dogs in the house – it would be difficult for the dog to remove her shoes on entering! So Rocha had a kennel at the foot of our outside back stairs. Feeding her was cheap as she enjoyed the boiled up fish heads, given to me on request by the local supermarket.

She did indeed produce her litter of five pups, two male and three female. It was wintertime, so she smoothed out a semi-circle in the snow for them, and was quite content outside. There was no problem finding homes for the males but the females were not generally wanted; two of our lady missionaries fell for the very attractive pup we had named 'Pudding,' because she was plump, black and white, and appealing. They called her 'Guinea' (perhaps because they valued her) and gave her a home in their flat.

When we had to leave for our home assignment, neighbours wanted Rocha but we had to have her spayed.

The twelve years in Sapporo were quite an adventure in themselves, interspersed by home assignment and holidays with the children.

Interlude

Stanmore Baptist Church, 1972

The flight

I HAD COME ON AHEAD FOR SURGERY (hysterectomy) flying to London via Cairo. A passenger alighting at Manila kindly agreed to post a letter for me there. Doug was puzzled, wondering why I was in the Philippines! We reached Cairo as a sandstorm was brewing. We were able to land, but the storm reduced visibility, preventing us from taking off again. We were accommodated overnight in the airport hotel. I joined a practically-minded Indian nurse, sharing a room, as neither of us wished to be alone in unknown territory.

The next morning, we went sightseeing with an organised group. The wind was causing the sand to swirl around cutting into our flesh, reminding us of a hailstorm. On the way a 'friendly' Egyptian offered to take our photographs. He persuaded me to stand with my back to his camel, instructed me to lean back – the next thing I knew was that the camel was on its feet standing with me on its back. I looked at the sympathetic faces of our group nearby and saw the expanse of the desert in the far distance. Deciding that I didn't want to be taken out there on my own, I slid off the camel's back landing on top of the photographer. He wanted payment for the photograph and I replied that he should pay me for the stockings I had ruined in the fall. I was relieved to rejoin the party.

We continued on to climb up the inside of a pyramid. Our guide took one look at our group, decided that I was the most feeble, grasped my hand and literally pulled me up the long climb of steps. On the way down he paused at a secluded turning and confided, 'I like the Germans.'

I assured him I was English – a pause – 'I like the English.'

I understood his meaning and explained, 'I am really quite poor but I can give you a little.'

He seemed satisfied with the amount and I didn't begrudge it. I was frankly glad of his assistance.

15. Sapparo snow festival – the 'buildings' are made of snow (see page 181)

16. Four of the Hirosaki lads learning English (see page 165)

17. Morning exercises at school English camp (see page 245)

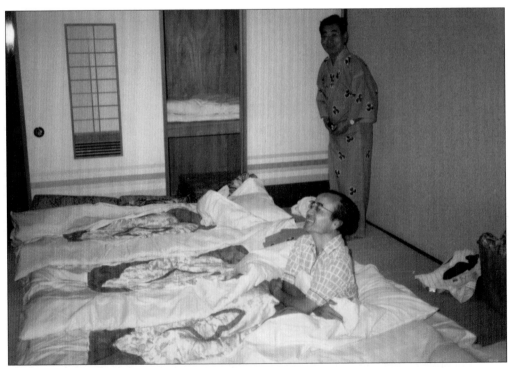

18. Sleep well! Futon on the tatami floor

19. Koganei Free Methodist Church old building (see page 233)

20. Koganei Free Methodist Church new building (see page 239)

21. Coming to worship – a founder member

22. Mr and Mrs Tsubomi with their well designed meal (see page 229)

23. *Author demonstrating cooking (see page 219)*

24. *Yoneko, third from right, tall because she could lengthen her wooden legs, with the Koganei church ladies (see page 220)*

25. The Pastor places the urn with the ashes in the church burial plot (see page 240)

26. A farewell gift to the author from Mr Tsutada, Bible college principal (see page 249)

27. *Author buying a nightdress at a street stall in Beijing (see page 252)*

28. *A father with two lads wanting his photo taken with Doug in Beijing (see page 252)*

29. Reunion with Irene Hope and the Kamada family in Sapporo

30. Goodbye at Narita Airport

The storm finally subsided and we boarded the plane for Heathrow. The calm of an English summer was a pleasant contrast to the sandstorm we had experienced.

John Caisley, our efficient and helpful OMF business manager, was there to meet me and take me to our OMF London headquarters in Newington Green.

The hospital

My friend Enid Crane was on leave in England from Nigeria, visiting a fellow student from her Bible School, and staying at our headquarters. She had learned, possibly from John Caisley, or perhaps from our church in Whitley Bay of my expected arrival. It was she who took me along to the Mildmay Mission Hospital, a small Christian establishment, and gave me her support as I prepared nervously for the operation.

I had visitors every day. Enid was the first.

'I know you are tired. I'll go away if you wish, or just stay here. You don't need to talk.' I was tired.

'Please stay,' I responded, 'and if I get other visitors please would you talk to them.'

Bill and Edna Lemon walked in. He had been Whitley Bay Church secretary and knew Enid well. It was great that they could catch up on Enid's news of Nigeria, while I rested.

Pastor Laing, the new Pastor of Doug's church dropped in, bringing me a word from Isaiah Ch. 43 'I will bring your children from the North, the South, the East and the West.' I don't think he had known that Grace, Michael and Richard were coming from different directions. Grace from North Wales, Michael from the West, and Richard from Japan, the East. He told me of an incident when visiting a church member in hospital and praying for her. Other patients were worried because they thought she must be dying if he was praying.

One couple, parents of a fellow missionary in Japan, explained that they were retired with no fixed routine, so prayed for God to guide them each morning – hence they came to see me. (Later I learned that, on his death-bed, he suddenly sat up and exclaimed with his last breath. 'It's really true!')

There was no day without someone calling in but surprise, surprise, when who should walk in unexpectedly but my fifteen-year-old daughter,

Grace looking charming. Although the school term had not ended, she had finished her O-Level exams and had received permission from Clarendon School to travel from North Wales to London to see me. This was indeed a bonus.

The young doctor assigned to my case came to examine me, drew the curtains around my bed and then we had a theological discussion for about twenty minutes. He had known me through a former girlfriend from Whitley Bay. There were two wards upstairs in the hospital. Our little group was constantly immersed in laughter. A young patient opposite me was a cheerful humorist. I had great difficult in restraining my laughter because it hurt my stitches. Should I have said, 'She had us in stitches?'

I got to know a patient in the other ward who was in the charge of the second houseman. She had been in the Salvation Army but had abandoned her faith, married an unconverted Anglican curate, and they both came into a new relationship to Jesus and served Him in Africa as missionaries.

The peace of the hospital was shattered one morning – a lady, who had just returned from very difficult circumstances in India working in a school amongst Indians, went berserk and had to be removed to a private room. My 'African' friend received permission to talk to her and prayed for her in tongues. I was in a slightly different position because she was not the responsibility of my doctor. I did at last go to her, talked and prayed with her, she confided that her fear was of going mad.

The hospital was plunged into gloom, a heavy spirit came over everyone and there was no laughter from our humorist. I made my way down to the other ward, to the lady from Africa, and said we must pray together. This we did, in the power of the Holy Spirit, praying for deliverance from the evil spirits. The atmosphere of gloom evaporated immediately and the wards were restored to their happy freedom.

The time in the hospital was a rich experience, the happy atmosphere, the kindness of the staff, shared troubles and joys, visitors, texts on the walls, daily prayers. When I think back on this period I am amazed at the detailed companionship and help I received all along.

I left for a short stay in a Worthing convalescent home where Michael came to visit me, and then back to Stanmore to meet Doug and Richard returning from Japan. Michael and Grace were reunited with us in the house the church had supplied.

The family united

Pat and Beryl Goodland drove to Heathrow with me to welcome Doug and DD arriving from Japan. (DD was the diminutive name that Grace had given Richard as a baby, not knowing it was the Chinese for Little Brother.) Doug and DD had travelled together from Sapporo, having bought a terrapin before leaving; DD carried it in a jam jar and was successful in taking it through barriers in Tokyo, Hong Kong and Bangkok airports. At Heathrow, he put the jar on a suitcase and, as Doug picked up the suitcase, the jar went flying, smashed into pieces but the terrapin remained unhurt; DD looked after it tenderly until we reached the house in Stanmore. It was a spacious semi-detached house, next door to Mrs Clinch, a pharmacist, who had been a founder member of SBC.

Grace and Michael joined us for their school holidays. We were all very happy to be together again as a family; DD had missed his brother and sister while they had missed him and us.

Our immediate need was for a car large enough for the five of us to travel to relatives, friends, churches, conferences and meetings, throughout the country. We agreed to pray for a suitable car and DD prayed, 'Please, Lord, may we have an Austin Cambridge like the one we had last time.'

Doug remonstrated, 'It's OK to ask for a suitable car, but isn't it a bit too much to specify the make?'

After church the next Sunday, a young man approached us on our way home with the question,

'Are you on wheels?'

'Not yet,' we answered.

'I've just bought a new car, and was going to put my old one in as part exchange. Then I thought you might be able to use it. It's fully taxed and has passed the MOT. It's over there.'

He pointed to a car parked just opposite our house – an Austin Cambridge!!

Was there a satisfied smile on DD's face? And did we feel rebuked, and grateful to God. The car did us well for the year of furlough, only stopping sometimes after about sixty miles: the AA, garage and knowledgeable friends, were unable to solve the problem.

We travelled north to visit my mother (sometimes brought her down to London to stay with us), and to my church in Whitley Bay, etc., and especially with frequent visits to Michael's school, Monkton Combe.

We had to make arrangements for DD also to attend the same school. He was accepted by the school, but a problem arose concerning the fees. The local education authority could no longer give grants to boys under eleven – DD was ten. We wanted him to have a year there while we were still home, and to be with Michael. We prayed for the fees. A member of OMF's Scottish Council, who hardly knew us, but knew our need, gave us a very large gift enabling us to cover the fees for a year. Michael was already established in Monkton, even if not too happy there. His own struggles made him particularly sensitive to the needs of younger boys, especially sons of OMF missionaries, and he was very helpful. He gave himself to DD whenever he could. We also had friends in the area with whom we could stay on our numerous visits.

The following is DDs comments about our separation.

'When we are home together, I am with you and see you all the time. When I am at school I see you on our school holidays and on your visits to the school. When you are back in Japan, I see you once a year. But if you should die, it would only mean the period before I saw you again would be a little longer.'

It was quite a profound observation but also indicated how separation was comparable to a bereavement.

Gracely had just completed her O-levels so we arranged for her to have the year with us, attend a local grammar school for A-levels, and trusted that someone in Stanmore would give her a home for her final year – Gladys and Ken Cuthbert, with one teenage daughter at home, offered to look after her for that year. She was a warm hearted capable Christian, he was a policeman, practical and kind.

It was a busy year for us, deepening friendships, visiting John and Gwyneth Watson, house parents for our children at Donnington Herst, a spacious OMF mansion where they looked after teenagers when their missionary parents were abroad.

The time was approaching for us to return to Japan after the year. We were taking the boys on their last half-term holiday to the Isle of Wight. Doug prayed fervently that the car would not let us down. No problem getting there, but on the way back to the boarding school it stopped. Doug said:

'See if you can stop another car to take the boys back to school while I see what we can do about our car.'

I stopped a couple's car 'I am sorry we are not going in that direction,' the wife explained, 'but my husband knows a bit about cars and will have a look at yours.'

As he got out of his car his wife said to me, 'He loves cars – he doesn't have a shirt without oil on it.'

He opened the bonnet and looked. 'I think it's the coil – just a minute.' He went to his own car and produced a spare coil. 'Oh dear, it's the wrong fitting, just a moment.' He returned to his own car, produced another coil, back to ours, and it fitted. Who would carry two spare coils in the boot of his car?

We continued on our journey with no further problem, praising the Lord for sending his servant.

While all this was happening, DD had been very anxious almost in tears.

'I'll be told off for being late back to school,' he told his father.

'If that happens, I'll take you out of the school.'

These words of assurance meant a lot to him, knowing the support Doug was giving him. Parting is never easy.

CHAPTER 7

Sapporo, our Headquarters (1973–1981)

The town and the snow

SAPPORO, THE CAPITAL OF HOKKAIDO, was a booming city of a million people. Doug and I were married there twenty years ago, in 1964. The roads were straight and paved unlike Hirosaki, streets built according to plan, north to south, east to west, buildings of concrete – wooden houses rare because they could not be insured, and were a fire hazard.

Hokkaido had been developed at the end of the nineteenth century as a defence against the Russians. The labourers were political dissenters banished from the mainland, and dispossessed Samurai; they suffered from the harsh winters while building the roads.

A language centre, several churches, a book shop, Bible College and headquarters were established by OMF, as most of our work at the time was here in the north.

Our flat was above the HQ offices, with housing for the secretaries at the side of the building. Snowfall was heavy for four months from the end of November, and snow tyres mandatory. The police would check the tyres. There was an unusually cold spell one mid-November before the date for changing the tyres. We had to drive to Asahikawa, about fifty miles. The road up to the town was covered with sheer ice. Cars were abandoned at the roadside, others were sliding uncontrollably backwards down the slope. We succeeded in continuing up the hill in our relatively heavy vehicle but would have been quite helpless had another car slid backwards in our path. We reached our destination, shaken, but safe, and returned to Sapporo by train.

Long, thick icicles hung from the roofs and would curve round, breaking windows. They resulted from snow on the roof melting with the heat of the house, then freezing, melting again and slipping down, finally falling from the roof. We had to break them off before they smashed the windows.

Driving in the snow could be treacherous. Drivers often carried 'helpers'. These were made of hinged metal and were put under the wheel of the car stuck in a drift, effectively providing traction to release the vehicle.

In the centre of town, household waste was used to heat under the roads, resulting in an area clear of snow. It was also used to heat the public swimming pool in the winter.

In February, Sapporo celebrated a snow festival. The army brought in snow to cover structures built of wood in the central 'green belt'. Different groups, such as colleges, students, department store employees, etc., would erect fantastic statues – legendary figures, historical themes, famous buildings (e.g. the White House), Santa's sleigh. Flowers trapped in blocks of ice were beautiful. The scene could be spoilt only if the weather turned warmer.

Further excitement came when Sapporo hosted the Winter Olympics. Doug and I enjoyed watching an ice hockey match, accompanied by an American friend who explained the game, and he himself entered the contest as an enthusiastic spectator.

Because of the cold climate, houses were kept warm and we buttoned up when going out. When Doug had returned from a trip to Tokyo, he often commented on how cold he felt there. The houses were not heated. I was reminded of the contrast between the north and south of England in a cold summer.

Day to day activities

Doug, as Superintendent, was involved as Pastor to the OMF missionaries, administration – visitors were frequent – from overseas, other missions, the quarterly 'Field Council', folk needing a bed. I was grateful to have a pleasant Japanese lady helping in the house, and a surprisingly large oven. I don't know where it came from; but to be able to cook a whole salmon in it was convenient and not time-consuming.

A fellow missionary had given me advice as to what to do as Super's wife: 'Be yourself.'

I followed this, enjoying preaching opportunities, teaching English to children, to university classes, to adult Bible classes, the ladies' cooking/Bible class, visiting.

Living in our street was Mrs Igarashi and her daughter, Mrs Imamura. We had met over twenty years previously when I lived in Kitami. Mrs I, a Christian, had brought her twelve-year-old daughter to my house. The daughter had never forgotten me because I had given her one toffee (see page 64) instead of the whole bowl. Now she was married with her own little girl, Yuko. She was not yet a Christian – she told me that her life was too comfortable to change, and, 'I wouldn't want to be wealthy. I enjoy hunting for bargains.'

She hesitantly asked me about one matter. Japanese people had started to use toilet seats – not just squatting.

'How does one manage with a little girl?' Yuko was only four.

I had a question for her. I had recently learned that the phrase I was using when offering someone something translated, 'You may have this if you wish' was coming across as 'If you are desperately wanting this, OK take it.'

I told Mrs Imamura what I usually said.

'Yes, that's OK,' she said.

'But would you say it?'

'Oh, no!'

'What would you say?'

'If you don't mind (if it's all right with you), then please take this.'

I found later that when I used this sentence my offer was generally accepted, where previously it had been refused.

The Japanese generally would be too polite to correct our language. Further, I had reached the stage of fluency where they would not realise I was making a mistake. They are forgiving when we make our first efforts.

Mrs I came to the Bible/cooking class but tried to avoid meeting me in the street. She told me that no matter which route she took to the shops, she would meet me face to face. An encounter to her was a challenge to belief in Christ.

When her mother was dying in hospital, she confided to me that she could not become a Christian just to please her mother. It was more than ten years later that she took her own step of faith and was baptized.

Primary school children

Looking out of our living room window at breakfast time, we could see hundreds of black-haired children hurrying to school, chatting to their friends. I longed to tell them about Jesus and prayed for an opportunity to start a regular Sunday School in our flat.

Tony Schmidt, a large warm-hearted accountant from South Africa, was willing to help although he was limited in language. We duplicated invitations to children from second to sixth grades (seven to twelve years), to come from 8.30 on Sunday mornings, to learn about the Bible, at a cost of about 50p a month. We gave them out to the boys and girls on their way to school two mornings.

Why charge for Sunday School? Some colleagues thought this was dreadful, but the reason was simple. Something offered free was considered to be of no value. The children's reaction was, 'This is great, 50p a month is a bargain. Let's go.'

Why second grade upward? The Japanese rarely discipline their children – young children and the elderly have the right to do anything they like. Discipline begins with school.

Further, second graders would be able to read. I would then be able to teach all grades together, especially as the material, stories of Jesus, was new to them. (And the first graders could hardly wait for the next year.)

The children responded eagerly as a queue formed outside the door from 8 a.m. When we opened the door they flocked upstairs into our living room, an enthusiastic group of curious youngsters, many sitting on the floor.

Tony was a great help – even though he read the register one week forgetting to mark it. His love for the children and for the Lord shone through. We were rewarded by the children's keenness and understanding. They sang with gusto, to my violin accompaniment, 'The true God, there is only one.' They could grasp the concept of one true creator God more easily than their parents who were accustomed to the myriad gods of Japan.

To the question, 'Are lies right or wrong?' I have rarely heard a child defend lies. The adult answer is usually, 'Lies are a convenience.'

I used the flannelgraph – with flannel covered pictures illustrating the Bible story. This kept the younger children happy while I explained the story to the older ones. Seeing the temptation of Eve, the class were almost willing Eve not to yield to the serpent – Don't do it! We used three-month courses with explanatory leaflets and pictures of the life of Christ. We came to the climax when Jesus asked the disciples, 'Who do you say that I am?' I asked the class – 'Who do you say Jesus is?' They replied, like Peter, 'He is the Son of God.' The story of the cross left them crestfallen. But far from questioning the resurrection, they declared happily – 'That's what ought to have happened.'

Church groups in England pasted Japanese texts (provided by OMF) on the back of old Christmas cards, often portraying the Christmas story. We received them and used them to reward the boy or girl who answered a question. One boy accumulated a large number and treasured them. His mother told us that the family was quite well off and the boy had lots of toys, but he valued these cards above all. He had earned them. When we gave the children little booklets about Easter and Jerusalem, he read his and commented, 'Then the stories we have been learning are real historical facts.'

We made folders with coloured cartridge paper to hold the weekly Bible story leaflet (produced by the Japan Sunday School Union) and a picture to colour. We printed the child's name in large black capitals, and gave them out at the start of each lesson. It was a tremendous help to us to know their names – an essential requirement when teaching. To know the name helps in discipline and in relationships. The attendance charts also helped in this and added interest. Week by week stars were put against the name of the child, but it was never a straight list. We had one in the form of a wheel, names at the end of the spokes, a circle for each week. Another a fish, the stars the scales, a cross, etc.

For Easter we arranged a special programme, borrowing the children's leisure centre across the road. Every detail seemed to be contested – as though some mischievous imps were playing tricks. The centre was normally closed on a Sunday but the authorities had agreed to have it unlocked for us. The possessor of the keys was nowhere to be found. We had to make hurried arrangements to use our office block. Slides we had intended to show and had placed on the stairs disappeared into thin air, but were finally discovered elsewhere. We managed to complete the pro-gramme in time to clear up everything before the start of the adult service, held as usual in our living-room.

Different colleagues helped at different times during our period in Sapporo. We divided the Sunday School into two groups at one stage.

Christmas was always a time of celebration for the children with nativity plays, etc. The summer holiday was an occasion for camps by the sea. I should have taken a group instead of sending them together with fellow missionaries, and strengthened my relationship with the children and their parents.

The Shibakawa family

It was a pleasure to meet up again with the Shibakawa family. They had helped me in language study in Kitami (see page 68). Rinya brought me the canary (Shadrach) after the loss of our baby (see page 105). Masayoshi, the eldest son was living in Sapporo, with his family, head of the timber business. After reading the life of Hudson Taylor, he resolved not to go into debt. This was an unprecedented step to take in running a business in Japan. He found the steady supply of wages, and no panic over debts, resulted in smooth, cordial relationships in the factory.

The tour

His mother had died and was buried in the father's private property in Kitami, on the 'Hill of the Cross'. The Buddhist practice is to have a ceremony after three years, but Mr Shibakawa Sr decided to celebrate with an evangelistic tour of east Hokkaido, staying in hotels at different locations and having Gospel meetings in each. Transport was in a fleet of seven taxis. This was very much a family affair: Doug and I felt honoured to be invited to join about twenty others. We were both asked to give evening messages alongside 'lay' preachers, old Christian friends of Mr Shibakawa Sr.

Mr Shibakawa Sr's daughter had married the brother of a Shinto priest. The priest was our companion on the tour. He was impressed by the testimony of the laymen who spoke at the meetings.

'You and I are the same,' he said to Doug. 'We are professionals, but this man is a Christian speaker and an ordinary businessman.'

Self-introduction is part of Japanese custom. At one church meeting a lady stood up and said, 'Mr and Mrs Abrahams, you won't know me but I remember you. You ran a Sunday School in Shizunai. My sister attended and brought me along. She left, but I continued and became a Christian there. I trained as a nurse, married a doctor, and we are together in this village to tell others about Christ.' The village was famous as the birth place of Yokozuna Taihō (the top sumo wrestler), his statue prominently displayed.

The taxi took us to a lake where the water was warm with hot springs. Bottles of milk were being heated in the sand. Two bearded gentlemen in *Ainu* costume were sitting on chairs at the lakeside with a bear between them. The *Ainu* are the aborigines of Japan, the few left living in east Hokkaido. Their features are very different from the Japanese – smaller, wide-eyed, hairy, more Caucasian. Traditionally they worship the bear. They are rarely seen, but dressed in their native ornate costume they attract tourists. They pose with their bear to be photographed for a price. I told them about our Christian *Ainu* friend, Mr Ega, from Shizunai. They knew him, were excited about our friendship, were themselves Christian – and *they* wanted to have a photograph of *me* with them.

Another stop, at a national park area, thirteen of us stood around in a semi-circle eating freshly roasted potatoes. Potatoes are a special product of Hokkaido.

It was a wonderful time of celebration – the joy and fellowship of Christians, and fantastic views in glorious weather – a gift God had given us, His thoughts towards us so much higher than ours.

The new wife

Mr Shibakawa had needed a wife to look after him. Masayoshia's wife, Akiko, frequently took the tiring six-hour train journey from Sappora to Kitami to look after him. But a second wife had been found for him from Shizuoka, a 'young lady' of sixty-three. She told me of her early experiences as his wife. They were at the airport, and he was laughing.

'Why are you laughing?' she asked.

'Because I have lost the tickets.'

'Surely that is serious, no laughing matter.'

'Remember,' he exhorted her, 'when any trouble occurs the first thing to do is to laugh.'

(Some years later he had arranged for us to meet him at a restaurant in Tokyo. We couldn't find it, then we saw him, laughing. 'There must be some trouble,' Doug and I said to each other.) The restaurant was non-existent!

Alcoholics rehabilitation

Mr Shibakawa was a help to us in establishing an Alcoholics Rehabilitation Centre.

When we first arrived in Japan, drunkenness was accepted in society. The drunkard was not held responsible for his actions or accidents. Public opinion mounted over the years; drunkenness was disapproved of but little was done to help the alcoholic. Hospital treatment was only a temporary respite. On discharge the craving returned, money and livelihood gone, only despair left.

Bob Cunningham, new to OMF Japan, had worked amongst alcoholics in Chicago. He had plans to set up a Rehabilitation centre in Sapporo. Doug encouraged him, having had a concern for alcoholics, who often made a beeline for him. Bob set up a temporary centre in his own home. When one of the men turned on him with a knife, the local police were called and were followed by a bevy of newspapermen. When Doug went down to see what was happening the journalist asked him, 'What are you doing here?'

Doug replied, 'We are about to have a Bible Study and Christian prayer meeting. You are welcome to join us.' The room quickly cleared.

That was just the beginning. One day Bob came to Doug excitedly, 'I've just found the ideal Japanese man to head up the work. He is a former alcoholic himself transformed through Christ. I'd like to introduce you. He is from the Hidaka (Shizunai region). His name is Utsunomiya.'

We had known him years ago and his brother and sister. We remembered the shock his family had received when at the funeral of his father, as the eldest son, he announced, pointing to the body, 'That is just my father's body. His spirit is with his creator. As a follower of Jesus Christ I cannot worship my father or offer incense to him.'

Doug had visited his home in the mountains, staying longer than planned because of a blizzard making the village snowbound. He spent several hours giving a general exposition of the New Testament to half a dozen men in their small room, all sleeping there on futons spread out on the floor. (See Doug's *Man and Missionary*.)

Mr Shibakawa helped us to find a suitable site (neighbours were worried about having drunkards nearby) not far from Fujino church, for which he had responsibility. When the work was up and running, he invited inmates to attend his church. He also offered them employment in his firm, meeting the need of former alcoholics who could rarely find work.

The book shop

He was on the board of the Christian bookshop and his business acumen was invaluable. He realised that with the activities of an able salesman the work was expanding too quickly for success. He said so, but acknowledged that, if the project was directed by God, it could succeed. We should have listened more carefully – he was correct in predicting its collapse.

The retreat

Mr Shibakawa Sr had built further on his plot on the Hill of the Cross, and established a centre for Christian retreats. We accepted his invitation to visit. Doug warned me, 'Be sure to be ready with some Bible message.' Mr Shibakawa does not ask you in advance. He announced, 'Mr Abrahams will speak tonight. Olga will speak this afternoon.'

On the day we were leaving just before breakfast, 'Olga will give us a Bible talk after breakfast.'

'She won't', countered Masayosi. 'They are returning to Sapporo on the 9.30 train from Kitami.

'Oh – Olga will bring the word, before breakfast.' I was ready.

The younger brother

Masayoshi told us the story of the marriage of his youngest brother, Riichiro. He studied chemistry in the USA under difficult circumstances when financial support from Japan was cut off. On his return with his degree from the States, his father and two brothers met him at the airport. They sat down at a table to discuss the future, when Mr Shibakawa Sr suddenly got up taking the brothers with him.

'We'll have to decide what to do with him. He has become too American.'

(We later asked Riichiro what he had done wrong. 'I'm not sure,' he answered, 'but probably I sat with my feet on the table.')

The decision was to find him a wife. Mr Shibakawa Sr was attending a Gideon rally. He approached a colleague.

'Do you think you could help us? My youngest son has been in the States for three years and has become too American. Would you be able to find him a suitable wife?'

The colleague, astonished, answered, 'My daughter has just returned after a year in the States. The culture has rubbed off on her also.'

They married and have 'lived happily ever after'.

Training a new worker

Maggie was struggling to learn Japanese – she was attending our small Sunday Service when unexpectedly a young American student joined us. She spoke Japanese fluently although she had been in Japan only a few months. She had been living in a student dormitory, fully immersed in both language and culture. Maggie protested to Doug

'That's what I need. I'm not getting very far in the OMF language centre.'

'OK', replied Doug, 'off you go.'

Mr and Mrs Shibakawa took her into their home; she joined in their 6 a.m. prayer meeting, and the activities of the Fujino church. Mrs Shibakawa looked after her like a mother when she was unwell. She and their daughter Kaori became firm friends.

Beethoven's Choral Symphony

Traditionally, Beethoven's 9th symphony is played every December throughout Japan. We had the pleasure of Mr and Mrs Shibakawa's company to celebrate our December birthdays by going together to listen to the Sapporo Symphony Orchestra's performance.

Visits

After we had moved to Tokyo, they welcomed us back to Sapporo to stay in their home. They entertained us royally but, on one occasion, trouble struck. Doug got a very bad asthma attack. We realised the cause. Their daughter, Megumi, now owned a very lively thick-haired poodle that had the run of the house. The dog was friendly but Doug is allergic to dogs' hair. He got through the night but after that Mr Shibakawa arranged for us to stay at a hotel.

The Kamada Family

Ten minutes walk away from us across the busy East 10 main road lived Mr and Mrs Kamada and their three daughters. The plaster house was well built and the arched windows reminded us of a church. Nothing on the outside gave any indication of their religious beliefs but inside showed the typical adherence of Shinto and Buddhism, usual in a Japanese household. In the first room, high up like a kitchen shelf, was the Shinto god-shelf (*kamidana*) symbolising the spirit of Japan and the Emperor with no idols. In an inner room, looking like an ornate lacquered cupboard was the Buddhist shrine (*butsudan*) honouring the family deceased, the photograph of the dead person plus a plaque inscribed with his posthumous name (given by the priest) occupied a prominent place in the shrine. Mr Kamada as eldest son had the responsibility of looking after his father's spirit although it was Mrs Kamada who offered up rice and water daily, reciting a prayer. Any special delicacy was placed before the spirit before the family received it.

The middle daughter, still at high school, had become a Christian. Away at a young people's gathering, an Irish missionary had told her about Jesus. She found that He was able to help her in her personal problems and, back in Sapporo, a compassionate Australian lady had befriended her and taught her further about Christ.

It was not easy to be a Christian in a Buddhist-Shinto home but she wished to be baptized. We always felt that a minor needed parental consent. So by arrangement Doug visited Mr Kamada. He was an upright, handsome police officer, very loyal to his country. Doug opened the porch door, called out 'Excuse me,' and removed his shoes in the porch as he was invited into the house.

He and Mr Kamada knelt on cushions at the low table while Mrs Kamada brought in green tea. Doug explained at length the step that Miho wished to take, that she would no longer worship at the family shrines, would come to church to worship God Sunday by Sunday, and would not marry a non-Christian. Baptism signified her faith in Jesus. Mr Kamada was adamant that he would always continue his worship of the ancestors but consented to his daughter's baptism. They bowed as they parted and remained on cordial terms.

Miho was baptized in the baptistry of North Glory church one Sunday morning. The water was a little shallow and had not warmed up but she had started on a path from which she did not deviate. Through her witness her two sisters also became Christians. Mariko, her older sister, told us, 'I was standing on a stool changing the water at the *kamidana*, when God knocked me down. I slipped and the water went flying.'

Miho was a skilled artist, excellent at calligraphy. She loved to tell the children about Jesus and was happy also broadcasting His name in the open air. After leaving high school she worked in a police office; she qualified in every category of driving – trucks and all. But her one desire was to bring others to know Jesus Christ, her Lord.

One day, Miho was having a pressing problem and begged me to come to her home to pray. We were kneeling at the low table when I prayed in the name of Jesus against the spirits that were troubling her. I had in mind trouble she was having at work. When we looked up she said to me, 'You see where we are sitting. The god-shelf is directly behind me. When we started to pray I was forcibly bent forward. As you prayed I was released. My problems were not connected with work.'

When the mother returned home she sensed that I had been there and prayed. This experience made me realise the power of the name of Jesus and also the spiritual conflict in the ordinary home.

Later Miho married Ralph, an OMF American. She struggled with language and culture at an American Bible School and returned to Japan with Ralph to plant a church in the Tokyo area. Ralph had travelled east to study Zen Buddhism but had discovered a Gideon Bible in his hotel room and become a Christian.

Toei Church and the barber

We returned from England for Doug to resume the duties of superintendent, voted in now by fellow missionaries. He endeavoured to visit all the eighty missionaries once a quarter, so was travelling a lot, sometimes preaching at different churches on Sunday mornings. John and Judy had filled in for us while we were in England.

Judy had been holding a small service on Sunday mornings in the living room for a few folk unable to worship at either of the nearby churches. I agreed to continue the meeting. At first only about five people came each Sunday. Miho was keen to come and bring friends when she could. I enjoyed preparing and bringing the Bible message and accompanying the hymns on my violin. Over the months numbers built up.

Baptism in the sea

Mr Morosawa was a plumber. He and his wife came with us to the Ishikari beach where we enjoyed swimming. They told us that it was regarded as unlucky to bathe there after mid-August. This could have been just one of the many superstitions rife in the land, but I reckoned it was probably due to a change in currents at that time of year. I love sea bathing – Mr Morosawa reckoned my character changed completely when I got into the water. It was at the sea that we had a baptismal service, a real church picnic. Doug spoke on Psalm 121: 'I will lift my eyes unto the hills.' He described the magnificence of the view from the mountaintop. Friends of the Morosawas were with us – we discovered afterwards that the lady was an expert mountaineer. (What Doug said spoke to her heart.) The area we had chosen for the baptism was a little rocky. Doug gingerly found his way to a spot that was of suitable depth. As he baptized Mrs H, he slipped and went under also – roars of laughter from the shore.

In the winter, we chose to use the local public baths for baptisms on a

Sunday morning before they officially opened. Miho's sister, Kumiko and Mariko met with us regularly; also Mrs Igarashi, the Christian lady I had first met in 1953 in Kitami.

Easter meal

Easter is the most important festival in the Christian calendar, celebrating the resurrection of Jesus from His death on the cross. 'Sunrise' services are usual. I arranged a special Easter service following the morning Sunday School. Easter eggs are popular, and Easter bunnies, but I couldn't see anything in the Bible about them. On the other hand, after the resurrection Jesus said to the disciples, 'Come and have breakfast,' and had prepared a meal of fish and bread. So, I went down to the fishmonger to buy enough fish for the church's breakfast. I explained what I wanted and why. The fishmonger was astonished. 'I've heard of Easter eggs, not of Easter fish.'

'Jesus died on the cross, rose again and appeared to His disciples,' I explained. 'On one occasion he ate fish with them, on another he cooked fish for breakfast for them, there was no doubt that He was alive again.'

I had a large oven and put all the fish in it before the beginning of the service. Alan Mitchell was helping in the church at that time and was scheduled to preach that Easter morning. His sermons usually lasted forty minutes – I calculated that the fish would be cooked just as he was finishing. After twenty minutes he seemed to be stopping. 'Oh, no,' I thought. 'The fish won't be ready yet.' True to form he continued for another twenty minutes. After breakfast we continued with a Communion Service – as the early church would have done. 'The Lord's Supper' was a meal.

The barber

A young barber called on Doug in his office one morning. 'Mr Osaka told me to come and see you,' he said. Mr Osaka was a Christian man running an English school in the centre of Sapporo. On the board outside the school he advertised not only the English classes but also Bible teaching. The barber had learned the Lord's prayer at an RC Sunday School when he was little. Now he had a problem – he thought it might be resolved through the Bible. He had had an affair with a young lady; she became pregnant and they destroyed the life. She was unconcerned but he felt guilty and sought forgiveness. He enrolled at the English School hoping to find release. Mr Osaka realised that his slow progress in English indicated that English was not his interest. So he sent him to Doug for Bible teaching. The barber, Mr Watanabe, did find forgiveness through Christ's dying for him on the cross. He came regularly to Toei church, and then brought along a hairdresser from the shop next door. She also became a Christian. It was no surprise to us when they decided to get married. (Later he went to Bible School, trained as a Pastor, served as Assistant Pastor at Toei church and then as Pastor in Kushiro, a foggy town in SE Hokkaido.)

The church had a variety of leaders. When we were in England for the year, Hugh Trevor took responsibility for Toei. On our return, the group was still meeting in our living room and they were needing their own premises.

Visible from our upstairs window was a vacant building. It had been renovated as a restaurant but the owner had become ill before the opening day. It was for sale.

'That sounds ideal,' was the general response. 'Could we afford it?' Hugh was enthusiastic and a man of action. We investigated the price; each member calculated how much they could contribute. If I ran a children's English Bible class in the building, Miho would take charge of the fees. Certain alterations had to be made but the church was well supplied with carpenters, plumbers, painters, etc. We bought the shop and soon had the services up and running. I enjoyed my particular assignment. I loved teaching English Bible and found a group of youngsters responsive, both to the message and to the English.

The downstairs room was renovated for services – pulpit, chairs, a background curtain, easy access from the street. Upstairs were two tatami mat rooms, suitable for the smaller children or babies during the services.

There was a special 'cupboard' in one of the rooms which we thought would be ideal for storing the ashes of Christians who died. After we had arranged the shelves we were disappointed to learn that housing ashes in a building of this kind was illegal. Where they will finally be interred is a matter of paramount importance to the Japanese Christian during his life time. No way do they want to be put in a Buddhist cemetery. In Toei church, Mrs Igarashi was the oldest member: her mind was at rest when she thought there was a place for her ashes in Toei church. Later we arranged to share with North Glory Church.

The family

One summer holiday, the three children came out to us via Aeroflot. Fog prevented the plane from landing at Tokyo, Narita Airport. Doug waited patiently for hours until the announcement came that the plane had landed at Nagoya and passengers would come to Narita by bullet train. The bullet trains arrived every fifteen minute at different platforms. By the time the three arrived happily from their adventures, Doug was exhausted with the heat and going up and down stairs every fifteen minutes.

'You needn't have worried, Daddy,' explained a calm Grace. 'We would have found you. I would have gone one way, Michael the other, and we would have left Richard here to look after the luggage.'

There was further delay because of a security alert. Richard managed to sleepwalk into the waiting area restaurant. I was unaware of the drama, waiting anxiously for their arrival in Sapporo.

We had a great time. I always asked God to give us a holiday in depth as it was always short. We had some time in our old seaside resort of Takayama and then some days in the building on Mr Shibakawa's Hill of the Cross in Kitami. There we had to keep the windows closed because of the insects, but the light attracted a wonderful display of varied coloured moths on the outside. We pulled the rope to toll the bell that had been placed there by Mr Shibakawa to pray for the people of the city, and explored the mountainous countryside around. We revelled in our family reunion.

Seasoned travellers Grace and Michael returned to England while Richard stayed in Japan to resit his A-levels for Cambridge entrance. I don't think he did much studying, but he was able to pay his way through opportunities to teach English, and become remarkably fluent in Japanese as well as learning to read and write it. He made numerous Japanese friends, sometimes communicating without words through music.

He got to know Mr and Mrs Watanabe well. Mr Watanabe, the barber, cut his long hair for him – a relief to us for he had been mistaken for a girl! One evening, we were all seated on the tatami mats in the Watanabes' flat for Bible study. Doug turned to Richard, speaking to him in English. Mr Watanabe expressed surprise that Doug should be so fluent in English! We entertained them at our home, introducing them to the English custom of dunking biscuits in tea; we gave them toasted cheese with homemade tomato jam. This they relished and it was what they wanted on subsequent visits. Our friendship deepened.

Visitors

Visitors were frequent.

Dr Theo Stöckle, a German psychiatrist, and Traugitt Stahli, head of Swiss OMF work, were having a meal with us when the phone rang. Margrit Bahler, a Swiss worker, was concerned about the need of finance promised in two months' time for the church building in her town.

'What's the trouble?' asked Mr Stahli.

'Margrit (usually law abiding) has committed herself to money she doesn't have.'

Doug explained. We all knew of the OMF policy of never going into debt.

'Just a moment,' Mr Stahli consulted his notes.

'That's no problem. The Swiss office can forward that amount.'

A letter had arrived for us from Grace in the mail that day. Grace indicated that in her gap year she would like to spend some time in Germany. Traugott translated the letter for Theo. His answer was immediate.

'She could come and live with us, help my wife and, if she wanted some extra pocket money, she could give a hand in my hospital kitchen.'

So it came about that she had a wonderful seven months with the Stöckle family, becoming fluent in German, although Miss Kobrak had advised her to drop it at school.

I longed to be able to speak German to communicate with Dr Stöckle, a man of wisdom and understanding. This was the only occasion they visited our home.

The cooking class in our living room was a regular event. Pattern – demonstration of a dish – the Bible study while cooking – followed by eating. The problem was one child who would jump off the chair on to the floor, causing disturbance in the office downstairs. A lady had brought some doughnuts she had cooked and offered them to everyone. Doug appeared at that point, sampled one and said in Japanese loudly, 'Olga, why have you brought out these stale cakes?!' Embarrassment all round.

Hospital visiting

Lorna had to have an operation in the Sapporo City Hospital. I visited her there and she stayed with us convalescing. I was required, as the nearest approach to next-of-kin, to receive from the hospital the part of her body that had been removed – I am not sure of the reason for this hospital regulation.

Lorna was my last visitor for a time. I had had to be tidy while my visitors were with me. So when she left, I put something on every chair to claim my independence.

Doug's itinerary

Doug was often away visiting pastors or missionaries. He was able to maintain a heavy schedule by staying in hotels, having a constant supply of funds for the purpose. This ceased when one of our home staff, not aware of the use, stopped that particular supply as seeming to be unduly large. This limited his visitation programme.

I was always pleased to have Doug back, getting everything in order for him. I realised that I wanted him home even if everything wasn't in order – to me a parable of our looking for the Lord's return whether or not we are quite prepared.

What more can I write of student Bible English camps, teaching English at a Catholic Girls' College, conferences, friendships, welcoming new missionaries, etc.? The R.C. sister in charge gave me freedom to present the Christian message, but I overdid it, and she asked me to limit it. I enjoyed the companionship of the German nun whose room I shared.

Furlough plans

We were again due for a year's furlough in England. Previously our programme had been arranged through our one deputation secretary in our central office in Newington Green and we had travelled all over Britain to conferences, churches and prayer groups. Now there had been changes in OMF so that Britain was divided into regions, each with its own office, and we were expected to live and work in the area we came from.

Doug's brother Ron had offered us the use of a bungalow he owned in Sandhurst. It sounded ideal but was just outside our assigned area. Correspondence with our Regional Director, our friend, a gentle, gracious Christian, became heated over the issue of where we were to live. We were confused, depressed, later realising that we were experiencing an attack by evil spirits, something that is rarely acknowledged in the West. We felt we were in a dark cloud.

The plan was for us to go to England via North America, crossing that continent by train or by car, and speaking at meetings and conferences as we travelled. We would be staying with old friends, associates, OMF prayer supporters and OMF staff. But first we had to obtain visas to enter the USA; it was more difficult than I had expected. At the American Consulate, the form stated, 'You must declare if you are or have ever been a member of the Communist Party.' Had I given it much thought I would have answered 'No,' for in fact I was under age at the time of membership, but other questions followed. Doug looked on in despair, as his naive wife was too honest. 'Were you active or passive?' asked the young Consul. Had he asked 'Were you an activist,' I would have answered, 'No,' as I had never been involved in demonstrations, shouting or throwing stones. I said that Communist members were always active. The very active nature of the student Communists had attracted me to the political party where the members knew what they were talking about, and did not remain passively silent. Further, at that time, Russia was our ally. Doug thought the Consul was doing his best for me and the two of us were not communicating. I was finally issued with a limited entry visa.

As we were preparing to leave Japan, Robynne, the director's secretary, and my helper and friend in the Sunday School and Church, gave me a text from Isaiah 55 v 12: 'You will go out in joy and be led forth in peace. The mountains and hills will burst into song before you and all of the trees of the field will clap their hands.'

Interlude

A wonderful five weeks across Canada

As WE REACHED NORTH AMERICA, the gloom we had been under vanished as though the evil spirits had left us. I read Isaiah 55 every day of our journey. It became part of me, especially verses 8 and 9, verses that have overarched my whole life: 'My thoughts are not your thoughts neither are your ways my ways declares the Lord. As the heavens are higher than the earth so are my ways higher than your ways and my thoughts than your thoughts.'

Our first hurdle was on landing at Honolulu where my visa had to be checked at a special desk, and stamped. We had wondered if there would be complications after my discussion with the Consulate in Sapporo. There was no further problem but I felt like a criminal.

We flew on to Los Angeles, met by the OMF representatives there and taken on to 'The Firs' Conference Centre in Texas. On our way back to the OMF (USA) headquarters, we saw the police checking cars. They were searching for Mexicans hiding in the boot.

We travelled up the western coast of the USA and crossed into Canada, relieved that as British subjects we did not need visas. I had felt uncomfortable with my limited entry visa to the States.

Leonard and Laura Street (see page 46) were now retired in Vancouver. They had lived for Christ in Lanchow, NW China, from 1931 until forced to leave in 1950. Leonard's thinking was profoundly affected by seeing the Muslim Chinese being mowed down by the Communist Red Army. Although their experiences amongst an unresponsive Muslim community coloured their approach, they came to Japan to open up the OMF work. They welcomed us to Japan in 1952 and acted as father and mother at our wedding. She had sent my mother a lovely letter in copperplate writing describing the ceremony and sharing her own feelings and loneliness in separation from her own boys. She had pioneered the first OMF church in Sapporo. Now we were staying in their well designed sheltered accommodation. They were hungry for news of Japan. We revelled in renewed friendships and memories of past association.

They escorted us to the railway station in Vancouver and said goodbye to us as we boarded the Canadian Pacific Railway train for the long 500-mile ride east to Calgary where another OMF retired director would meet us. We relaxed on the reclining seats of the spacious carriage and enjoyed the journey chatting to other passengers. The lady in the opposite aisle was making macramé, the yarn suspended from the luggage rack. The friendly informative guard passing through the carriage stopped to greet us – he was from Cullercoats, the town next to Whitley Bay where I had frequently swum in the safe bay and fished from the pier. He invited us to go on the roof of the train and see the view from the 'bubble car'. We ventured up the steps and found, as he had said, a perspex 'bubble' with seats and looked out on a magnificent panorama of the Rocky Mountains. There was an occasional whistle-stop as the train pulled up at an isolated platform. Gophers looking like squirrels were sitting up at the edge of the line as though they were begging. Banff was the main stop on the route, a centre for tourists exploring the Rockies. Snow was still lying on the mountain-side but a fellow passenger told us 'there has not been enough snow this year to water the crops when it melts and runs down the mountain.'

This remark gave Isaiah 55 v 10 and 11 extra meaning: 'As the rain and the snow come down from heaven and do not return to it without watering the earth and making it bud and flourish so that it yields seed for the sower and bread for the eater, so is my word that goes out from my mouth. It will not return to me empty but will accomplish what I desire and achieve the purpose for which I sent it.'

God compared the snow and rain to His word from His mouth coming down and accomplishing His purpose. I realised that when God promises something there may be a period before we see the fulfilment. The promise remains poised until the appointed time.

I can't even remember what meals we were given on the journey, how long or when I slept, only that we had an unforgettable, pleasurable time, rocked by the motion of the train. The Canadian Pacific Railway is a remarkable feat of engineering.

At last we stopped – Calgary – as promised OMF retired Director, Marvin Dunn, welcomed us. He showed us the Prairie Bible Institute, a training spot for many OMF missionaries while we stayed in Calgary.

From there we went to the home of Allen and Anna Iddings who knew us, had retired from the Philippines and now lived in an isolated homestead in Alberta. They introduced us to life on the Prairies. Their nearest neighbour was forty miles away so the occasional visitor was always welcome. He was a jack-of-all-trades, electrician, car mechanic, farmer, etc. Alberta was rich in oil. What looked to us like milk churns on the road off the highway, he told us were containers for oil collected regularly. Dotted across the open countryside we saw and heard the steady beat of donkey engines, ceaselessly pumping oil. The Iddings introduced us to a Japanese student. Doug was able to talk to her and give her his Japanese/ English Gideon New Testament, leaving himself without a Bible. At our next stop, where Doug was preaching, our host produced a Gideon Bible but Doug left it behind in the church. And at our next stop, the second host gave him another Gideon Bible.

Ruth Dueck was a lively fellow missionary and friend of ours in Japan. She had first come to fill a gap in our office as a book-keeper but it was not her line and she struggled. Released from that job she showed herself as a gifted worker, able in the language and a help to others as she had had experience living with many siblings. We were delighted to meet her parents, visit their farm and appreciate the support they gave to her. We stayed in the home of her pastor, the Rev Harold and Edna Berg. Doug spoke at their church and we joined in singing some of the hymns in German. It was a reminder that Canada has been populated by different races from Europe, keeping their own languages and customs.

Next it was the English area.

In Winnipeg, we called in on a couple who we had known in Stanmore Baptist Church. They had emigrated to Canada but retained their English culture. We enjoyed the meal at the dining room table, laid out British style, knives and forks held at the same time. Nostalgic – talk about SBC, their children and their experience of Canada.

We stopped for a meal at the spacious, welcoming home of a widow, an OMF supporter – it was a large caravan. She was a first rate cook and we were afraid we might overeat. It was my turn to lead our brief daily prayer time. I smiled as I had come to verse 2 of Isaiah 55: 'Listen, listen to me and eat what is good and your soul will delight in the richest of fare.' We freely enjoyed our hostess's rich fare and thanked God for it.

Our informative OMF representative drove us through the extensive but thinly populated province of Saskatchewan. The straight wide tarmac roads carried little traffic. During about an hour we saw three cars coming from the opposite direction. 'It's the rush hour,' Mabel, our humorist, retired, fellow missionary remarked. Over the car radio came the voice of Billy

Graham, 'It is a sin to read while driving.' Drivers would put the car into automatic and read from a book propped up on the steering wheel.

Our next overnight stop was Thunder Bay on the north west corner of Lake Superior. We were scheduled to continue our journey by Greyhound coach round the coast of Lake Superior. Mrs Hogarth, our hostess declared, 'That is a very long journey, you will be tired out. Spend today with us. We'll buy plane tickets for you.' The generous booking was made. Later the telephone rang, 'There is fog over the south-east of Lake Superior. If you can,' said the voice, 'we would advise you to wait until tomorrow.' This we couldn't do. We had to keep to our schedule. We flew right over the Lake from NW to SE and landed safely at Sault Ste Marie. The Rev Barnett, pastor of an OMF member's church, was waiting for us. Although he wasn't wearing a kilt he looked every bit a Scotsman – we were entering the Scottish area. 'Has the fog cleared?' we asked. 'What fog?' he replied. 'It has been lovely weather here all day.' He concluded that the plane had been overbooked, so the airline had tried to persuade some passengers to wait until the following day. He took us to his home. 'I hope you won't mind being in the basement,' said his wife. We had visions of an English basement, not the luxurious guest room we found at the bottom of the stairs. Everything we could possibly want was provided, a shower, tea making facilities, toaster, etc.

From Sault in Ontario we were heading for Toronto. What next? Could there be any more surprises and blessings? There were . . .

Victor and Helena Morrow, elderly and experienced, pastored a church in Bruce Mines near Toronto. He had been Governor of Jamaica, she a missionary in Africa with the Sudan Interior Mission. We were booked to speak in their church, but the area was so sparsely populated that we wondered if there would be anyone there. 'Wait and see,' he assured us. Cars poured in from the surrounding district and the church was packed. Distances count for little in Canada. We asked one man whose hobby was fishing, 'Do you fish nearby?' 'Yes, just forty miles away.' Significantly for us personally they told us, 'Here in this quiet spot, we have learned secrets of prayer. We keep records of those we are praying for. We will pray for you on the date of your birthday each month, i.e. the 4th and 24th but if you ever have a particular need, let us know.' Several months later we did, and valued their help (next section).

Our Canadian OMF headquarters was in Toronto itself. Here we were able to relax, launder our clothes in automatic washing machines, and meet old friends again. David Michell, with his wife Joan, was now Home Director for Canada. He had been appointed as Director in Japan but unable to return because of Joan's health. He was an exceedingly capable and interesting person. His parents had been many years in China, were Australian but OMF representatives in New Zealand. David had studied at London Bible College (now London School of Theology). He had been interned as a six-year-old boy by the Japanese in China and written his story 'A Boy's War' relating his adventures at the time. We had had holidays with him in Takayama, Japan, and he had looked after Doug as mid-husband with Grace and Michael when I gave birth to Richard. He took us to Niagara Falls on a blazing hot 4 July. We were amongst thousands gazing at the falls, watching a little boat with passengers surrounded by a rainbow as the sun caught the spray. Niagara marked the border with the USA. The car number plates showed that every State in the union was represented – it was American Independence Day!

Amongst our former colleagues in Japan was the intrepid, very elderly lady, Miss Taylor. She was a classics graduate who had taught Latin in China to CIM children, including David Hayman. When missionaries were expelled from China, she came to Japan to continue teaching OMF children, not classics, but elementary subjects to six to ten year olds. She found elementary arithmetic harder than Latin.

Who would we be surprised to see next? We were going to a conference at 'Fair Havens', a Christian camp. When we heard the word 'camp', we expected to see something fairly basic. In fact, it was a magnificent site, more like a luxury hotel. We noticed folk dressed up for the evening meal so Doug put on his best summer suit and I dragged out my kaftan. We had been told the meal was to be a smorgasbord but we didn't know what that was. Long rows of tables were laden with food for us to help ourselves; roasts were carved on the spot, everything was delicious. Our only problem was a limit on how much we could eat. We were amazed at how much some of the Canadian men did eat. We were surprised to discover we knew the main speaker, Geoffrey King from England. He had been the pastor of the church I attended in my training days in London in 1950 – a great preacher, well known for the long index finger he pointed, his emphasis on baptism, and his dislike of any interruptions in the services.

His Bible exposition was unusual. At that time, 1977, the popular view was that the 'end times' and the appearance of ten kings was a reference to the European Union. Geoffrey King's interpretation was that the opposition to Israel would come from ten surrounding lands. This seemed unlikely in 1977 but plausible in 2007.

We were excited to meet Don and Winnie Morris again after many years. They had arrived in Japan, engaged, shortly after we had and also had to continue their long engagement until they had been in the country for two years. We were together in language study days in Karuizawa and, later, they were in the next village to us in early days of marriage in Shizunai. Our lives closely knit, prayer days together, children of similar age and holidays in Takayama. They were the first house parents at the OMF school at Nanae. Barbara and Grace became and remain close friends. Their son, David, with Michael, John and Danny were all the same age, thought they were special because they were all left-handed. Bill Pape had performed our wedding ceremony, then theirs and, later, for their daughter, Barbara's, in Canada. Grace saved up enough money in College to go out to Canada for Barbara's wedding. What a delight to be able to see one another again. They drove us from Fair Havens to their holiday home in the lake. I say 'home in the lake' as we had to cross a plank over the water to their front door. Joy and nostalgia again as we reminisced.

Wilma had lived in the house next to the tennis pavilion in the next street to ours in Earsdon where we had known each other as school girls. She had married Ronnie, the boy next door. They had emigrated to Canada. Don contacted them by phone and Ronnie told him where to meet him on the road and then led us to his home. Ronnie had made ceramics his hobby and, on retirement, built a workshop on his extensive property. Life was much more fulfilling for them than it could possibly have been in England. Wilma was teaching in a technical college and they were enjoying the vast openness of the country. Regarding our visit she said, 'It's just as though you have come down from the sky,' – an unexpected pleasure for both of us after thirty years.

What next, could there be any further adventure?

Meeting up with Oswald Smith of the People's Church in Toronto was special. Doug had admired the Pastor, seeing the church growing over the years and sending out and supporting scores of missionaries.

Doug and I both spoke at the Japanese church in Toronto, which was divided into older and younger groups. Those born in Canada knew very little about Japan and spoke only English.

We finally said goodbye to our Canadian friends from the OMF headquarters who took us to the airport and we boarded the TWA plane for Heathrow fully expecting that to be the end of our breathtaking days in Canada. The plane was overcrowded, no seats for the children. After about an hour's flight over the Atlantic, a voice came over the loud speaker, 'This is your pilot speaking. One of the engines has overheated, we have had to jettison some fuel so we will be returning to Toronto.' Passengers on one side of the plane had seen the engine catch fire. I felt quite calm until we landed and were greeted by the Press enquiring who had been hurt? Then I became anxious. All the passengers were taken to a hotel for the night and given instructions about departure the next morning. On landing safely at Heathrow, the passengers cheered the crew. This was the end of our exhilarating five-week journey, but we had a permanent record of where we had stayed as I had carried our visitor's book with us and had asked our hosts to sign.

A difficult home assignment

Depression

The plane landed us safely at Heathrow airport. We had had an exhilarating time in Canada, filled with unexpected memories and much joy. It seemed that we came down to earth with a bump in England, back under the dark cloud of evil that had troubled us as we were leaving Japan. We could not shift the deep depression. Many people were praying for us. In particular, Louis and Nancy Gaussen, friends who had spent years in China, wrote making suggestions, but 'This sounds serious – both of you – we'll be praying for you.'

Then we wrote to the couple in Bruce Mines, Ontario, who had told us, 'We have learned certain secrets of prayer here: if you have any particular problems let us know.'

After several weeks we sensed freedom at last. From Mr Gaussen came a book-mark with words of scripture 'You shall be above only, you shall not be beneath,' and a letter saying, 'we knew this was for you: tell us how it happened.'

And from Bruce Mines, 'We have been praying against the spirits and for you since we received your letter. We sense that the depression lifted for a while and then came down again but now you should be completely free, we have bound the spirits and claimed freedom also for your children including your son in Edinburgh.' And so it was.

The bungalow

Ron and Gwen settled us into the bungalow in Sandhurst that had belonged to Gwen's mother. With three bedrooms, there was adequate room for the children on their holidays. It was the only occasion we had not been near one of our supporting churches. Our immediate neighbour was a friendly Scotsman, Jock, who had retired from Hong Kong, and owned a large gentle dog. Doug sometimes took it for a walk through the fields. Sandhurst was, of course, well-known for its military connections. Jock told us about the dogs trained for the forces. Sometimes they did not reach the required standard and could then be sold privately. One of the soldiers had bought such a dog and ordered it to get on to his bunk when he was away for a short time. When he got back the dog refused to let him on the bed. Jock was a good neighbour to have, full of adventure stories, especially of Hong Kong, and the need for construction workers to 'appease the dragon' before continuing their building. With full Scottish hospitality, he came across on New Year's Eve to share his whisky. Doug was away but he offered it to me. I politely declined, saying I didn't drink whisky, so he passed it on to Michael and went back to the house to get wine for me. I drank it thankfully (even though I am TT).

The car

As usual we needed a car to take us to meetings, conferences, churches, schools, friends and relatives. A friend in the motor business had found an Allegro for us. The tyres were flat by the time we got home, and we should have returned it, but kept using it hopefully and trusting the friend who had sold it to us. I don't think we had one journey without there being some fault. We were so weary travelling that we could do nothing when we got home and felt unable to make even nearby visits. We lost friends as a result.

Visitors

Apart from our children and my mother staying with us, we enjoyed visits from old friends.

Jonathan, son of our friends and fellow missionaries still in Japan, was a welcome and helpful guest (mending broken hinges). He had started at Monkton Combe School a year after Michael. Michael's friendship had meant a lot to him, especially when at the relaxed quarters of my brother Graham (see below). Breakfast in our house was a moveable feast. We had finished when Jonathan came into the kitchen-dining room.

'Make yourself at home,' I invited him.

'As a matter of fact, I feel at home here,' he volunteered. 'All the Japanese things around the place and . . . the clutter!'

Win's mother, sister, and son, Chris, all called on us. It was her mother from Whitley Bay who had wept when she thought I had become a nun. She was visiting her other daughter in nearby Guildford. Chris was in the army, training as an officer, an enthusiastic young man, later killed in the Falklands War. Our children enjoyed visiting him.

When my mother was staying with us, Esther and Albert Kimberly came to see her. Esther had been related by marriage to Mam's brother Tony and had shown exceptional kindness to her, looking after her in their home in Rugby when Mam was not too well.

My cousin, Norman Rutherford, drove us around the area: he had had a stage career and was now responsible for drama on the BBC.

'Why did *Dad's Army* (our favourite sit-com) not continue?' We asked him. 'It was brilliant.'

'The stories were all based on true events,' Norman explained, 'we ran out of material.'

Mam had always had a welcome in Barnes when she stayed with Norman's wife.

Most visitors gave us notice of their arrival but this custom seemed lost on the Japanese. One teenage girl whom we had known in Sapporo arrived unannounced on the doorstep with her friend.

A visit from a policeman did not cause us so much surprise. When we had been driving in crowded traffic through Streatham, an elderly drunk staggered across the road, oblivious of the cars. We saw him bump into a vehicle in front of us and land on the bonnet. No way could the driver have avoided him. We stopped a little way on, Doug went back to give the driver our address as eye-witnesses. I was out shopping when the police called at our house. Doug told him how unavoidable the accident had been. We don't know what our neighbours thought seeing the police arrive. Doug said to me, 'I'm glad you were out. Our stories might have been different.' It reminded me of the authenticity of the accounts of the resurrection of Jesus: the variation of the accounts proved there was no collusion.

Visitors from OMF were always welcome. Frank Snow, our area superintendent welcomed us, renewed fellowship with us, and arranged our deputation programme. Fred and Margaret Collard, old friends, were house parents for our children in our absence. Grace and Eustace Govan, from Edinburgh, were amongst those who had prayed for O.M.F for years. (We worshipped at a church in Fort William decades later. The minister told us that he knew OMF well – Mr Govan had led him to Christ.) Theo Stöckle, whom we had met only once in Sapporo when he invited Grace to his home, was studying English in Bournemouth. He was another welcome visitor, but he still struggled with the English language.

Grace

Grace was studying at Oxford Polytechnic for a Diploma in Catering and Hotel Management. She had learned to drive before our arrival and helped us on our travels. The course included practical placements. Now she was training at St George's Conference Centre, Windsor Castle. It was a section of the castle that the Queen let out for clergy conferences. The practical demands were not great, but she had a close view of the 'Garter Ceremony.' At the gates of the Castle was a police check. She explained that she was working there. The policeman looked at our family 'Who are all these?' he asked. We were allowed to enter. Cars are not normally permitted in the castle grounds. As we drove through we were aware of eyes upon us, wondering who we were. (Did we look dignified? We felt important.)

For her twenty-first birthday, a friend introduced us to a nearby exclusive restaurant that never advertised. It was suitable for the occasion and the five of us enjoyed a sumptuous meal, with waiter service.

Graham

My brother was now living in Midford Castle – not quite as prodigious as Windsor. It was owned by an authoress who wanted a chef, especially an expert in cooking curries. Graham had lost everything in Beirut when his house was burnt down in the conflict in Syria and was separated from his wife. He answered an advertisement in *The Times* for a cook at Midford Castle. The authoress had converted the stables into living quarters: Graham was happy to live a Bohemian-type bachelor existence, brew his own beer, make nettle wine, and cook whatever was required in the house up the stairs.

But, where was Midford Castle? In Somerset, a stone's throw from Monkton Combe School where Michael and Richard were pupils. They were able to walk through the fields from school to visit Graham with no question about obtaining permission to visit their uncle. The relaxed atmosphere of the 'stables' suited both boys, escaping from the routine of boarding school. My mother sometimes visited him there and we also called in as a family on occasion.

Unfortunately, the owner decided to put a lawn in front of her window, which meant it was on top of Graham's rooms. This caused excessive dampness that gave him arthritis; he couldn't climb the stairs and had to leave. He decided to move back to Earsdon and live as Mam's carer. This was his position when we returned to Japan.

Richard

Richard was still at school at Monkton, enjoying being with us on holiday.

Michael

Michael was studying chemistry at Edinburgh.

For the Christmas holidays we planned, with their invitation, to visit the Stöckle family in Germany, near Frankfurt. (I was ashamed to be badly prepared for the exchange of presents.)

We travelled by car: I was confused at a roundabout because of the unfamiliar left-hand drive; and on the autobahn I thought I was keeping to the speed limit until I discovered that '60' meant not less than '60'. I learned through the indications from other motorists.

The Stöckle family gave us a wonderful welcome (especially as they were preparing to move). Theo took Doug to see Heidelberg – my energy had gone. The simplicity of the Christmas tree, decorated with stars made from straw, Christmas presents all made by members of the family, gave a peaceful spirit of worship.

A short walk through the woods brought us to the hospital. Dr Theo was at pains to emphasise that it was a mental hospital, not an asylum. He expected his patients to get better and leave. There was a beauty, too, in the design of the hospital itself. The corridors ended in curved corners; the thick windows in the section for more dangerous patients opened with metal fretwork for safety instead of bars.

Patients had made a cross by pasting spent matches on to a board – not only was it effective but also indicated the control the patient had.

Back in England we had wondered whether the time had come for us to stay to look after my mother. During the year she seemed to be getting more and more frail. Problems had arisen in Japan which required Doug's return. We were staying in Earsdon with her, when our plans to return were made. Then she fell and broke her arm. Doug decided to go ahead, leaving me to look after her until the arm healed. Michael came to keep me company – he being the most compassionate of the family. I realised that he ought to be with his friends in Edinburgh: which linked into Mam's view that I should be with Doug. Graham arranged to leave Midford Castle to come as carer, when I returned to Japan. As we were preparing for him, Mam slipped and broke the other arm. The doctor could hardly believe the X-ray as it was the mirror image of the first.

Graham arrived and I returned to Japan. Two weeks later she died aged eighty-nine. Graham was devastated. He had been in the house when she had called out, and tried unsuccessfully to resuscitate her. He resented the Christian ceremony that my pastor, David Neil, kindly conducted in Whitley Bay cemetery. John Caisley who represented me and OMF was a great help to Graham.

Delayed return to Japan

Doug was already in Japan, continuing his responsibilities of superintendent, when I returned. He was away in Singapore when I received the news of my mother's death. The shock did not hit me immediately but two friends, Roslyn and Irene, gave me much support. Roslyn gave me pills with the instruction: 'These will calm you, take one when you need it and stop when you are over the shock. They are not addictive.'

Irene offered to come and keep me company until Doug returned. I did not think it was necessary but accepted her offer and was glad that I had. I had not been aware of my own emotions.

I had a lovely letter from my mother which she had written after I had left England but it reached me after the news of her death. Her expression of love and appreciation warmed my heart. In clear handwriting, she gave an account of what she had been doing, without any illness, of visitors, Graham taking her despite the snow to the hairdressers, the doctor's letter to arrange for a hearing aid, Graham shopping and cooking for her. I have treasured the letter.

My memory of my last period in Sapporo is hazy. We kept in touch with our children through tapes as well as letters, coming over loud and clear on our tapes was the incessant ticking of the cuckoo clock plus the half hourly cuckoo call.

We celebrated our silver wedding anniversary with office colleagues and Japanese friends in the OMF offices.

Our annual holiday in England was the occasion of Grace's wedding. At first we had been concerned that in her college days she was sharing a house with another girl and two young men, Adrian and Andrew. Mixed digs came as a shock to us. We were greatly helped by a newly arrived New Zealand couple who assured us that this was now quite usual and often safer than accommodation in hall. When Grace graduated she found employment as a hospital caterer in Everton and Adrian helped needy young people connected with a church in Everton. They became engaged. Their wedding was a triumphant service led by Fred Collard who had been house-father to our children when they were at school. We were delighted to meet up with Adrian's parents, at their request, before the ceremony. Grace washed my silk wedding dress and looked a charming bride in it.

Conferences by OMF were held every year in Japan. An unusual one was where the main speakers were two American psychologists and their wives. They enabled us in a very short time to get and appreciate one another's needs and gifts.

Problems accumulated for Doug. He was increasingly stressed and half way through our term it became obvious that he could not continue to lead the OMF team. He resigned the superintendancy (probably too suddenly) and Bill Fearnehough took over the job (also suddenly). A gradual handover would have been easier. Bill and Sheila moved into our flat above the office, while Doug and I rented a flat across the road, carrying on with our church work (Tooei), with fellowship with Mr and Mrs Watanabe, the three Kamada sisters, and others.

We were there when our General Director, J. Oswald Sanders, visited. At the meal in our flat we had inadvertently omitted to open the new ketchup tube. Putting us at ease, JOS assured us that he could manage it. He did! squirting a large quantity of tomato ketchup over his smart grey suit. A stage whodunit could not have asked a more realistic blood-stained body. Fortunately, an obliging dry cleaner agreed to restore the suit in twenty-four hours.

There remained the question of where we should go after our next home assignment. Doug had for some time felt that as OMF we should give some help to Pastor Haga of Tokyo Koganei Free Methodist Church. Pastor Haga had given his time unstintingly to help OMF and was chairman of the committee sending Japanese missionaries overseas with OMF. It was possible that we should spend our last term in Japan associated with his church in Tokyo. Meanwhile we needed the refreshment of Home Assignment.

Recuperation

Stanmore Baptist Church had always been a source of encouragement and spiritual refreshment for us. In cooperation with our Regional HQ in Watford, they had arranged for us to use a house in Mill Hill loaned to missionaries on furlough by Lady Laing. Stanmore was going through difficulties and splits, the minister was asked to resign, so the church asked Doug to preach on Sundays for three months. This would refresh Doug, as he would not be involved in frequent journeying and it would be a benefit to the church to have continuity in ministry.

The house was spacious and quiet, situated at a reasonable distance from SBC but not so near that visitors would be constantly dropping in.

Michael had just graduated in chemistry from Edinburgh University and we wanted him with us again. Job applications were frustrating at that time for recent graduates. The rejections came with the explanation that forty young graduates had applied for the same post. He took temporary work, grossly underpaid, with the local greengrocer. But his advice to Doug was wise, 'Decide on a series to preach on. Don't just look for something Sunday by Sunday.' Doug followed this and taught from the upper room discourses, John 13–17. The restrictions on Doug's movements affected me, in that a church I was closely linked to, who supported me, and had invited me to talk furlough after furlough apparently was refused. (I think this must have been to spare Doug.)

The split in SBC was severe. I felt concentrated group prayer was needed, so I approached several ladies from SBC with whom I had previously close connections to join me in Mill Hill to pray into the situation. We agreed to confidentiality, a promise to be open with one another, and to be united in our purposes.

'Should we ask the Lord for a specific matter where we could see the answer and confirmation of His hearing and responding?'

There was gloom over the church.

'Let us ask for a smile on the face of the church secretary?'

At the next church prayer meeting, the secretary was at the piano.

'Do you know this hymn?' Doug asked.

'Oh yes,' he answered enthusiastically, his smile stretching from ear to ear.

Some of our ladies exchanged grateful looks seeing the answer to our prayer. God was with us.

One of our meetings was interrupted by an unexpected visitor. It was Lady Laing herself, calling to enquire about the well-being of her tenants. She was delighted to hear we were praying together.

Grace called in frequently. She was experiencing difficulties and needed us.

It was good to be in a large house, especially for our family parties with Ron and Gwen and their children and spouses.

Doug baptized Ted and Vera McAtee at SBC. This was followed by lunch at their house, largely cooked by their daughter Angela. It was there that Michael and Angela met, and later married.

We had to help Michael to search for accommodation before we left – but we ourselves were too ignorant on such matters to be of any help. He finally moved in with Jonathan and Mary Highwood, former school friends.

In all it was a happy home assignment, but packing to return was a scramble. Ron and Gwen decided just then to visit us, as also did the Revd Butler, whose son was joining OMF. Grace and Adrian came to take us to stay overnight with friends near Gatwick Airport but had been delayed because of a smashed windscreen on the way to us.

And so back to Tokyo.

CHAPTER 8

Final years in Tokyo (1982–1986)

The city

OUR LAST FEW DAYS IN ENGLAND were full, the final day frantic. Grace and Adrian drove us at last to the home of Peter and Jill Hazael by midnight, not for the relaxed evening we had planned. Friends from SBC handled the final clean up of the house in Mill Hill. The next morning Peter came with our Michael to see us off at Gatwick Airport.

The flight to Hong Kong was remarkably smooth. We had a relaxed five days there, seeing familiar sights, crowded streets, the lovely view of the harbour from the peak, but a changed skyline with high rise buildings.

Then we flew on to Tokyo, to be met by old friends, and to new experiences working with the Koganei Free Methodist church.

Tokyo was very different from the city we had first seen in 1952. It was now a thriving prosperous metropolis, embracing whole areas that had previously been independent cities. Koganei, to the west, was one of these, gobbled up by the giant municipality. Some of the roads were narrow but the new highways had been built over the houses and high rise buildings. They looked like long winding bridges supported with many steel reinforced concrete legs, often built above existing roads, canals, rivers, etc. I asked my friend Mr Suzuki if he could tell me how these highways had been built. This was his reply:

> Today I received from the Metropolitan Highway Corporation their reply to my questionnaire. According to their reply, the construction work of the oldest highway in Tokyo started in 1959 and the newest one was completed in December 2007. It therefore took nearly fifty long years to complete the present highway network. About 60 per cent in area of Tokyo highways are built above existing road, canals, rivers and other public spaces that require no expense to acquire. The most of the rest of them were built above land newly required by clearing away existing buildings. In this case land and the highways are used for various purposes such as car parking, playgrounds and warehouses. Since most of the Tokyo highways are like high bridges; in some cases highways were built above existing buildings.

(I myself even saw a highway using the roof of a long building as part of it.)

213

At junctions, on the highways, drivers politely took turns to join the main lane. A new word to us was *juutai* meaning traffic jam. In Hokkaido we had learned *konde iru* meaning crowded. Cars were everywhere, but because of the lack of space no one was permitted to own a car who did not have a parking lot for it. Owners of plots of ground were making a small fortune renting out areas for parking. Air pollution was high.

High rise buildings – fifty or more storeys – had been built to withstand earthquakes. Cross, vertical or massive steel reinforcement was added; rubber cushions were provided beneath the buildings and earthquake energy was absorbed with dampers. The building would sway but not collapse, resulting in an alarming though not dangerous experience for those on the upper floors. Earthquakes were expected. Walking on moving ground outside felt eerie. Inside we quickly pushed open the sliding doors, knowing that the earthquake could twist the runners, jamming the doors. Concrete buildings and walks by law had to be built with steel reinforcement – even garden walls. One earthquake which shook us had caused damage through the collapse of a garden wall – the owners had to observe the building regulations when the wall was first built but had ignored them on the extension. We were all issued with instructions as to what to do in the case of a major earthquake. Tokyo was ready in anticipation, the bay measured regularly was found to be shifting slightly. In fact, the predicted quake later hit unprepared Kobe with loss of life and the destruction of homes and infrastructure.

Modern electric railways criss-crossed the city; different lines under different management. Some were owned by the department stores and the railway station was inside the store. Especially interesting to us was the 'Seibu' line owned by the company who also had their own baseball team, the Seibu Lions. We often enjoyed watching matches in the evening, held in the open stadium at the end of the Seibu line. On one occasion, in the calm of a summer evening, pleasantly cool we sat with Japanese enthusiasts. In a nail-biting finish, bases loaded, the last man in on his third stroke hit a homer. Even I leaped up in excitement shouting 'we've won'. Celebration continued in the Seibu department stores – all the shop assistants wore headgear with the team's logo, a lion.

The line we usually used to Koganei station was the *Chu oo* line (Central). Our problem again was to know the words – express, semi-express, slow, and where the train would be stopping. Finding ourselves going past our station or letting a train go because we thought it would not stop where we wanted, became part of our learning experience. Trains were always packed. At the rush hour railway employees literally pushed passengers on to the trains. In the winter many passengers were seen wearing a small, white surgical mask. This not only limited the spread of germs, but also was convenient for keeping one's nose warm on cold days – at least that's what I found when I wore one.

Sky Mansion

There were many apartment blocks. We lived on the ground floor of a five-storey block known as 'Sky Mansion'. 'Mansion' was the usual word for a flat, so we did not expect great luxury. The forty flats were of the same design; five rooms, a bedroom, two living rooms, a dining-kitchen room, a bathroom. Furniture was sparse and not needed as the walls of the room were cupboards with sliding doors, appropriately known as *oshiire* literally 'push in'. Bedding could be 'pushed in' during the day and anything else that had to be tidied away in a hurry. The Japanese designation of the size of the rooms was always by the number of tatami mats, so the living room and bedroom had six mats each. Normally the mat is one yd × two yds but we found out that the tatami mats for flats were smaller. We had ordered a bed (beds were now available in the country) and the shop gave a design showing how particular beds would fit in a six-mat room. When the bed arrived we discovered that the diagram had been for standard size rooms, not for apartment sizes. It did go into the room, leaving no space for anything else; not even a little table. We did, of course, have the *oshiire*; on one of the walls. Sky Mansion was on the corner of a busy intersection, traffic lights controlling the cars, but at the red lights the cars outside the block were stationary with engines running so air pollution was considerable. Our flat was at the furthest point from the lights.

Nearby was one of the many parks of the city and a walk into Koganei church was through lanes between pear orchards. Every so often were small stalls, unmanned, with fruit and vegetables priced, and a box for the money.

Koganei Free Methodist Church

We never met Mrs Milikan, the foundress of the Koganei Free Methodist Church but she was highly respected and her example followed by Pastor Haga and church members. She and her husband had been missionaries to Japan before the war, left in 1927 to educate their seven children but responded to the call of General MacArthur in 1946 for missionaries to fill the spiritual vacuum left by the cessation of Emperor worship. General MacArthur was Commander of the Allied Forces of Occupation and the virtual ruler of the country.

The mission board accepted their offer but then Mr Milikan died. Mrs Milikan was prepared to go ahead, but in no way would her mission board accept responsibility for a sixty-one-year-old widow to live alone in the turbulent conditions of post-war Tokyo. Undaunted, she applied directly to General MacArthur, sold her house and arrived by herself in Tokyo. This was around 1950 when the city showed all the signs of the devastation of the war.

She rented a shack in downtown Tokyo, invited mostly high schoolers and students to study the Bible in English, and started a Sunday service in her home. One of her first students, Shoji Mikami, later became a leader in the Gideons, an international organisation placing Bibles in schools, hotels, hospital, etc. He brought a student from a Buddhist home, Tadashi Haga, to the group. The number of believers outgrew the premises. One Sunday morning Mrs Milikan announced, 'I am not giving a message this morning. We need bigger premises. I have no money, you have no money, we must pray.' This was the start of the Koganei Free Methodist Church built in 1953. The believers prayed and gave. One couple postponed their wedding for a year to give their money for the building. Another lady had no money of her own but was given cash to buy a long bread roll for each member of the family for lunch. She bought four instead of five, did without her lunch and gave the price of her roll to the church. We met these people and other founder members when we joined Pastor Haga and the congregation of 200 in 1982.

Wooden building

A plot of ground suitable for the church was found in Koganei City, a quiet suburb of Tokyo. An attractive wooden building was erected with an attached manse. Mrs Milikan sent Tadashi Haga to study at the Immanuel Bible College, Yokohama, so that he could return under her leadership as pastor of the church and to continue there after she retired or died.

Pastor Haga, fluent in English, was an able preacher with a concern that the world would know about Jesus Christ. Concerning Koganei he would say, 'We are grateful for the 200 believers but what about the 2000 outside.'

Because of his known interest in worldwide missions, he was recommended as the first Chairman of the Japan Home Council of OMF, sending
Japanese missionaries overseas. His wife, Aki, also of a Buddhist background, had attended the Immanuel Bible College and was his fellow
worker. The Free Methodist group believed in women's ministry.

Later two or three OMF missionaries were sent to help at the church in
Koganei. When Mike and Valerie Griffiths left us from Hakodate in 1960
for student work in Tokyo they lived near Pastor Haga and worshipped
with his congregation. Bill Fearnehough benefited from meeting the
Christians there during his first period of language study from September
1963. A year later, Pastor Haga officiated at his marriage to Sheila. Grace,
aged eight, with Bronwen Griffiths were bridesmaids, dressed prettily in
green. Grace was nervous so I told her she was just a green leaf beside Sheila
the white flower.

By 1982 there were other church workers employed. On Sunday
mornings, we would walk through the pear orchards to the service, remove
our shoes at the entrance and step into slippers provided. On the blackboard
was a list of members who would be absent that morning – e.g. Mrs B
visiting family in Hokkaido, Mr C in hospital, Mr D called away on
business, etc.

Inside the church we sat down towards the back but if there were
unoccupied seats at the front we were ushered forward. The choir led the
singing, ably assisted by a young gifted organist. Usually we knew the hymn
tunes, the words were written in the phonetic script so we could sing them
even if we did not always know what we were singing.

After the service we had lunch together – often a bowl of noodles. This
was followed by separate group meetings – the young people, the mature
men, and the ladies divided into the Ruth group and the Naomi group.
This was an age division that worked very well. For mothers with young
children, not able to get in on time or disturbed through the hour, were
together in the Ruth group. Older women preferred quieter undisturbed
sessions starting on time, in the Naomi group. Deacons met later in the
afternoon around 4 p.m. Doug and I were invited to attend, Doug did so
but I declined largely because of lack of stamina.

Small house meetings were held during the week, half a dozen to a
dozen ladies at different homes. Doug and I both sometimes spoke at these
meetings.

We attended the mid-week prayer meeting. The first half hour was led by a deacon, perhaps talking about what had happened during the day, rarely spiritual and then there was a Bible message from the pastor followed by a time of prayer. A church worker carried a roving microphone and, as soon as anyone began to pray, the microphone was brought across. I found this a little daunting but it was excellent that everyone could hear. Finally we split up into groups of three, shared problems and needs and prayed aloud in the threes, about personal matters that would not call for the concern of the whole church.

Sky Mansion neighbours

We could hardly believe our address – Sky Mansion – Kodaira City, but there we were, living in a block of forty flats. 'Mansion' is the Japanese word for flat or block of flats. Mr and Mrs Ishikawa, church members, were glad that we could occupy their flat while he was posted to Hong Kong for three years. She hoped I would continue the Bible study she had started with some of the ladies. Many of the forty flats were occupied by families with young children. Mrs I introduced me to some of them immediately – introductions are essential in Japan. They also invited me to join in their activities and to visit their flats.

Mrs Miyahara was our next door neighbour, with two little girls. Being on the ground floor we had gardens adjoining and got to know the family well. She was always particularly helpful to us. They moved shortly before we left Japan and invited us for a meal in their new flat. Unfortunately, we were seated on newly laid tatami which triggered Doug's asthma, limiting the time we could spend with them.

Mrs Kokame lived on the fifth floor with her two children and husband. She had chosen the daily climb up four flights of stairs, for health reasons. Her doctor had assured her that the air was less polluted higher up but she had found she was still affected by the exhaust from traffic at the busy intersection. If her husband was going to be late home, he would always phone to let her know. One Christmas Eve, she answered the phone, looking forward to hearing he would soon be back, to receive a shock – he had had a heart attack and died. She was devastated. He was quite a young man, no indication of ill-health, leaving her with two small children. She needed a picture for the family altar. The only one she had of him was their wedding photograph. This had to be used, a copy being made just of him. I visited her flat where the altar was set up with his photograph central, and joss sticks available to burn, offering up incense to his spirit. While I was there, others came in to offer condolences, and burn a stick. One lady asked Mrs Kokame what I was doing there. She knew I would not offer anything to the spirits, and explained that I had come to express my sympathy. Certainly everyone in Sky Mansion felt deeply for her sudden loss. We attended the Buddhist funeral, a time without hope, where the incantations of the priest were incomprehensible.

I became friendly with Mr K's mother from Hiroshima where he had been born. We went together to see a film based on a book by the nationally well-known Christian authoress, Mrs Miura. It was a story of fishermen from southern Japan at the time when the country was closed to outsiders. They had adventures and hardships in different countries, finally reaching Hong Kong. There Dr Gutzlaff, a missionary to China, befriended them, learned Japanese from them, and translated John's Gospel. They were very helpful in giving the most suitable words, 'In the beginning was the Word and the Word was with God and the Word was God.' The fishermen gave him the most honoured word possible for the verb 'to be' *gozaru* not *aru* or *iru*. The British attempted to repatriate the men, but the Japanese refused to have their own men back because they had been out of the country. The ship approaching the land to repatriate them was fired on. The fishermen finally managed to get back secretly. The film was moving, portraying the hardships and emotions of the sailors; Japanese and English were both used, according to who was speaking, i.e. the fisherman spoke Japanese, their Canadian captors or the British in Hong Kong spoke English, and captions were in English and Japanese. This brought realism to the film and ease of understanding bringing the story to life.

I often spent time with Mrs Matsubara. She had an albino son. He was known and accepted amongst the Sky Mansion children although he looked odd with fair hair, pink cheeks and pale eyes amongst dark haired, 'yellow' skinned, dark eyed Japanese children. Mrs Matsubara did not dare to risk having another child in case it was another albino. Anywhere she moved to she ran the risk of her boy being ridiculed, and feared his starting school. She wanted to receive the Christian message but did not want to be different from others.

Mrs Suchi was outgoing, friendly, and helpful. She invited Doug and me to play tennis with a group of the ladies who usually went to the club together. She had joined in our cooking/Bible class. The ladies took turns in demonstrating a recipe, and I still have recorded in my own cookery book her recipe for 'rice coquille'. Interestingly, the younger Japanese wives could not cook rice without a rice-cooker (I could). Another lady was surprised that I didn't have a microwave oven. This was a contrast with my early days in the country when the Japanese did not have ovens and were impressed by my rotary egg beater.

Mr and Mrs Tsubai helped Pastor Haga in the work of the church. Mrs Tsubai came along to Sky Mansion to help in the cooking class, sometimes looking after the children, sometimes helping with the Bible talk.

One day there was a ladies' lunch in the church with a special speaker. The group of about ten ladies from Sky Mansion set out (to the surprise of the janitor, who wondered what attracted so many at once). Mrs Haga welcomed us all to the lunch and introduced the guest speaker, Yoneko.

Yoneko, a failed suicide

Yoneko was an attractive, happy speaker, on the tall side. She smilingly told us that she could easily alter her height by moving her wooden legs.

We were spellbound as she told her story – as a motherless teenager she had thrown herself under a train, was miraculously rescued but had lost an arm, two fingers of her right hand and parts of both legs. 'But look I have three fingers,' she said, making a paper crane as she spoke, folding the paper with one hand, holding it against the upright piano with the stub of her other arm. In hospital three young Christian men, Bible students, visited her and told her about Jesus and His love for her. 'I didn't want to hear,' she continued, 'but, one night in great despair, I called out to God, "Help!" I slept. In the morning I woke to feel a wonderful peace and hope permeating my body. One of the young men helped me to know more of God's Son, and to walk again. Then he proposed to me. How could I possibly inflict myself on anyone? Finally, I agreed. I learned to use the body I had, three fingers to cut up vegetables. My husband refused to help me – not because of lack of sympathy, but from confidence that I would succeed. And now, we are a happy family with two lovely girls, and knowing the love of God and His presence in our lives. I wish and pray for that joy for you all.'

The Sky Mansion ladies were deeply moved. I don't think there was a dry eye amongst us. But their response was, 'That was a moving and true story. But we have not attempted to end our lives, so we do not need to ask for God's help.'

On Sunday mornings the parents liked to lie in but the children were up and lively. I wanted to start a Sky Mansion Sunday School for them and a number of the Koganei Christian ladies were willing to help. We had just three months before we were due to retire but we invited the children for 8.30 a.m. on Sunday mornings. I designed the programme to give the essentials of the Gospel in twelve lessons, with memory verses, Creation, Adam and Eve, the Birth of Christ, incidents in the Gospels, Crucifixion, Resurrection, Pentecost. The helpers were dedicated teachers, who produced colourful visual aids. One girl who missed the first two sessions thought that God was the spirit of her dead grandfather. I was so thankful to have this short time with the children before we left Japan.

Kabuki

Pastor Haga was chairman of the OMF Japan Council for sending and supporting Japanese missionaries. Mr and Mrs Nojiri, formerly pastor of one of the related churches was already in Thailand. Once a month we met with others to pray in the OMF office attached to the church. Emiko was secretary but found the position extremely lonely as she worked by herself in the office. She gave us an unexpected and wonderful present – two tickets for the front row of the balcony of the Kabuki theatre.

Kabuki and Noh are the best known traditional Japanese theatre forms. Noh is more serious and sophisticated; the actors masked; Kabuki was developed for the common people. The scenes portray ancient stories – intrigue, clan loyalty leading to suicide, battles and samurai; the costumes are ornate, vividly coloured, the stage scenery spectacular, e.g. the sea shown as blue water with waves constantly moving, or the complete darkness of night as skeletons appeared. The classical Japanese language (like Chaucer's English to us) is hardly understood by the general public, so at the reception tape recordings in Japanese or English are available for a deposit of about £1. These give the story of the play as it unfolds. Our English tape enabled us to follow the plot and enjoy the acting and singing. Soldiers who were 'killed' would show their death by lying down on their back with their feet up in the air – expressive, understandable and amusing.

The interval was an opportunity to leave for a meal. Doug and I had our refreshments but were late back for the second part. The theatre was very dark with skeletons appearing on the stage. We edged along the extra seats in the crowded aisle, feeling our way. I was behind Doug and a lady indicated there was a seat beside her that I could use until the next break. Doug had no idea what had happened to me as we were both watching the skeletons. He crept forward, groping, and his hands landed on the back of a lady's neck. She didn't move! With the end of the skeleton scene and light again in the theatre we were able to return apologetically to our own seats in the front row.

The actors have been all male since 1629, when it was thought that in the interests of propriety women should not act. Female impersonators are the biggest stars now. Ennosuke, the leader of the theatre troupe when we were there, was especially known for his rapid change of costume during scenes, seven times an act.

Weddings

Doug and I were engaged before we sailed for Japan. My language teacher, a Christian young man, asked me 'Did you choose each other? I don't know how you do it. I am so glad that my parents will find a wife for me.' Post-war (mid-twentieth century) girls were given greater freedom – they were at last allowed to refuse their parents' choice, although we do know of a Christian young woman who had to leave home because of her father's anger at her turning down non-Christian young men, suitable to her family's status.

Normally an older couple would act as 'go-betweens'. On request, they would search for a compatible match. For example, a bank manager and his wife would look for a bride for a young employee. She would need to be the right sort of person for the bank. Both sides would be vetted, common interests looked at, family backgrounds and birth signs examined. Any girl born at night in the year of the Tiger would have little chance of a good marriage, since that birth sign indicated a bad-tempered, aggressive character. The go-betweens would arrange for the couple to meet with them. This was known as an 'honourable look and see' (o-miai). The couple would sit with downcast eyes, hardly speaking. Their CV, interests, education, etc., with photographs would be exchanged. When the wedding took place the bank manager and his wife would accompany bride and groom at the ceremony, often performed at the local Shinto shrine conducted by the Shinto priest, although the legal procedure was at the city office. Christian weddings were conducted in churches, arrangements beforehand being handled by the churches.

The wife of a university professor told me that she and her husband were often asked to find partners for former students, because of difficulties these students had in finding partners.

Another friend told me of the disappointment she had had when her daughter's apparently good choice turned out to have a drink problem. 'It's my fault,' she said regretfully. 'I should have employed a private detective to investigate beforehand.'

In our time in Tokyo we witnessed a number of weddings, although I seem to have very little remembrance of them. Shortly after our return to Tokyo, Kumiko Kamada was married in Sapporo to a young Christian of her own choice. I attended the wedding while Doug witnessed the marriage at the same time in Koganei of the daughter of our friends, Mr and Mrs Matsuura. It is normal for the couple to give presents to the guests and to charge them for attendance. The wedding breakfast may be a small carton of food for each guest, attractively arranged and put in each place. The colour of the contents and the meaning of related words are significant. Red snapper is usually included. 'Red' denotes congratulations and good luck. The word *tai* (red snapper) resembles a word for congratulations. 'Chestnuts' sounds like a word for victory. The Japanese are fond of puns, and this is borne out in the contents of the box. The guest is expected to take home his box with anything left.

Any relative or friend invited, but unable to attend, is sent a carton, attractively wrapped in a *furoshiki*, a colourful cloth wrapper. I remember Doug bringing me one from a wedding he had attended when I couldn't.

We enjoyed the somewhat unusual ceremony for Yumi Naito and Professor Goto. We had known her and her parents in Hokkaido; and also of her deep affection for Mr Goto. They asked us to accompany them as the go-betweens but assured us that it did not put us under any obligation. At her request I played my violin, solo, at the reception – very nervously. They were determined to set up a Christian home. Later we visited his mother in Tokyo. They welcomed us and tried to persuade us to stay the night – but we had to escape quickly. The house was filled with cats, some of them settled decoratively on the shelves round the room. Doug's asthma reacted immediately and we struggled home.

An unexpected phone call

One evening I answered the phone. 'Are you the Mrs Abrahams who used to be in Hirosaki? I was called Itō. Do you remember me?'

There had been three Itōs. The speaker had been on fire for the Lord in high school, then on graduation had wilfully married a keen member of a militant Buddhist sect, both convinced that in no time the other would change religions. Instead, ceaseless quarrels and finally divorce.

Then this letter arrived.

'You must have been surprised by my sudden phone call yesterday.'

She went on,

I was so happy I couldn't stop crying. On the phone I was reminded of one thing after another – playing with Grace, visiting your home in Hirosaki with my parents and sister, evangelistic meetings, the English Bible class and your giving me the name Joyce, Moya Camp – all kinds of things. Last time we met I was still at high school. Now I'm over thirty.

For a long time my heart was separated from God and I didn't pray. I ran away from Hirosaki to Tokyo. At first I had a part-time job with a telephone company, saved a little money and trained as a telephone operator. For six years after leaving Hirosaki, day after day was dark and painful. I couldn't sleep at night. I worked hard, taking no holiday or rest like others, to get really tired. But it was no good. Mental problems and bodily sickness are quite different aren't they? Further, I remembered the cute little two and a half-year-old son I had left behind. When walking outside I found my heart pierced, and tears would well up at the sound of children's voices. At night, under the blankets, the years were fearful as though I had fallen into hell.

Four years ago I met my present husband. At that time he had a son, but his young wife had died a year and a half previously of cancer. In this too I was fortunate. Perhaps because he had lost his mother and was lonely, the little boy took to me from the beginning. Now I have a baby girl, so we are a family of four.

My parents and sister have moved. When I visited them we often talked of you. I've always remembered you. Once again I thought I would like to meet you. Although there was a church near my present home, it seemed different. When I married in Hirosaki my many Bibles, cards, etc. were all burned; I didn't have any, but wanted to read the Bible and sing hymns again.

Then a wonderful thing happened. Into my letterbox came a pamphlet from a Gospel church. It was an introduction to the home and circle of a German missionary, Mr H, who had worked in Nagoya for twenty-five years. I quickly went to visit him and was able to discover your address and telephone number – hence yesterday's phone call and today's letter.

Mr H has just returned from furlough and came back to Nagoya in August. He wanted to start a new work, so looked for a house in this area.

He'd only been there a month. It's only ten minutes away by car. There are only three Christians so far but he has plans for a Sunday Service, Sunday School, Middle School English, German, Ladies, etc. The first meeting is on 15 November. Mrs Abrahams, aren't I blessed? Surely I'm the Prodigal returned.

I've got a new start. When I told my husband about it he was pleased. 'Very Good.' Suddenly my body is renewed and has come to life again. I'm having a busy time, taking my two-year-old daughter along with me.

I'll have to stop there. It's past midnight. Yesterday I prayed again after ten years. I've had to ask forgiveness for many things and am only about half way through. After I've prayed, surely the sky will be clear.

To my second parents,
Mitsuko Akita

And in a later letter . . . 'My husband is also coming with me regularly to church with our little girl.'

The Immanuel Bible Training College

Dr David Tsutada

'God's ways are higher than our ways.' Isaiah 55 v 9

Dr David Tsutada was born into a respected Japanese Christian family of diplomats in Singapore, then a British colony. His ambition was to become high up in international diplomacy, representing his country. He set sail for England, an accepted student at the London School of Economics, excited about the prospects of success in his ambition. On the voyage he met with a medical missionary returning to the UK from India. Lengthy conversations about the Christian faith caused him to think deeply and to declare himself a believer in Jesus Christ as Lord of his life. He gained the qualification he needed for diplomatic service but had so grown to love the Lord Jesus as to choose to follow Him and introduce others to Him. He returned to Japan, disembarking at Yokohama. On the quayside to meet him were a group of his family and friends and a pastor standing on his own. He greeted the group and then left them to join the pastor. It was a declaration of faith.

During the war he was imprisoned for his stand as a Christian. His success in making Jesus known to other prisoners upset the authorities. They placed him in solitary confinement for six months until his release at the end of hostilities. While he was isolated, Japan winning victory after victory, God gave him a vision of what he would do later. The vision was for worldwide mission. He concluded that missionaries to Japan had failed to teach one important aspect of the Gospel – to go and tell others. He was to start a missionary society with three main principles: (1) reliance on the Bible, (2) no dependence on foreign funds, (3) to spread the message of Christ throughout all the world.

Out of prison, Japan defeated, he fulfilled the vision, establishing the Immanuel Bible Training College in Yokohama to prepare students to lead churches in Japan and many other countries. He himself was an outstanding Christian leader. It was to this college that Doug and I were introduced.

The principal, Joshua, was the second son of Dr David Tsutada, of whose other children, one was a pastor, one a pastor's wife; two daughters were members of the Immanuel Mission.

Dr Joshua Tsutada had trained in India and taught in a Bible College there. He was a man of drive and enthusiasm; we loved having discussions with him, especially as his ideas were formed through international experiences, not limited by those of Japanese culture. He was an international speaker with excellent English. In telling us of being one of five speakers at a conference when 'contextualisation' was the popular trend, he had virtually contradicted the previous speaker by saying contextualisation was unimportant; all that was needed was to 'get totally sanctified, and live it out.' We were taken aback because we heard 'get totally sanctified and leave it out'. The Japanese language has no short 'i' pronunciation!

The College was co-ed but the sexes were not allowed to mix in any way. The boys were forbidden to speak to the girls. I found this a problem in teaching English conversation. In the twentieth century it might have appeared a little extreme but I reckoned that it was to the advantage of the girls who would not have had practice in leading a Bible study had they not been separate. The women were trained to lead churches, in twos. We asked which was the fastest growing church in the denomination. No doubt – the church pastored by a daughter of Dr David Tsutada.

No-one was permitted to speak at meal times, sexes separated. Nor were they permitted to put the heat on in the classrooms unless the temperature dropped below 15° – a staff member could – this was training for difficult circumstances they might have to face.

Marriages were usually arranged by the staff who knew the background and personalities of the students. One former student told me he knew who he wanted to be his bride, so declined the first suggestion of the staff, and finally married his own choice.

Doug and I went to the Bible College once a week on different days. We had to get two trains, usually crowded. We followed the advice to hold on to the vertical pole and not stretch up to the straps, which would be more tiring.

I had small classes for English. I met experienced American missionaries Mr and Mrs Johnson each week in our staff room. They were both musical and brought Gospel messages to different church groups through hymns, he singing, she accompanying. The drink of coffee with chocolate stimulated us through the morning. Occasionally I gave the talk, in English, in the College Chapel, always with pictorial illustrations, so that those with little knowledge of English could follow it.

Both Doug and I found the atmosphere in the Bible College refreshing. The students were all dedicated to serving the Lord Jesus Christ.

When Michael and his wife, Angela, visited us, I took Angela with me to see the College. My four girl students asked her questions. One was 'Do you get on with your mother-in-law?' Angela tactfully replied, 'We are just getting to know each other'.

1983 and Michael's wedding

1983 proved to be a year of meeting new people and enjoying fresh experiences. Richard was studying engineering at Birmingham, but 'home' to him was where we were. With OMF help we gave him, for his twenty-first birthday, the fare to join us for six weeks of his spring holiday. (His course required him to spend the summer in Germany.) He was already fluent in Japanese and felt relaxed with us.

There were about eight churches in the Free Methodist group which had started in Koganei. Mrs Milikan had taught that a church must plant another church and send missionaries. The pastors and church workers met periodically for discussion and prayer. We were able to meet them, sitting in a circle, the men in the upper semicircle, the women in the lower, strictly in order of seniority. I found this hard to take, so at the meal table I said to a junior church worker, 'I'm not sitting there' and took a 'lower' seat.

'It's no good,' she responded. 'They'll just think you are being humble.'

I had to accept the cultural pattern of the country.

Although we visited the various related churches from time to time, I spoke regularly at the Ome church to the women. Mrs Matsunaga was the pastor. She had spent two years as a missionary in Taiwan, married a gracious Taiwanese doctor, and returned to run the Ome church while her husband continued his medical practice in Ome. He endeared himself to his patients, several of whom became Christians through his life and witness.

I enjoyed the half-hour train journey from our home through the countryside to Ome, the company of the cheerful, well-built pastor and the meeting with the ladies who gathered. The return journey was straightforward unless I got confused with the terms, 'express', 'semi-express', 'every station', and missed a train because I thought it wouldn't stop at Koganei.

The first branch church from Koganei was established in 1958 in a small village in another suburb of Tokyo, then a small village. This was the town where Mr and Mrs Suzuki lived. We had first met them in England. Mr Suzuki was a businessman and a member of Stanmore Baptist Church was working as his secretary. She introduced us and Doug baptized him. His wife, already a Christian, was delighted to meet us and to converse in her own language. Their two boys were at school in England.

Now we were living quite near to them and meeting frequently or telephoning. Their house was approached by narrow, winding, well paved roads on steep slopes; they had inherited it, a more spacious dwelling than occupied by an average family.

In August we received a surprise phone call from Michael, telling us of his engagement to Angela. They had first met in her parents' home when we had a meal together after Doug had baptized her mother. Vera and Ted, her husband, had been childhood friends in Wales, he had come to London for work and was a capable police superintendent. Vera had delayed her baptism because of fear of water. They had prayed for us for years. Ted commented concerning his future son-in-law, 'I prayed for him before he was born.' The wedding was planned for December. Koganei church folk insisted that we attend.

We flew to Heathrow and stayed with John and Anne Doulton, lovely friends from SBC The Rev David Walker officiated at the ceremony in SBC. Richard contributed by singing with his guitar. The reception was held at the nearby St Anselm's church hall. Angela had made the wedding cake; the photographer developed the pictures quickly so that we could take them back to Japan. She was a beautiful bride and a great daughter-in-law for us. We had a busy time meeting many old friends and were tired ourselves before boarding the plane back to Japan via Anchorage.

I looked forward to a sleep on the flight, but that was denied me at the beginning of the journey. Sitting next to me was a young lady in distress. She was a Christian and unloaded her story on me. She had injured her spine by jumping too high on the trampoline and hitting the ceiling. What was more devastating was a discovery lately, in her twenties, that the family she belonged to had adopted her. She felt she no longer belonged to them.

When we reached Anchorage the weather conditions were so bad (fog and ice) that we could not land at the Anchorage air terminal. We circled around for some time, then told we were landing at the military airbase but that only the passengers disembarking could leave the plane, transit passengers had to remain on board. We had no chance to stretch our legs nor to see the special crafts or souvenirs from Anchorage. Our friend of the journey left us there. I must have slept soundly for the rest of the journey to Tokyo.

Christian homes

Mr and Mrs Tsubomi

Mr and Mrs Tsubomi were an unusual elderly Christian couple, with Christian children and grandchildren. Mr Tsubomi was very hard of hearing; when he and Doug talked together after a church service Doug had to shout giving the impression of a quarrel. The meal we had in their home was colourfully displayed with each item on its own small dish: yellow egg, red tomato, green spinach, etc. rice bowls and green tea, and the hot damp cloth by the side for us to wipe our hands before the meal. Japanese rice is cooked so that the grains stick together; it is much easier to eat it with chopsticks than the Chinese kind with the grains separate. Japanese chopsticks are also pointed at the ends so it is possible to spear the food. (I have never been able to manage jelly with chopsticks.) The wooden house was small and for heating they had a *kotatsu*. That is usually a table over a pit in the floor with smouldering charcoal and a blanket over the table covering the thighs of those kneeling round it sitting on their heels. Mr and Mrs Tsubomi had made alterations for comfort. I think the heating was with electricity rather than charcoal; but we did not have to sit on our legs. We sat comfortably with our legs down in the 'pit' and didn't need a blanket. (If you want to understand the difference, try kneeling down and sitting back on your heels. How long can you manage?) The wooden table top was about a yard square, the food placed for each individual.

We knew them as an elderly couple, the wife doing most of the talking. Perhaps forty or fifty years ago Mr Tsubomi, the orphaned son of a doctor, was working in a car manufacturing firm. The fact that his father had died made it more difficult (under Japanese custom) to find a wife. But a doctor friend of his father's hunted for a suitable bride. He knew Mrs Tsubomi's family and suggested that the daughter might be suited to him. According to custom, she was shown his photograph.

'It didn't matter which way up I held it,' she explained twisting her fingers up and down to demonstrate 'I couldn't make it out, and turned down the proposal.'

The approach was made twice more. Her mother finally said to her,

'You had better accept, people will be asking who do you think you are!' Reluctantly she agreed and went off to Tokyo as his bride. As she left, her mother handed her a small parcel, wrapped in a decorative cloth saying,

'If the marriage doesn't work out you know what to do.' The cloth contained a knife to kill herself rather than bring disgrace on the family by having a break-up of the marriage.

Adjustment to married life was far from easy. For the first two years, she and her husband did not speak directly to each other. Communication was only through his mother. One day she went along to the Free Methodist Church in Koganei, heard of all that Jesus had done for her, invited Him into her life, and found a new joy and peace. Her life was changed.

Her mother-in-law heard her singing in the kitchen.

'What was that you were singing?' she asked aggressively.

Timidly she answered, 'It's a hymn I learned at church.'

'Well,' came the reply. 'It seems to have done you some good, you've been different lately. I'd better come along with you and see what it's all about.'

So the two ladies came to attend church together, both of them believing in Jesus. Mr Tsubomi could hardly escape their determined witness and he also joined the church. Although this occurred many years ago, Mr Tsubomi, now retired, wanted further Bible teaching from Doug. We all sat round the square wooden table with open Bibles and revelled in joyful discussion.

Mr and Mrs Yamamoto

Mr and Mrs Yamamoto had postponed their marriage for a year to give their savings for the building of the first Koganei Free Methodist Church in 1953. He was now an elder. Japanese Christian culture put the pastor above criticism and women in a subsidiary position. If the elders wanted to suggest a correction to the pastor they would say to Doug, 'You tell him, we can't but you can, you are older.'

If I wanted to make a suggestion, I would make it to Mr Yamamoto, a man on the diaconate, as it would carry more weight that way, because of my being a woman.

We were honoured by an invitation to join their family for the traditional New Year's meal. Usually only family members would take part. The main dish was a thick red-bean soup with glutinous rice beaten to a powder. Beating the rice was always undertaken by the men at the end of the year.

On arrival Doug had parked our car by a verge. Later, as it was difficult for me to get in from the verge, Doug drove off intending to give me space. I was left standing. Mr Yamamoto ran after Doug banging on the car window.

'Haven't you forgotten something?' he asked. Doug looked round the car, puzzled: he couldn't see what was missing. 'Your wife!' volunteered Mr Yamamoto.

New Year's Eve is celebrated by most Japanese in going up to the Shinto shrines and making a prayer to the gods. The families also expect everyone to take part in worshipping the spirits of the dead ancestors in the house god-shelf. Christians often arrange New Year Conferences to avoid worshipping the spirits and without causing confrontation with non-Christian relatives.

New Year greeting cards are delivered by the post office from New Year's Day. The post office issues numbered cards, and the lucky numbers receive prizes. Cards posted before the end of the year are kept at the post offices until New Year's day.

Mr and Mrs Gohara

Mr and Mrs Gohara had had heavy hearts since the death of their three-year-old little girl. She was standing with her mother, waiting to cross the road, when a lorry came along and she ran in front of it, Mrs Gohora helpless to stop her. We used to have a ladies' meeting in her home, the photograph of the daughter prominent. They had three other children. The nine-year-old boy whom I called Gordon attended my English Bible Class in the church. If the class was noisy, I would say 'Listen, listen.' Gordon was able to repeat 'listen' with perfect pronunciation. This was remarkable because the Japanese language has no 'l' or short 'i' or final 'n'.

Mr Gohara told us of his concern over taking part in the rites for the village gods. In his home there was no observance of Shinto or Buddhist ancestor worship. But the whole local community once a year, would join together in honouring the village 'god' and tidying up the surrounding area. If he boycotted this he would lose his credibility and be cut off from any effective Christian witness to neighbours.

Mrs Gohara played the *koto*, a traditional Japanese musical instrument, a horizontal harp with thirteen strings. She used it to accompany Christian words.

Mr and Mrs Matsuura

We had known Mr and Mrs Matsuura years ago when we were living in Sapporo and travelling to Otoru to build up a small church. I was also teaching English in a girls college and in the Otaru Commercial College. Mr Matsuura had an important position with the Ministry of Education and had been posted to Otaru to take responsibility for the Commercial College. They were members of the Koganei Free Methodist Church; Pastor Haga probably asked them to help us in establishing the Otaru church outreach. They came along to the small group of believers each Sunday, their daughter playing the organ for the singing.

Now, back in Koganei, he introduced me to the Keimei School to teach English. This school was established especially for returnees from abroad with Christian backgrounds, who would not easily fit into the general Japanese educational system, but I failed to motivate the small class of uninterested lads.

Later, on one of our journeys to England, we met again in Hong Kong where he had been sent for a time. They helped us to buy jade in the Hong Kong market: they knew its value and could ensure we were not being cheated.

In Koganei, Mrs Matsuura spent much of her time looking after her husband's mother, who had become senile and would wander off, not knowing where she was.

They looked forward to life after his retirement, but sadly he became ill and died just after he was free of work.

Mr and Mrs Saga

Mr and Mrs Saga always gave us a welcome to their home. He was a retired bank manager and very grateful to Doug, as it was Doug's talk before we left for England last time that had convinced him to put all his trust in Christ. We sat on the tatami round a small glass-topped table while Mrs Saga was up and down bringing us cups of green tea, biscuits, cake, etc. and Doug was teaching bald-headed, cheerful Mr Saga. Mrs Saga was so hospitable that Doug finally said to her, 'This teaching is for you also. Don't keep getting up and down.'

On our next visit, she obediently sat still until her husband turned to her, 'When are you going to bring in the tea?'

'The teacher told me not to keep going in and out,' she protested. But we did finally get the tea.

The new church building

The Koganei Free Methodist Church, erected in 1954 in the leafy suburb of Tokyo, was an attractive wooden structure loved by the Christians, several of whom had contributed to the cost. But now, in 1984, it was too small for the congregation, a fire hazard, and out of place amongst the well-built high rise department stores around. Was it time to pull down the much loved sanctuary and pastor's dwelling and replace it with a more solid and spacious church?

The subject was discussed at length for several months. Everyone was expected to express an opinion but in Japan greater weight is always given according to seniority. Final decisions depend on consensus, not on majority voting.

When the Annual General Meeting was convened, the decision to pull down the old building and construct a new two-storey church was taken. The ground floor for worship was to be flat from the front of the room rising towards the rear, with underfloor heating. The pulpit was to be placed in the centre at the front with two coloured glass panels on either side behind, the pastor's special wish. Behind the back of the auditorium, a glass panelled room for mothers with children would give the opportunity for the mothers to hear and observe the service without the children causing any disturbance.

The pews were of four wooden boxes joined together. We had all been asked to try them out for comfort and height, but with a warning, 'The Japanese are getting taller. Bear in mind that the seats may be too low in a few years' time. Decide now, but don't complain later.'

One important matter exercised the members. Mrs Milikan had put so much into the building of the first wooden church that it seemed wrong simply to demolish it. So some of the original wood was used to make a small room for P.A. equipment, etc., and designated as the 'Mrs Milikan memorial'.

The entrance was spacious with room to hang coats, toilets available, and the blackboard to give details of absent members. An imposing staircase led to the upper floor.

Upstairs was one large room that could be divided into several smaller ones, each with folding chairs and tables, and a kitchen.

During the reconstruction we met for worship under the huge canvas covering set up by the builders over the church, car park and builders' workshops.

At the A.G.M. it was announced that Mr and Mrs Tsubai, who had assisted Pastor Haga, were leaving to take up responsibility at the Ome church.

Pastor Haga had been in some pain which his doctor had said was heart trouble. Following the A.G.M. while he was preaching, an eminent heart specialist observing him said to his wife, 'That man's problem isn't his heart.' The specialist did not normally attend church but he was unable to practise for six months so had come to the service with his Christian wife.

He knew he would somehow have to get Pastor Haga to another doctor but could not be seen to overrule the first doctor. He succeeded in obtaining a second opinion. The new diagnosis was unequivocal and devastating – stomach cancer. And what was to happen to the plans for the new church in the absence of the one man responsible, the Pastor? Pastor Haga was definite – 'Continue as planned, you have the Abrahams to help.'

Pastor Haga was in hospital immediately. The whole of his stomach was removed, besides other attached parts. When visiting him Mrs Haga wondered if this would be their last time together. The operation was successful but left him frail and thin. He was glad to have Doug preaching in his place.

It is the custom in Japanese hospitals to release the patient for one day before deciding on final discharge. Pastor Haga came to the church but was hidden at the side behind the pulpit. As Doug concluded the service, he called on the Pastor to pronounce the benediction. He appeared in his white hospital gown, like Lazarus coming from the tomb, went into the pulpit, raised his arms and gave the final blessing. The congregation had not known he was there and their applause was spontaneous and moving.

He was finally discharged and took up his duties again with great courage. It was during this period that he had hoped to go with a church group to Thailand and asked me to go in his place.

A trip to Thailand

God's ways again, higher than ours.

'Would you be willing to accompany a group to visit our friend, Mr Nojiri and his family, in Thailand, and take my place as interpreter?'

This request from Pastor Haga was like a bombshell, yet a privilege. He had planned to lead a party to cement relationships with Pastor Nojiri and his family, missionaries with the OMF from Tokyo Free Methodist Church. The dates 30 June to 9 July 1984 would have enabled him to go directly from Bangkok to Singapore for the Conference of OMF Home Director Chairmen.

What had caused the change of plans? In April he had undergone the life-threatening stomach cancer operation. He came through the operation successfully, but was weak, limited in what he could eat, and thin instead of rotund.

So I joined our group of six, setting off for our adventure in Thailand. Young Pastor Tokuda, of a sister church, took overall responsibility. A younger man leading gave greater freedom to the team. An older man would have taken a more authoritative position. Mr Endo, a young working man from Pastor Tokuda's church came to take slides for the first part of the visit. Miss Hayashi, a bright artistic student, Mrs Fukunaga, mother of the Koganei missionary secretary, and Mrs Makita a small, neat, intrepid widow, and I, made up the six.

We were warned that Thailand was hot and we needed cool and colourful clothes, not the drab shades that were regarded as smart in Japan. On 30 June, Pastor and Mrs Nojiri with their two young boys met us at Bangkok Airport and took us back to their home, Klong Chang Church where Thai

Christians had prepared a meal for us. We sat on the floor at a long, low table. Each of us received a plate piled high with rice. The other dishes were brought in and placed on the table so that we could help ourselves. Omelettes, meat and vegetables, pineapple curry were amongst the many dishes set before us. All were delicious and not too peppery especially for foreign guests. We learned something of our programme, as well as information on Thai culture, e.g. 'when sitting on the floor, tuck your feet under you.' 'Don't drink water that has not been boiled,' was a constant warning, 'even for washing your teeth.' 'Take care not to eat uncooked vegetables: the rivers are used for everything, and even fruit such as watermelon can be contaminated.'

The three young members stayed in the church. Pastor Nojiri drove us three older ladies to the relative comfort of the OMF mission home. We were delighted to be welcomed by Makino and Izu, a Japanese couple with OMF, whom we had known and valued for many years.

As the next day was Sunday, Pastor Nojiri drove the three of us back to the church to join in their Sunday activities – a morning Bible study, Thai-led, followed by the morning service and communion, a meal together then afternoon sharing recent experiences, etc. After a short rest came a visit to a housing estate and the flat of a Christian family, and then supper at a Thai-Japanese-Chinese restaurant as guests of Christian Thai Jan Pen and her Chinese husband. Then, in the evening, we went to a house meeting in a poor Thai home – sitting on the floor being careful not to show our feet which would have been extremely rude. It eased the discomfort to sit with one's back against the wall; then we returned to OMF where we met another Japanese missionary, Mr Irizuki.

What a first day! Hardly a day of rest! I reckon we all slept soundly.

Monday was more relaxed. We were introduced to Thai culture at the 'Rose Garden'. The programme was designed for foreigners – Thai dancing was fascinatingly graceful, dress many coloured. Our hearts were in our mouths as we watched the dancers hopping over rapidly moving poles, boxing, and engaging in sword play; a demonstration wedding was also enacted for our entertainment.

We ate our evening meal at a Thai restaurant. Thai food is spicy, but usually the hot sauce is served separately – fortunately for me, as the meal could be eaten without the sauce. Buddhists don't kill, the Muslims are the butchers; the Buddhists are quite happy to eat what has been killed.

The Bangkok Bible School was our next day's focus. Dr Timothy, the

Principal, was from the Philippines and spoke perfect English. As I was talking to him in English, Mr Nojiri joined us and started to interpret for me into Japanese!

In the evening I had a long chat with Isaac and Eileen Scott, OMF director of the work in Thailand, Laos and Vietnam. Their daughter, Joy, was a special friend of Grace, and they also were very fond of her and knew of her situation from Joy.

Wednesday, our friend Mr Makino escorted us round the city. He showed us three universities. In one, to go up by lift we had to stand to one side otherwise it would not move. Rather scary at a height! We also saw the palace of the king of Thailand who is deeply loved and respected by the people.

The emerald temple is one of the many temples in Bangkok – named for the bright green image of the Buddha in the temple. Ironically, Mrs Makita was not permitted to enter as she was not 'suitably' dressed. She was wearing an immaculate trouser suit – but no women are permitted inside the temple wearing trousers.

We took the boat-bus down the river, seeing houses on stilts on the banks, women doing their laundry in the water, saffron clothed monks waiting for the 'bus' and the floating market with fruit and vegetables displayed on little boats.

On the Thursday, Mr and Mrs Nojiri escorted us to the house and church of Mr and Mrs Watanabe, Japanese TEAM missionaries. It was situated in a new housing estate, and much more comfortable than the Nojiris'. We saw the Japanese school and attended the Japan Christian Fellowship meeting. We were disappointed that a storm prevented us from going to see a Thai silk factory – Thai silk is excellent, inexpensive, attractive, long-lasting – and a prison-shop.

Friday was a day of rest – shopping.

Saturday we went up country about 100 miles north to visit Manorom hospital, an OMF hospital in the rice fields. Mrs Nojiri escorted the older ladies in the air-conditioned bus, while Mr Nojiri accompanied Mr Tokuda, Miss Hayashi and Miss Lek in the van. A rickshaw was good transport to the hospital from the bus stop. Nurse Jean Anderson, in a wheelchair, showed us round the hospital. Meeting with Jean was a bonus for me. We had trained together in Newington Green, hoping to go to China when the door closed. Jean was a nurse, but shortly after reaching Thailand she became paralysed with polio and unable to walk. Although she bravely attempted rehabilitation, she had to accept the rest of her life in a wheelchair. She was a cheerful Irish lady. When visitors, or patients, saw her sitting in the chair, they first reckoned she was lazy; when they realised that she could not walk, their admiration took over, and a sympathy which made them accept her more fully. She described her conversation with leprosy sufferers:

Jean: 'Why do you think you have contracted leprosy?'

Patient – a hesitant pause.

Jean: 'You think it's because of something bad you have done, don't you? Perhaps in a previous life?'

Patient, sadly: 'Oh yes. That must be so. It is a punishment.'

Jean: 'That is not the reason. But let me tell you about the one true God who loves you' . . .

Thai custom was for family members to come to the hospital and look after the everyday needs of patients. Christian services were held regularly in the waiting rooms.

We spent that night at Manorom Guest House.

On the Sunday we went to services at nearby Uthai. The building was airy, with a roof but no walls built in spacious grounds. The grave of a pastor killed in a motorbike accident was in the grounds, but as far as possible from the church and pastor's home, for the people were not free from the belief that the dead man's spirit might come and haunt them. There were a number of lepers in the congregation, the disease halted but the body still disfigured – elastic bands holding spectacles in place where noses were damaged, fingers shortened.

We visited the home of Grace Harris, a former China missionary, with whom Akemi, from Koganei had worked, hoping also to be a missionary to Thailand. By van we went to the hills overlooking the plains, viewing the uplands of North Thailand, then back to Bangkok, Miss Lek accompanying the three ladies in the bus. Miss Lek was an educated member of Nojiri's church and explained the position of women in Thailand. As in all Buddhist countries, the women are given a lower status than the men, but our Japanese group were astounded to learn of the job opportunities for women in Thailand. Miss Lek told us that the women university students were usually more diligent than the men and were able to advance according to their qualifications.

Young Thai-men are often temporarily in monasteries for a variety of reasons, sometimes financial or for training. The monks are seen in their saffron robes receiving rice or gifts offered so that the giver will obtain merit. In the bus I had thought one monk was being polite, but I found he was moving so that, hopefully, no woman would sit beside him or, if unfortunately she did, she wouldn't touch him. Had she touched him both would have become ceremonially unclean and would have been required to undergo elaborate cleaning rituals.

A spirit house outside a bank

Spirit 'houses', usually fawn, sometimes with a streak of silver or gold leaf can be seen everywhere – outside banks, offices, schools, houses, etc. When the Nojiri children attended the local Thai school they were required to bow before the shrine on their way in. The fact that they were from a Christian home did not exempt them. Mr Nojori said the only way to avoid the worship was for the children to be late.

Our Japanese group agreed that the spiritual battle could be seen outwardly in Bangkok but that the same conflict existed in Japan though hidden, where the god-shelves and shrines were inside the houses.

I returned to Tokyo realising something of the wealth of experiences I had had in Thailand living in four cultures simultaneously – OMF, Thai, Japanese and British.

Building the new church

The church continued all its regular activities for seven months in the prefabricated covering set up over the car park and garden. Pastor Haga though weak, weary and still losing weight, continued to preach powerfully. His body was slowly strengthened through careful diets and the avoidance of his favourite drink, coffee.

The heart specialist, whose observation had saved the pastor's life, continued to attend services with his wife. One morning he sat entranced, on the edge of his chair, as the Pastor spoke from Ezekiel 11 v 19. 'I will remove from them the heart of stone and give them a heart of flesh.' This was so much like the language used during heart operations. If, during the transplant, the surgeons were successful, the new heart was soft and referred to as a heart of flesh. If they were unsuccessful and the new heart hardened, it was referred to as a heart of stone. Deeply moved though he was, his own heart remained as stone: he was unwilling to receive the heart of flesh Jesus offered him.

When the church was at last erected, the rubble cleared away and the interior equipped and decorated, Pastor Haga and the believers were anxious to advertise it and bring new people in. The plan was to show the film *Chariots of Fire*. A hundred members of the church distributed 30,000 leaflets in the area. We were delighted when 300 people packed into the building. About 100 of these were students who were required by their university to see the film. The story of the Olympic runner, Eric Liddell, gripped the audience and, to the Japanese, his refusal to comply with the wishes of the British Crown Prince because of his loyalty to Christ, was almost beyond their conception.

Mr Suda's funeral

Mrs Suda had been planning to come to Thailand with the church group but had to withdraw because her husband was seriously ill. He had been diagnosed with cancer a year before but, according to Japanese custom, he was not informed. Although his wife, daughter and brother were Christians he was too involved in State affairs. Japan is dependent on imports of oil: during a critical period Mr Suda had travelled to Iran and obtained oil for his country. Now, in hospital in Koganei, he expressed a desire to have the Bible read to him and in the final days of his life trusted in Christ. We prayed that the Lord would raise him up to tell others of his new found faith, but that was not to be – he died.

His funeral was a triumphant proclamation of the story of Christ, His death and resurrection. The new church was packed for the wake, and for the funeral service the next day. The neighbouring supermarket agreed to the use of their car parking facilities for the scores of cars bringing mourners to the church, including high-up government ministers, honouring a man who had been of great service to his country. Such a gathering could not have been held in the old humble wooden structure. Pastor Haga, still very weak, was not willing to forgo his responsibility of conducting the service, nor miss the opportunity of telling so many people who had never heard of Jesus Christ, Son of the one true living God, crucified for them, risen from the dead, and ascended to heaven, where now Mr Suda himself had gone.

According to custom, certain periods of mourning were observed during the following days until the ashes were taken to the church burial ground. Koganei Free Methodists owned a plot of ground in the Fuji-en Cemetery (*en* = garden). Christians don't want their ashes, or those of their family, to be placed in the Buddhist temple grounds, the usual location. It is important to them that the church owns a burial plot. A large group of ladies from the church set off for Fuji-en in a private mini-bus, with Mrs Suda, her daughter, Pastor Haga and others. It seemed to be a happy church outing as we picnicked in the beautiful extensive garden of Fuji-en. The companionship amongst us was rich.

The opened tomb revealed several urns containing the ashes of former Koganei Christians. In a short service, Pastor Haga thanked God for Mr Suda, asked blessing on his widow and family, and put the urn on a shelf alongside the others. It was a strangely moving occasion: the widow was not alone but surrounded by supporting friends, all of us knowing that Christ had died for us and death was the beginning of everlasting life with Him.

The 'Pension' and the 'Pilgrimage'

A short cool summer which had been forecast, turned out to be a long hot one, and Tokyo can be very hot and humid. We had not left Koganei for cooler holiday resorts unlike most missionaries in the city and received approval from the Pastor for our 'dedication'. Despite air conditioning in the flat we remained lethargic, and then discovered there was little church activity, and that the pastors also were inactive during the period of intense heat.

We wondered about a short escape to the southern coast of Honshu, away from the heat and pollution of the city. Mrs Haga gave us the phone number she had found from a list of 'pensions', small boarding houses. Doug rang up, asking if accommodation was available.

'Well,' came the reply. 'I wouldn't want foreigners staying here. What would you eat?'

'We've lived in Japan for thirty years,' Doug reassured the proprietor. 'We speak Japanese and are very happy with the meals you produce.' Somewhat reluctantly he agreed to take us.

We drove through busy crowded roads on the outskirts of Tokyo and then to the refreshing atmosphere of the coast. We reached the pension situated above a picturesque bay with rocks, tall cactus plants and the sea. The water was ideal for swimming, clear and cool. The accommodation was simple but adequate, and the meals enjoyable, not fancy. We cemented a friendship with the owner.

The following year Richard joined us again. He had finished his finals at Birmingham and had obtained a job with BP at Moorgate from September. We booked accommodation for a few days again at the pension. The landlord was delighted to receive us. Most Japanese use the pensions as stopping places as they tour the area and rarely return to the same one. Our return, with Richard, indicated how much we had appreciated our first visit. Especially fascinated by the little blue fishes visible in the clear water as we also swam. DD loved the place.

We returned to Tokyo where DD was very much at home, fluent in Japanese and travelling to different parts of the country meeting with friends. He was company for Doug while I was away on my trip to Thailand. He returned to England to start work at BP – quite an adjustment for him.

In the autumn, Michael and Angela joined us for about a month although they were still having problems finding a house in England. We and they realised that if they were going to visit us it would have to be soon as we were due to retire in a year. Everything was new to Angela although her father had visited Yokohama as a merchant seaman at the end of the war. For Michael, he was returning to his roots.

Angela explored Yokohama on her own. She also came with me to the Bible School where four of the girls I had been teaching asked her questions.

'How do you get on with your mother-in-law?'

With great tact and wisdom, Angela replied, 'We are just getting to know each other.'

For Mike it was a fantastic pilgrimage to old places of his childhood, and an introduction for Angela.

We drove northwards, stopping first at the modern university town of Tsukuba where our friends Frank and Betty Nowell were living. They had supervised our OMF mission home for a period. They were delighted to meet us again and welcomed us with open arms.

Continuing on we visited our holiday resort, Takayama. It was out of season, the beach deserted, but Michael and I had a nostalgic swim in the sea. Not far from Takayama is the tourist attraction of Matsushima (Pine Tree Island), with many small islands in the sea, each with at least one pine tree growing on it. The city of Shiogama is nearby. Here we enjoyed the hospitality of Professor Watanabe's family, in their large house. He had been studying in Swansea when David Bentley-Taylor befriended him and introduced us. The family were Christians but one member had wished to keep the huge ornate god-shelf, enshrining the dead, that dominated one of the rooms. The rest of the family did not wish it to be kept. The Shiogama Baptist Church had been built on grounds near a copse of trees left in commemoration of a Christian group trying to escape persecution but had been caught and martyred on that spot centuries previously.

Continuing northward we reached Aomori Prefecture, the northern part of Honshu. The pastor of the Aomori city church greeted us warmly – he told us how three neighbours who had been opposed to the Gospel had now believed. Aomori was the town where our three children had been born and Mike saw the house of his birth. We wandered once again over the extensive Hirosaki Park, dominated by the ancient castle keeps. Here Mr Katagawa, the struggling manager of the Christian Book Shop, opposite the University, met us. We had worked with him so closely years back. He was moved almost to tears as we parted with prayer.

From Aomori we had to take the ferry to Hakodate. From there we went the short distance to Nanae School where Michael's primary education had started. It was a reminder of the cost of separation for parents and children, plus the care God gave us all and the sense of being one big family – the children together in the school as brothers and sisters, parents sharing the sadness of separation, and all the OMF members, including the single ladies, were as aunts and uncles to the children.

On to Sapporo and many friends. The Shibakawas put us up in a hotel. Their church, Fujino, was thriving and Mr Shibakawa was still involved in the Alcoholics Rehabilitation Centre, supervised by Mr and Mrs Utsunomiya, fellow Christians of thirty years ago. It was a delight to meet up with the Kamada family and their three Christian daughters. We called in on our OMF headquarters where we had lived for twelve years.

We had a meal round a large table with the Kutchan pastor and believers, including Mr and Mrs Doki, first fruits of Doug and David Hayman's bringing the message of Christ to the town.

On our return to Tokyo we admired the beauty of Lake Towada reflecting the reds, yellows, oranges and greens of the trees in autumn splendour.

We said goodbye to Mike and Angela at Narita Airport, with many memories.

Increased activity

Friends in England often met Japanese and sent us their addresses. Usually this came to nothing, but Mr Kuroda was an exception. He was an English professor, studying further in a Teacher's Education College where Pam Dowman was also studying. She wrote to us. We were able to meet him and invite him and his wife to a meal. She was a little nervous because she did not have her husband's knowledge of English but was reassured when I spoke in Japanese. We also enjoyed our return visit to their house. They were Christians: he told us that his father had worked for the Imperial household, had maintained his Christian faith in this strongly Shinto establishment and that, when he died, members of the household had attended the Christian funeral in his church.

Japanese schools arranged camps in the summer for their pupils. I was invited to the Keimei one. We slept on wooden floors on very thin futons. Early morning exercises to radio music and instructions started the day. This was fine for the children who were used to this daily routine but I felt quite stupid trying to follow the instructions and do the exercises with the children. One group of children were from a Buddhist school and would not kill a fly, mosquito, spider or any other insect, in accordance with the Buddhist teaching of not killing.

Mr and Mrs Shea, a young Chinese couple, had moved to Tokyo. We had first met them when he was a post-graduate chemistry student in Hokkaido University, and baptized them in Tooei Church. He was in the process of buying a car, but had to find a suitable parking spot for it before ownership was allowed.

Barry and Jan Potter were near neighbours: we had welcomed them to Japan on arrival and seen them established in the northern city of Asahikawa. Now he was putting in his weight with the Pacific Broadcasting Association based in Tokyo, sending Gospel messages by radio throughout the country. Jan was looking after her growing family, struggling to make ends meet with the food she bought for them – American style, not English. She was an excellent typist but could not meet Pastor Haga's needs because he required typing to be done immediately. Barry was very busy with the radio work and language learning, so was not able to attend all the meetings that would have seemed obligatory to the Japanese. We celebrated Christmas at the other side of Tokyo, with Hugh and Margaret Trevor and family, the Potters and family and Ruth White. Koganei church had meetings on 19, 22, 23, 24 and 26 December – Christmas Day was free.

Both Doug and I found ourselves busy with speaking engagements – at the branch Free Methodist churches, at the numerous weekly house groups, and with other Christian groups in Tokyo. The ladies International Women's Group included largely American ladies. I enjoyed telling them how I became a Christian and so became known as a speaker.

Classical concerts at the NHK (BBC) hall were of a very high standard but we preferred the concerts we had attended in Sapporo – easier to get to, not so crowded.

We spent many hours with the Suzuki family visiting them or on the telephone. Mrs Suzuki was suffering from a post-operative infection. He and his son came to the monthly English service at Koganei where Doug was usually preaching. Both had excellent English.

The church workers changed. Mr and Mrs Tsubai had been great friends. She came to my cooking/Bible class, often helping with the children, and got to know the mothers. Mr Tsubai was always cheerful and prepared to do any chores, like driving for Pastor Haga. When they were posted to Ome and Pastor Haga was in hospital, Doug took the church services more often. The two girls, Akemi Honda and Rie Sakurai continued as helpers. Rie had appreciated the Revd Tsutada's lectures at the Bible School and his personal experiences of dealing with demonic forces in India and continuing in Japan. We were together with Rie when a young woman asked to be delivered from spirits that enabled her to tell fortunes. We were able to help in Jesus' name. She told us, 'The spirits have left me, but they are still hovering around, above us. They are saying "Please don't send us away, we like it here".' She asked us to take the 'charm' she had been given from a temple and keep it until she wanted it destroyed.

Akemi had longed to become a missionary with OMF to Thailand. This required a fluency in English. I taught her for a time: she responded and studied hard but was very disappointed when she did not reach the required level to be at ease in the language. Pastor Tokuda had an interest in her and they agreed to marry. This was a colourful and lively ceremony in the new church building with a very happy and beautiful bride. We were astonished at the speech given by another pastor speaking of Pastor Tokuda, not praising him but emphasising his shortcomings. They later went as missionaries with the Free Methodists to Bolivia – not an easy assignment, but they loved it.

At the Koganei ladies' rally, I spoke on John chapter 3 v 16, 'For God so loved the world that he gave His one and only Son, that whoever believes in Him shall not perish but have eternal life' using a teapot cover, a cake tin and a bathing costume as illustrations. The cake tin, familiar to Japanese ladies, to illustrate creation, they would not throw a cake away but would be disappointed if it was not satisfactory; the teapot cosy – I had made it so it was important to me; the bathing costume, perishing.

At Christmas time I spoke to a group of seventy mothers of kindergarten children. This time I wrapped a small present, not very attractively, in brown paper, telling them the contents and offering it to anyone who would come and get it, illustrating God's gift to us in sending Christ at Christmas time. One lady hesitatingly came forward and accepted it. She was delighted that she could keep the gift. The Japanese on the whole are more concerned about the wrapping than the content.

Farewells

The year 1985 was our last full one in Japan – Doug at sixty-five, me at sixty due to retire. We took the opportunity to escape the heat of Tokyo in August and enjoy the relative coolness of Hokkaido to say goodbye to many friends there.

We were booked to fly from Haneda airport to Chitose in Hokkaido. That same day a Japan Airlines jumbo jet crashed into Mt Fuji. It seems that the plane, on a domestic flight from Haneda to Osaka, lost a chunk from the tail-end possibly including control machinery. It went off course just over our pension, headed north, and the pilot sent the message that the plane was out of control. One of the four survivors out of 520 was a stewardess flying as a passenger. She was able to give an account of what happened. It crashed into woodland on the mountain. We were thankful to land safely in Hokkaido.

Doug was due to preach at Shibakawa's church in South West Sapporo on the Sunday. Mr Shibakawa had booked us into a hotel. We watched the TV at leisure, including Tchaikovsky's piano concerto. We could have watched the 'Giants' baseball team on another station but we had our loyalty to the Lions, the team we had seen in action. (The door lock of our hotel room was out of order so we found ourselves locked in!)

Our trip included three mornings swimming in the sea – and getting sunburned; time at the Hokkaido churches conference; at a hot spring resort; a visit with Alan and Elaine Mitchell to the Kamada family; welcome at Kutchan; the OMF conference at a lake, with a farewell to us; three days in Kitami staying in Mr Shibakawa Sr's home on his eightieth birthday. At eighty he was as alert as ever, but finding his legs not carrying him as they used to; and we were able to say goodbye to some I had known thirty years before – and back to Tokyo.

I had started a Sunday School in our home with several Japanese ladies, but without the permission of the Pastor. He reprimanded me strongly in Japanese – in English he would have been more gentle. By way of reconciliation, Mr and Mrs Haga took us for a day ride round Mt Fuji, visiting the four lakes, and then to a very special raw fish restaurant. We saw the carp and trout swimming in tanks, assuring us that the fish we ate was fresh.

In October we received the news we had been waiting for – Roslyn Sarah Keal had been born on the 1st of the month, our first grandchild. Grace sent us tapes to hear her first cries. We were surprised to find ourselves moved by the sound.

At the beginning of December the Pastor arranged for a church workers' retreat to the Izu peninsula. Eight of us fitted into the eight-seater car. We drove round the coast past the 'pension' we loved, and stayed one night in another pension. The scenery was fantastic – beautiful coastal scenes, steep hills, temples and, outstanding in the morning, fog had frozen on leaves and flowers, giving a fairy-like Christmas picture. This was unusual as the Tokyo area rarely experienced snow or frost (though I remembered one unusually cold spell when we did have snow, even as late as April in Tokyo. I saw a shop keeper trying to remove ice in front of her shop by pouring boiling water on it. I should have stopped and advised her to use salt!)

The church elders took us out for a special meal one evening. We went through an archway into the restaurant grounds and then into a tatami room with low benches round ash trenches with glowing charcoal. Outside the windows were water channels. The raw food came along on trays on the water; we received it through the windows and cooked it over the charcoal. I remember the frogs' legs that were very tasty. The disadvantage of the system was the smoke from the burning fuel choking us.

Our farewell in the church – Doug and I were both preaching – giving our experiences, and a missionary challenge.

Pastor Haga had arranged a farewell meeting for us with our past associates in a room in central Tokyo. He did not know how the meeting would go. Among the guests were folk we had known years ago and more recent acquaintances. Lionel Thomson from 1955, Lt Col Fuji, Sapporo, and others were Principals of Bible Schools of varying denominations, but some we had known as students. Pastor Haga invited the guests to give their memories, which were heart-warming but that was the whole programme, non-stop. The Lt Col told how Doug had tried to introduce him to Jesus and, although interested, he preferred the girls. Lionel spoke of many past memories of his early days in Japan with us in Shizunai. So it continued round the circle. We were cheered, touched, exhausted. From the group, Pastor Haga gave us an ornament of Mt Fuji – a cloisonné, decorated with enamel inlaid in compartments formed by small fillets of metal. The plaque was of red enamel, Mt Fuji standing out with streaks of white, indicating snow. It was 15cms by 20 cms, quite heavy, with a stand to support it.

As it was our last year in Japan we had a large number of visitors.

Mr Nakagawa and Mr Tanosato came together to say goodbye. Both had become Christians during our early years in Shizunai. Mr Nakagawa, a former boxer and criminal, had spent many years as a pastor. Mr Tanosato, from the village of Samani along the coast from Shizunai, had gone to Bible School unbeknown to us and then continued as a pastor in a small church.

The General Director of OMF, J.O. Sanders, spent three days staying with us in Koganei and celebrated his eightieth birthday – royally fêted by the Free Methodist Church.

Doug was tour guide round Tokyo for Andrew and Joy Pickin – Joy, the daughter of our friends David and Dorothy Highwood, had been at school with Grace and Michael.

Nanabu Kubota and Mr Ishikawa, just engaged, called on us for marriage guidance. He was a younger brother of the owner of our flat. She was church organist, and singer, and it was she who had 'interpreted' for me at the children's gatherings in the church when all thirteen had become Christians. Apart from answering their questions, we were able to pass on to them our bed which we could not take with us.

We spent much time with Yumi Goto and her brother and sister-in-law, Mr and Mrs Watanabe. She, Mrs Watanabe, was having mental health problems. I calculated that we met with fifteen Japanese with such problems that year. Some of the problems were caused by evil spirits although such spirits were not acknowledged in Japan.

From England we learned that Richard was ill. Also, that a riot on

Broadwater Farm, North London, had resulted in Doug's nephew's house being burned down and the family of four escaping with police help.

We met so many friends during the year that I must have left out many names.

At our farewell from the Bible School we were given a plate-clock and matching vase, still in our kitchen. Principal Tsutada gave us an encouraging quotation from the Bible, Psalm 92 v14: 'They will still bear fruit in old age, they will stay fresh and green.'

It had been a great year of Bible verses for me. At the beginning of the year Doug preached on, 'God's exceeding and precious promises'. I asked for a promise a day through the year – and received them.

Goodbye to Japan, but our hearts remained there.

Interlude

To London via Beijing

WE WERE PREPARING TO LEAVE Japan permanently. This involved packing and taking all our possessions to be shipped or given away, and sorting out our hand luggage for the journey. In 1952 I had bought a bicycle in Hong Kong. It had served me faithfully for thirty-four years. Would I get it back to England? I called at the cycle shop opposite our flats.

'What do you do with the crates the new bicycles come in?' I asked.

'We have no further use for them,' the owner replied. 'We just throw them away.'

'We are going back to England. Do you think you could use one of them to crate my old bicycle for shipping?'

They obliged.

In 1983, we had bought an oil painting in Nathan Road, Hong Kong, of the junks approaching the harbour. It reminded us of ourselves moving together to our final destiny. We rolled it up to bring it to Tokyo where we had it framed. The framed picture was too long for any of our cases; it got special treatment. Other pictures, scrolls, presents, etc., fitted in our cases within the OMF weight allowance.

Next we had to book our flight. Doug enjoyed visiting different travel agents. We wanted to book a reasonably priced flight to London but we also wanted to go via Beijing and spend some time in China. There were many tours from Tokyo to Beijing to Tokyo but we wanted Tokyo – Beijing – London. At last Doug discovered an unpretentious travel agent who booked us on a Pakistan Airline to London via Beijing, disembarking on a Monday and picking up the equivalent flight a week later.

He also arranged for us to stay in the Beijing Toronto Hotel. After this was settled we learned that several Beijing hotels had been overbooked and guests were sleeping in the lounges. Oh dear! What should we do? I rang up the Tokyo booking office.

'We hear that Beijing hotels are overbooked,' I said. 'If the hotel were under Japanese management we would not be concerned.'

'You don't need to worry about the Beijing Toronto Hotel,' came the reply. 'It *is* under Japanese management.'

We did not book any tours from the hotel because we did not know how much energy we would have after all the packing and farewells. We informed our children, and SBC who had a house for us, re our time of arrival.

Our final preparation was to pack suitable warm clothing for the cold of January in Beijing.

Pastor and Mrs Haga and Steve and Evelyn Metcalf saw us off at Narita Airport.

Beijing

The flight was uneventful. We reached the comfortable Beijing Toronto Hotel, not too exhausted.

One of our suit cases was falling to pieces. At a local department store we bought another, the shop-assistant making sure we obtained one in good condition. We noticed it was 'Made in Taiwan.' At the time, relationships between China and Taiwan were strained but perhaps this did not affect business.

Breakfast in the hotel dining room was buffet style. Doug helped himself to fruit salad and started to eat it before noticing there were pins in it. The waitress was frightened and full of apologies. Doug was reluctant to report it, knowing that the staff could get into serious trouble. Afterwards we thought that she had used a bowl for the pins and Doug had picked that particular bowl for his fruit salad.

We had exchanged Yen with Chinese currency – Yuan. But the Yuan travellers receive is of much greater value than the ordinary Chinese Yuan. Equipped with Chinese money we decided to explore the town, first by bus.

'Where can we get the bus?' we asked at the reception.

'You need to go by taxi,' came the reply. 'Foreigners never take the bus.'

'We would like to have a ride in a bus,' we insisted.

So we were shown the bus stop. A very full bus, concertina-type with two sections joined together, drew up. We got on the bus and offered the conductress the lowest value note we had. She was troubled to give us the right change. We had not realised the difference between the 'foreigners' Yuan and the ordinary Chinese citizens Yuan. We had given her the equivalent of £10 for a 2p ticket.

Getting off the bus we walked along the busy streets. Bicycles were everywhere. An accident had occurred with a collision between a car and a bicycle. The heated argument between the driver and the cyclist brought a crowd of onlookers, moving their heads to right and left as the quarrel developed.

Further down, in a side street, we passed a number of stalls in the open air, the owners calling us to buy. We passed one rather large Chinese lady (most Chinese are small) selling cloth and clothing. She called to us but we walked on. Returning along the same path, I indicated that I would like to buy a nightdress but Chinese clothing was too small for me. She gesticulated that she had something large enough, raising her arms and demonstrating how fat she was herself. I did buy two cool nightdresses from her – all this charade-fashion as we could not communicate in Chinese. They were excellent, very roomy and not expensive. The exchange had been entertaining.

Using my camera resulted in curiosity from passers-by. One gentleman with two small children was happy for me to take their photographs.

There were four places we wished to visit – the Summer Palace, the Great Wall, a theatre with Chinese acrobats, and a Peking duck restaurant.

A taxi took us to a Peking duck restaurant, clearly designed for the Chinese, not for tourists. We sat down, British or Japanese fashion, at an empty table. The waiter approached us and asked us to fill up another table. The tables were filled one by one as people arrived. At our table were two school girls and a couple with a child. The school girls wanted to practise English and I helped. Doug communicated through the written Chinese-Japanese characters. They kindly showed us how to tackle the Peking duck, spreading the black sauce on a pancake, adding the salad and meat, and folding it over. The meat was tasty, the company interesting, and an experience we appreciated of a genuine Chinese restaurant.

Another evening a taxi took us to a theatre to see acrobats performing. Once again it was not designed as a tourist attraction. The seats were hard, the audience enthusiastic and the performers brilliant. We wondered how we would get a taxi back to the hotel, but the taxi driver who had brought us was waiting – accident or design? Whatever, we were grateful for the end of a thoroughly enjoyable evening.

No visit to Beijing would be complete without a walk on the Great Wall. A train took us to the start of the wall. We bought oranges from a mountain of oranges on a stall by the side of the road. As Doug started to peel his, the vendor's commanding finger indicated where he had to deposit the peel – no dropping it on the ground. We walked some distance along the wall seeing the road ahead winding through the mountains. Certainly it was an impressive structure but at the cost of thousands of labourers' lives and incredible hardship.

A huge picture of Mao Tse Tung dominated the government buildings overlooking Tiananmen Square.

We joined the throngs in the Square, through the gates into the Forbidden City and the Summer Palace. History of the Chinese Emperors' culture of those times was now preserved for all to see. The Summer Palace had been the summer resort for the Empress Dowager Cixi around 1900; a large amount of silver had been designated for the Chinese navy, but she used it to reconstruct and enlarge her palace. As it was supposed to be for shipping she had a 'ship' made of stone built on the lake. We saw this in January when skaters were enjoying the frozen water.

Returning to our hotel by bus, we missed the turning for our street and continued to the terminus.

The driver indicated to a student on the bus that we needed help. The young man spoke in English and directed us to the bus to take us back to the hotel.

We attended a Chinese church on the Sunday. An elderly Christian pastor spoke to us there. We sensed a degree of uneasiness.

On Monday our adventures in Beijing came to an end. We boarded the Pakistan Airline plane for London.

CHAPTER 9

Retirement (1985 onwards)

A summary of retirement

WE RETIRED FROM JAPAN AGED sixty (me) and sixty-five (Doug) expecting to have about ten more years to live. I had not yet grasped that God's ways were higher than our ways, and His thoughts above ours. Our next very full twenty-five need a whole book.

We spent time with our children again, at Richard's wedding, and with our seven grandchildren.

The churches welcomed us – Stanmore Baptist providing accommodation near the church; West Green Baptist giving us a grand reception with other friends invited; Whitley Bay Baptist anxious to hear from us. We met old friends who had prayed for us for years.

We had wonderful holidays – abroad in Tunisia, Yugoslavia, Singapore, France, Switzerland, the Moselle Valley, Jersey, USA, Japan, and in Britain at Teignmouth, Wales, Whitley Bay, Ponteland, Cambridge and Fort William.

Continued links with Japan included visits from Miho, Watanabes, Pastor Hosokawa, Pastor and Mrs Haga. With Valerie Griffiths, my friend and colleague in Japan I had Japanese Bible Studies with ladies living in the area. We also became friends with Mr and Mrs Takahashi.

Funerals were inevitable – close friends from SBC – Carol Hewitt, Ron Daykin, John Doulton. Doug's sister-in-law, Gwen, my brother Graham, Edna and Bill Lemon, Arthur Caiger, David Highwood.

Amazing and unexpected was my being returned as Councillor for Wemborough Ward in the London Borough of Harrow.

Links with Cambridge were renewed. In 1998, the women's colleges commemorated fifty years since women had been admitted as full members of the university. The Christian Unions also met to remember the joining of the men and women's CUs. Phone calls from present undergraduates to link with alumni are occurring yearly. A request came for information about the war years in Girton; the chemistry group of 1946 was featured in their magazine, *Chem@Cam*.

Beyond our wildest dreams was a three-week visit to Japan in the autumn of 2003 to join the Jubilee celebrations of the Tokyo Free Methodist Church. God showed us how His ways had been beyond ours when we had lived there.

And much more, and a caravan . . .

Adjustment to UK

Stanmore Baptist Church had bought a three-bedroomed furnished house for our use. I was glad to be able to settle in one place and not have to move any more. We realised later that this was a mistake. We had changed, the country had changed; we should have waited a year before making any final decisions re location. Deputation work continued for several months; we tried to readjust to England. The readjustment was more difficult than our adjustment to Japan. I think this was because we had expected to learn the culture of a foreign country, but thought we knew our own.

I found shopping somewhat intimidating. I had been used to the weights in Japan *mōmei*, then kilograms. When the Japanese changed to the metric system they used scales graduated to both. Not only that, the greengroceries were sold by the 'mountain', the amount piled on a plate. I could see the quantity of beans I was buying, or how many tomatoes. Back home I did not know if I should ask for 2 ozs, 2 lbs or 20 lbs.

At Christmas in Japan, many shops, or shopping precincts, offered a ticket for every 100 yen spent. Ten tickets gave a chance for a lucky dip. 'I'm so sorry,' said the owner, 'you haven't won anything'. Then he would hand you a small packet of tissues. It was a good free present. I missed this. (On one occasion I won ten crates of Coca Cola with tickets I'd received from purchases. Never mind that I don't like Coke.)

In Japan outdoor shoes are never worn indoors. We continued this custom in our own home, though did not feel we could impose this on visitors.

We missed the *ofuro*, the Japanese bath where one soaks up to the neck in hot water.

We continued to use the Japanese greetings when leaving the house and returning. *Iite mairimasu* I'm going. *Itte irrashai* go. *Tadaima* I'm back. *Okaerinasai* welcome home. There is no English equivalent – we just come and go, without a greeting.

I missed the Japanese courtesy. I had to get used to shaking hands instead of bowing.

Cherry blossom is of special significance in Japan partly because the flower appears before the leaf, and especially in the north where there is no other greenery, the blossom in Spring brings a sudden blaze of white. On our return to England we realised what a wealth of blossom there is on trees we have in this country.

Many things had crept into English society that saddened us. Freedom of speech was being gradually eroded and lack of truth called 'political correctness'. The much loved children's toy of my youth, the golliwog, banned, blackboard called chalk board, etc. I did not receive an answer to my question as to who decided these things.

I addressed the school assembly at my old school and used a scroll with calligraphy drawn by a Japanese Christian friend. It read, 'I am (the) way (the) truth and (the) life', explaining that there is no article in the Japanese language but the message is clear that there is only one way to the Father. Afterwards the senior mistress told me that the assembly is supposed by law (1944) to have a Christian message, which I had given, but that was not usually carried out. The decrease of Bible teaching in schools was disturbing. The use of first names for staff lack of respect for the teacher, poor discipline, and mountains of paperwork augured badly for the future of the country.

Drinking habits were also alarming. In Japan there had been increasing pressure against drinking although it was very common, because a man had not been regarded as responsible for his actions while drunk. In my youth we avoided going out between 10.00 and 10.30 at night when the pubs spilled out. Drunkenness was looked upon as shameful. Now in England supermarkets shelves were stacked with bottles, young men and women drank to excess.

Ward Councillor

In my teens I was interested in politics, but living in a foreign country, Japan, I was unable to enter into political affairs – I didn't even have a vote. Back in England I received a brochure through the door concerning the newly formed Social Democratic Party; it suited to my views. I joined. Then there was a merger with the Liberal Party: hesitantly I signed up for the merged Liberal Democrats. I supported Laurence Cox, an established scientist, at a by-election in our Ward, and then came the full council elections.

Laurence and Ann Diamond, a local housewife, were standing as candidates; we needed a third person for the Ward.

'You wouldn't think of standing, would you?' Ann asked me.

'No,' I replied, 'I might.' (I had answered her question thinking the Japanese way – wouldn't you? No, I would. Yes, I wouldn't.)

So it was that I was interviewed by the Lib Dem party group, to approve my suitability. I was free to mention matters on which I disagreed with their policy; there are rarely any members who agree with everything. But I did say I felt a little old at sixty-eight to start.

So we canvassed the Ward. On the day of the election at the polling station I was sitting beside my rival Conservative candidate, Paul, a professing Jew. We discovered that our views were amazingly similar. He was P.A. to Lord Brain of the House of Lords, and later he arranged for Doug and me to observe a debate in the Lords, sitting in the privileged section, 'below bar'.

In the morning of the poll, I had prayed, 'Lord, I am sure You want me to stand for election but I'd like to run away. But if this is Your will, please may I have a good majority.'

As we watched the votes being counted in the evening, we saw our pile getting higher and higher. Laurence, Ann and I were all returned. I had 1,815 votes. Was this God's sense of humour? He had answered my prayer for a good majority but 1,815 was Waterloo – had I 'met my Waterloo?' (Ann's was 1,805 – Trafalgar). I should have been dancing for joy. I was just overwhelmed and sorry for my rival, Paul. He graciously said that although he himself was not elected he was very glad that I had been.

Becoming a councillor was a shock to my system: I started on a steep learning curve. The Lib Dems had the largest number of councillors but not an overall majority. It was a difficult time with half our own party on the council for the first time and the Conservatives and Labour determined to discredit us.

I had our own party group discussions and council briefing sessions to put forward my views. There was one occasion on which I found myself strongly opposed to the group's decision. It involved financial advantage to the council but removing a group of residents from their accommodation. My Christian friends joined in prayer re the situation. The night before the main council meeting, at the housing committee, all parties agreed to support the move. My Lib Dem fellow councillor, Brian, rang me up, 'It's no use, Olga. Labour and Conservatives have both decided to vote for the motion. Only a miracle could defeat it.'

The next day, at the full council meeting, two of our members were missing, reducing our numbers, and the Conservatives did a U-turn, the motion was defeated. A miracle?

A year later, a Tory councillor explained, 'We did a U-turn to embarrass you'. I felt disgusted that people's lives could be affected by party political rivalry of this kind: yet I rejoiced that God could intervene.

Clive, a Christian Conservative councillor, had wanted a prayer meeting of the Christian councillors. We were able to start this. As an Anglican he celebrated Ascension Day. A new mayor was due to take office and the present mayor to retire. But Clive realised that the change was scheduled for Ascension Day, a religious holiday. So the change was postponed for a week. During that week the mayor, Mr Hamlin, died. The death of the mayor in office called for a lavish ceremony for the funeral.

Council meetings tended to be long drawn out occasions. One evening I got home at 2 a.m. to find myself locked out. A sleepy Doug slowly descended the stairs and opened the door saying, 'I don't remember locking it.'

On another occasion, at 2 a.m., I found the street flooded. A phone call to the Civic Centre security resulted in immediate action and the discovery that a drain was blocked through planks having been thrown into a stream.

I enjoyed the responsibilities as Ward Councillor – I could help individuals and have direct access to the Civic Centre staff from whom I always received a courteous response. Road problems, paving stones, constructing a pedestrian refuge. I was particularly pleased that I was able to arrange for a crossing directly to Stanmore Baptist Church. I thanked the engineer who replied, 'We don't often receive appreciation for what we do.'

Phone calls were not infrequent, especially from Jewish ladies, thinking with a name of 'Abrahams' I was also Jewish. I referred such callers on to Ann, who was Jewish.

A distressed widow contacted me because the grass-cutting machine used in the field next to her house had knocked against her fence and broken it down. My reporting this to the Civic Centre department brought an immediate response and repair.

We had a surprise visit from Mr and Mrs Watanabe from Tokyo (see page 248) and the Koganei Church. She had recovered from mental health problems and now he was a social services worker. Britain was ahead of Japan in this field: Mr Watanabe wanted help and guidance from us. It was

Saturday when the Civic Centre was closed, but an official from Social Services opened up the Council Chamber and spent considerable time with Mr Watanabe explaining what we did.

I celebrated my seventieth birthday in the Members' Lounge of the Civic Centre. Michael and family were in the States but Grace and Adrian with their two girls, and Richard and Christina and their boy and girl, came along. The cousins enjoyed playing together in the lobby off the lounge. The Civic Centre caterers arranged a finger buffet supper. The guests included about thirty from the Council and thirty from the church, and they gelled well.

Laurence's wife, Oenone, was an opera singer and sang accompanied by Valerie King, an accomplished pianist originally from SBC. Grace and Richard both sang with guitars – Grace said to me, 'We aren't going to sing immediately after that professional performance.' There was a break between.

For a main speaker, I had at first asked Lord Alton then Simon Hughes, both Christian Lib Dem politicians. Neither was able to come but willing to find a deputy. Then I realised the ideal speaker was Valerie Griffiths with whom we had worked in Japan. She made a brilliant speech giving an account of my life and finished by asking, 'What made an atheistic science student finish as a missionary to Japan? For the answer ask her out for coffee to tell you.'

Friendships made during my time on the Council are precious and have remained. I was exhausted and, I think, ill before the end of the four years and didn't feel fit to stand again.

I continued as governor of a local high school until Doug, at nearly eighty, had a heart attack.

The mayor, Mr Kiki Thammaiah and Mayoress, graciously attended our twenty-first anniversary of the founding of the Sheltered Housing Complex, Paxfold, founded by Revd Patrick Goodland, former pastor of SBC, with others.

On a visit to friends in Harrogate, we met with the Mayor (Lib Dem). The contrast of the American officer's car with the mayor's car was highlighted by the contrast in the heights of the men. We had been told that a photograph was to be taken in the square. Electric powered cars were being promoted.

Tony Benn came to Harrow for the unveiling of a plaque commemorating Clement Attlee who had lived in the area. Afterwards we were able to chat to him in the Civic Centre – an unusual politician.

All past members of the Council are invited to special occasions, e.g. the opening service for a new mayor, Remembrance Day service, and are notified of funerals of former members – so I hope many will attend mine when the time comes.

Back to Japan

May 2003

We always enjoyed welcoming Japanese friends to our home but none more than Pastor Tadashi Haga and his wife, Aki. Despite advancing age and ill health, they both remained enthusiastic and energetic, looking on mishaps as opportunities for new experiences, e.g. a foggy day – 'Oh good, this is just what we learnt about in our text books.' Pastor Haga knew the OMF staff at our UK HQ and had visited us previously but, on this occasion, he had a special invitation for us:

'In September, the Tokyo Free Methodist Churches are celebrating our fiftieth Anniversary,' he told us. 'We would be delighted if you could join us.'

We were excited at the prospect. Of all our thirty-four years in Japan we had spent only four with Koganei Free Methodists, but that four-year period had been very special for us, learning more of the culture and enjoying times with mature Japanese Christians in an established church.

Questions arose in our minds – could we undertake the journey back now, aged seventy-eight and and eighty-three? Would we remember the language? Our memory for names was deteriorating also; our hearing poor, and our stamina low. Tadashi and Aki didn't feel these facts were relevant and persuaded us to come.

September 2003

We booked our flight from Frankfurt to Narita. A week before we were due to leave, a chest X-ray revealed a shadow on my lung. The consultant was persuaded to let me go, arranged for a further check on return, saying 'There can't be a great change in three weeks.'

There was a long wait in the queue at Heathrow but I enjoyed chatting to a young African man, away from his Christian home and uncertain about his own faith. At last we boarded the plane for Frankfurt where we eventually unravelled the route to our plane for Tokyo through the labyrinth of corridors and escalators. We finally got there for the long haul ahead – we had a good sleep on the flight.

When we reached Narita airport, Mr Suzuki and Pastor Haga were waiting for us. Pastor Haga was to take us on the two-hour drive to his flat in Koganei. The roads were wide and the high rise buildings obscured Tokyo Tower, which no longer dominated the landscape. To us it was a new scene, unlike the Tokyo we had left twenty years previously.

Pastor Haga, on retirement as Pastor, had wisely decided to move away from Koganei to another area but within easy reach of the church. In so doing, he avoided interfering with Pastor Miyakawa, or people bringing problems to him.

The flat was new. Tadashi and Aki were proud to house us, the first visitors to stay with them. They showed us into our room with a double bed, but the toilet and bath required explanation! The toilet seat could be heated, the water temperature controlled, and it could be used as a bidet. The bath water temperature was thermostatically controlled; the washing machine beside the bathroom in excellent order. Aki had put washcloths out for us, 9 ins. × 2 ft, nylon not towelling.

We slept well. Breakfast was a full meal including salad and tea. A church member and excellent cook, Mrs Yabana, had remembered that we liked *inarizushi* – rice dipped in vinegar and a sweet powder, enclosed in a dry tofu skin; she had sent a supply round for us.

After breakfast we had a time of Bible reading and prayer together, taking turns in reading aloud. I always struggled, focussing on the syllables that gave the pronunciation at the side of the characters. Tadashi returned to his bedroom to test his blood sugar level and then give himself the necessary injection for the control of his diabetes. There was always a spirit of prayer and praise.

Celebration of the churches' Jubilee

Pastors, church workers and former associates gathered together for a banquet in a hotel in central Tokyo to celebrate the Jubilee of the Tokyo Free Methodist churches. As we arrived we were greeted by Japanese friends of twenty years ago, some just delighted to see us, others wanting to share their struggles.

Pastor and Mrs Nojiri were present. (I had known them in Koganei, and had met them again in Thailand where they had gone with OMF.) They were a very godly couple, with good English, but not sufficient to enjoy the general conversation when groups of English speaking missionaries chatted together. They could not share their profound understanding of the Bible and Thai culture. They had returned to Japan and pioneered a new church in the Tokyo area. Then they returned to north Thailand to head up a Japanese church.

When they returned to Thailand, Tokuda and Akemi with their two children took over the growing church in Japan. We had known Akemi very well during our four years with the Koganei Free Methodist Church. She had been employed as a church worker there, had hoped to go to Thailand with OMF, and had lived a short time in rural Thailand. Despite her efforts and mine, she could not reach the proficiency in English to work with OMF in Thailand.

Tokuda had been with me on the church ten days' visit to Thailand to Pastor and Mrs Nojiri in 1982. He had wanted to marry Akemi. We had been guests at their wedding in Koganei church in 1984. They spent several happy years as missionaries in Bolivia. Back in Japan with their two children, running a small church, they were struggling, even distressed. Akemi rushed to greet me and unburden her problems. Tokuda shared his concerns with Doug, who hadn't recognised him at first because of a dark, bushy moustache.

For the celebration we were all seated at large, round tables, about eight to each table. We were served as we listened to a variety of speeches, telling of the growth of the churches and outreach. Doug and I were the last to give ours. (I wished we had been earlier, as I am always nervous before speaking and would have enjoyed the meal more. Mrs Haga explained to me that we were the least important of the speakers.)

Because of one valued American lady present who had contributed much to the growth of the church but did not understand Japanese, Doug and I were asked to speak in English with an interpreter. This posed no great problem, the interpreter was excellent, but at one point I accidentally broke into Japanese. She was taken aback; we all laughed and continued as before.

I spoke a little about our connections with Pastor Haga and the Free Methodist Church although we had had only four years working with the Koganei church. Pastor Haga was chairman of the OMF Japan Council for sending out Japanese missionaries. He had spoken at our conferences in Hokkaido. A young woman who had become a Christian when I spoke on

John 1 v 28 at her Presbyterian church in Hakodate in 1987, had trained at Bible School and married a member of the Koganei church. He became a pastor in the north. It was she who confirmed that I had been dismissed from the young people's meeting at her Presbyterian church in Hakodate because I believed in the resurrection (see page 130).

Exhilarating, enjoyable, exhausting, well worthwhile – we still remembered faces and the language – then back to the comfort of the Haga's flat, ready for our next adventure.

Lake Kawaguchi

The Conference over, Pastor and Mrs Haga took us to a luxury Western-style hotel by Mt Fuji. He knew the Christian proprietress.

He had arranged for a group of four lively widows whom we had known well, to make up the party of eight. He drove us in his eight-seater the seventy odd miles to Lake Kawaguchi, up a good road, with lovely country scenery of fields and trees, to the Lake. We stopped halfway for a snack of noodles at a traditional noodle café, charming with polished wooden tables and chairs, the brown decor of old Japan, and quiet for us to have free conversation.

On arrival at the hotel, we were welcomed by the Christian owners, shown our rooms and the lobbies with cushioned sofas where we could chat with one another.

We gathered in the dining room for the evening meal, seated on padded chairs at an oblong table covered with a green tablecloth. I cannot remember what we had for supper only that it was refreshing and tasty, certainly not raw eggs or raw fish.

We slept well on comfortable beds. Breakfast was served in the same dining room but the table covered with a pink cloth. After breakfast we lined up for our group photograph, taken by our hostess.

The big attraction of the resort was the Ukai Music Forest Museum, the brochure prepared in English as well as Japanese. We paid to enter and received the brochure giving us a map of the museum, with details of each section. Doug and I were glad to be given the English version, with a clearer plan of the grounds in colour. (Japanese version black and white.)

We went into the concert hall and sat down to listen to classical music, with show cases with automatic orchestra, self-playing violins, a reproducing piano and mechanical figures.

In the large auditorium, an organ as the background, a string quartet played in the centre. Pastor Haga took me down to meet the quartet, introducing me as also a violinist. Groups came from all countries to perform in this concert hall, especially the Prague quartet.

We visited a 'salon' where there was a realistic-looking bird, perhaps a peacock that could be heard by listening carefully. Behind was a large mirror. I have an expressive photo of Pastor Haga, leaning with his ear close to the bird to hear it, plus the reflection in the mirror, and also a photo of our ladies round the bird.

On the outside of the organ hall was a clock tower overlooking a lake. An automaton in officer's uniform emerges from the clock on the hour and at the same time fountains spring up from the lake. It is hard to get a photograph of the soldier because he is obscured by the spray of the fountains.

The area was vast and interesting, but we lacked time to sit in the small church and enjoy the view of the Lake Kawaguchi and Mt Fuji.

We left the Ukai Museum to queue at the dolls museum. The dolls had all been made from old clothes and scraps. Peter Pan was cute dressed in black but with bare arms and legs, squatting pensively leaning on a sack. A red pointed feathered cap adorned his auburn hair. Another doll was of a little girl kneeling against cushions, resting her head on a quilt possibly asleep, with a paper crane at her foot.

We sat on a bench and relaxed in the sunshine waiting for our bus to pick us up.

Not least we enjoyed the spectacular scenery of the Lake itself, mountains in the background, blue or shimmering white water, the setting sun reflected from the surface, little boats by the shore, and yellow flowers in the grass.

The display in a souvenir shop near the hotel was a picture in itself, the ladies pleased to serve us, appreciated their own environment and souvenirs. We bought half a dozen posters of Mt Fuji.

Back to the hotel, to the eight-seater, the end of a dream trip, magnificent scenery, musical history, congenial company, and spiritual input daily from the pastor. It had been a stimulating and refreshing few days, unlike anything I had previously experienced in Japan.

Hokkaido

Mr Suzuki saw us off from Haneda Airport for the hour's flight to Chitose, Hokkaido. Irene Hope met us at Chitose and guided us to the waiting train for Sapporo. She had arranged for us to have lunch at Sapporo station with Ruth Dueck who had come the two-hour rail journey from Asahikawa specially to meet us. The whole of Sapporo station had been modernised. We had to be guided round the individual tables of the café area. Although we had spent twelve years in the city and had known it fifty years previously when the smoke from the steam engines covered the city with soot, it was now strange to us. A leisurely meal with Ruth and Irene enabled us to catch up with one another's news. When we had travelled through Canada we had spent a few days in Ruth's area meeting her parents. She and her sister had visited us in London. We knew the city of Asahikawa where she was pastor of a church – an unusual position for a missionary, but what the believers had wanted. When she had arrived in Japan in 1970 we had welcomed her to work as the accountant in the OMF office but this was not the right job for her. She came from a large family and was very capable of helping a group of fellow missionaries.

The meal over she left us to return to Asahikawa while Irene directed us to the Sapporo Grand Hotel. She had booked rooms for us there, knowing that our time and energy were limited. It was all we could have wished for – grand indeed – in the centre of the city, good meals available, comfortable quiet bedrooms and a spacious lobby area suitable for meeting and talking to friends. It was a busy three days.

Mrs Watanabe (see page 192) had travelled the four-hour journey from Kushiro to save us the time and effort of the long journey. Her husband was occupied with other pastors and regretted not being able to meet us. They had been a hairdresser and barber when they became Christians during our time in Sapporo at Tooei Church. After we left Japan, Mr Watanabe trained as a pastor at the Hokkaido Bible Institute, helped for a time at Tooei church and then took up the position as pastor of a small congregation in Kushiro, a foggy fishing town in south east Hokkaido. We had continued to keep in touch with them, prayed for them over the last twenty years. She told us about their personal lives, their two children; we felt the continued affection we had for one another.

Mr Shibakawa met us in the lobby in the afternoon. We were surprised for, although we had very much wanted to meet this dear friend, he had told us that he had to be in Tokyo that day for a medical check. He had made the extra effort to get back to Sapporo to see us. We chatted in the lobby for some time; he mentioned his medical problems and was eager to accept Doug's offer to pray for him there and then in the lobby. His son was now running their timber business, and his wife, Akiko, had succeeded in founding a kindergarten for disabled children. She herself was a teacher of the deaf. When they married he had promised her opportunity to develop these skills and at last there was the fulfilment.

I was having supper with three ladies, so Mr Shibakawa took Doug out for a seven course raw fish meal.

I had asked Irene if she could contact these three special ladies: Mrs Sagawa, Mrs Imamura and Mrs Kubo. We dined together in a secluded quiet corner of the hotel restaurant where we were able to talk freely without disturbance. Mrs Sagawa had been a near neighbour in Sapporo and with other ladies we had held a Bible Study group in her home. She had put up the text, 'The Lord is my Shepherd' in her home. Her husband had questioned her because the word for 'Lord' is the same as that for 'husband'. 'What does it mean? My husband is my shepherd.' She had moved to another part of Sapporo, joined a thriving church and clearly showed her faith. She looked as young as ever.

Mrs Imamura (see pages 64, 181), I had first met when she was a schoolgirl. I received a photograph of her baptism plus a tape recording of it, when I retired to England. She explained that although her mother was a Christian she herself felt she could not be baptized just to please her mother, it had to follow a clear conviction of her own. After her mother's death she reached this point. She had continued attending church for some time but stopped because of the autocratic approach of the pastor. Mrs Sagawa urged her to meet with other Christians and not be put off by demands from the church.

Mrs Kubo had helped me with the housework in the busy time when Doug, as Superintendent, had frequent visitors. She was a quiet, lovely person, an excellent house-help, steady, reliable and understanding. She did not have an easy life. She had never trusted in Christ. The other two ladies urged her to do so.

The ladies insisted on paying for the meal. We were glad we had been able to meet after so many years. Mrs Imamura gave me a beautiful brooch, four sky blue enamel petals on a gold background, three pearls in the centre. It had been her mother's, my friend.

The following day Irene picked us up in the mission van to take us to the prayer meeting of the Sapporo language students and missionaries. I gave a brief Bible talk to all of them, in English (we had been using

Japanese in conversation so far). Our friend, Melville Szto from Singapore, was leading at first, then we broke up into two groups to learn the problems and triumphs of individuals, and how the Sapporo churches were progressing. Most of the group were new to us.

Irene took us on for a meal with those we had known before. Pat and Tony Schmidt had spent a period in Canada (see page 182); they were unhappy with the apartheid system of their birth country, South Africa. We had enjoyed working closely with them in the Sapporo office, a warm-hearted, hardworking couple.

We had welcomed Melville and Salome Szto, from Singapore and Indonesia on their arrival in Japan. They had worked very humbly alongside Pastor Takemoto learning much from him, especially concerning the culture and methods of a Japanese church.

Ingrid, a German lady, was now married to a Japanese widower and continuing to help in the church in Otaru. Doug had greeted her with a handshake when she had first arrived in Sapporo – afterwards realising that this would be the accepted greeting in Germany.

After the meal, Irene drove us to see the building that had been bought for our new offices, 'The Red House'.

Next, she ran us over to the Kamada household (see page 189). The house itself had been enlarged to three stories to accommodate Mariko's family and not leave Mr and Mrs Kamada on their own. The sisters, Mariko and Kumiko were also there and gave us a very warm welcome. They had prepared food for us. I think it was pizzas but the 'girls' quickly removed it when they realised we had already eaten. Miho was away in America, disappointed that we could not see her and her husband, Ralf, on our visit to Japan. Mr and Mrs Kamada were in excellent health. The main living room on the first floor was dominated by a new large Shinto god-shelf. Mr Kamada, now retired (and not a Christian), had remained adamant that while he was alive the Shinto shrine, symbolic of Japan, would remain in place. Mariko and family lived on the second floor. She called her footballer high school son to meet us. He was on his school football team with a strong Christian faith and had refused to take part in the ancestor worship carried out before the matches. Her eldest daughter had declared her faith by going to her Aunt Miho's church in the south to be baptized. Once again we were deeply moved by the warmth of their welcome and sheer pleasure at meeting us again after twenty years.

There were other people and churches we would like to have met – the

Eastern Glory, Glory churches, cooking class ladies, etc., and there was no possibility of our travelling to Kitami.

Doug was able to spend some time with Pastor Yahiro and learn of the growth of OMF churches in Sapporo. What we had known as struggling groups now numbered hundreds, with new buildings and forward vision. As Doug and Mr Yahiro prayed together they both broke down in tears remembering the past.

The next morning we took our booked seats on the express train for Hakodate. It was a journey we had frequently travelled. I wanted to enjoy the view of the countryside, with colourful autumn leaves, and to glimpse at the towns we had known – Otaru, with the spectacular rocky coast line, Kutchan where Doug had lived for a year and a half, Mori, one of the first OMF stations, and Hakodate itself where I looked forward to seeing the peak of the mountain as we approached. To say I was crestfallen would be the appropriate expression as the crest of the mountain was shrouded in mist.

Mr and Mrs Uchiyama were at the station to meet us and take us to the church we had founded forty-four years earlier. In 1959 Doug had baptized Mr Uchiyama in hospital (see page 130) where he was ill with advanced TB, not expecting ever to leave the hospital. Now, 2003, he was still alive, strong in faith despite many setbacks, his wife having died. Similarly, he lost his son, a promising young doctor, with a sudden heart attack. His daughter cared for him, giving up her own career. He came to England to thank the congregation at Stanmore Baptist Church for sending us to Japan so that he had found the joy and salvation of Jesus Christ. On his return the churches found him another wife of similar faith and he introduced us to her. Sadly, he had some disagreement with the original church – we did not discover the cause.

They stopped at a restaurant to 'treat' us to a raw fish meal, before taking us on to a meeting of Hanazono Church, with Pastor and Mrs Shinada. We sensed a coolness in the atmosphere on our arrival. As we met together, Mrs Shinada prayed for me: 'Lord, you know how much Mrs Abrahams had wanted to see the mountain. Please clear it.'

We spent some time with Pastor and Mrs Shinada whom we had known for many years. He had helped us in our pioneer days in Hakodate, had spent some time in England, and had been principal of the Hokkaido Bible Institute before moving to a church in Tokyo. Things did not work out as he had hoped on his return to his native Hokkaido but he had developed plans to educate children who had dropped out of school because of bullying, and to put the former OMF school at Nanae to use for this. Judith Spear had taught OMF children at Nanae but was back in Nanae assisting in the thriving, growing church in that town. This was the school where our children had attended.

We said goodbye to Mr and Mrs Shinada, expecting that we would see them in the morning at the airport. Mr Uchiyama drove us back to the hotel where we were to spend the night.

We reached the hotel safely but realised that Mr Uchiyama's poor sight was endangering his driving. But we thanked him for bringing us to the hotel and said goodnight.

About 9.30 p.m. the telephone rang. It was Mrs Shinada. 'The mountain has cleared. If you are not too tired, and would like to go to the peak, we can drive you up tonight.'

We were tired but thrilled at the unexpected opportunity.

They brought us extra clothing as the top of the mountain is always cold. We bundled into their car and followed the traffic and police instructions up the winding mountain road. The traffic has to be controlled because of the narrowness of the road allowing for cars to go up or down, but not at the same time, and the route is popular. We reached the peak at last glad of the extra garments, and looked out on the magnificent night scene of the city studded with lights, and the deep blackness of the sea at either side of the peninsular. Back to the hotel.

The following morning they called again to take us to the airport where we had time to talk at length, Doug with the Pastor, I with Mrs Shinada, discovering their hopes and disappointments. As our plane was signalled we said goodbye to them and to Hokkaido.

It had been a wonderful time of seeing how God had worked out His plans, greater than ours.

On arrival at Haneda airport, Mr Suzuki was there again to meet us and to take us for a restful stay in his home.

A welcome to a friend's home

Mr and Mrs Suzuki were excited to have us as guests in their home. The fact we were on given name terms was an indication of close friendship. We had first met the family when he was working as a businessman in London.

Mr Suzuki had arranged with Pastor Haga to borrow us for a few days. His wife spoilt us; she was an excellent cook and fed us lavishly; we rested on beds in the spacious bedroom, had the use of the toilet off the bedroom, washed in the shower or soaked up to the neck in the Japanese style *ofuro* (bath), or with less water in it, washed with soap English style in the bath, all thermostatically controlled. She did our laundry for us.

When we lived in Koganei, 1982–85, we had visited the family. The younger son was very shy, would greet us with the minimum of courtesy, then disappear to his room upstairs to study and avoid us. The older boy was adjusting from his English education to Japanese culture.

Now in November 2003, they were a happy family. The older son, full of faith, was leading an international congregation in Tokyo with his violinist wife. Mr Suzuki was occupied interpreting and translating for his son's international congregation.

The younger son was also a pastor, his church meeting in his parents' home. His wife had had no Christian background but had been drawn to Christ through reading *Polyanna*. Their daughter was growing as a Christian and a delight. They all came to visit us.

Mr Suzuki showed us around the city, a clean suburb of Tokyo, with high rise department stores from which we could look down on the well-kept streets. We had a meal in a restaurant. When we asked the waitress if we could take her photograph, she thought we were wanting her to take ours. Later we had a walk through the park, chatted to a mother and child and took the photo of all of us. A small tent in the park indicated a family having a day out. There was a sumo ring where Mr Suzuki and Doug posed as sumo wrestlers. It was a happy, refreshing and relaxing time after our busy schedule in Hokkaido.

Mr Suzuki drove us back to the Haga's flat, calling in on Pastor Tsutada on the way. He went to a lot of trouble finding Tsutada's church. But we were delighted to meet this man again, he had meant so much to us at the Immanuel Bible College. Now he was Pastor of a church on the edge of the rice fields.

From Pastor and Mrs Haga's home

Back in the security of the Haga's flat, we thought most of our surprises would be over, but there was more to come.

'Taki' was the name by which my friend Nurita, a neighbour in Stanmore, knew Mr Miyazaki who owned a delicatessen near Koganei. He had trained in Germany with her son, had been a great help to him. Nurita was fond of him; they contacted each other each Christmas. Mrs Haga had already visited him at our request. Nurita had asked me to take him a small present. I think it was the Lord's Prayer decoratively written. Mrs Haga was pleased to accompany me. We reached his shop on a busy street corner, his cakes and biscuits beautifully displayed in the window. Dressed in his white apron and chef's hat he welcomed us. He left his assistant to look after the shop and took us upstairs to talk freely and without interruption. He was delighted to receive the card from Nurita, plus my explanation of the words. When we concluded with prayer, he reverently removed his cap and said 'amen'. As owner of the shop he was tied to the business, doing the cooking himself, so could not get out to the church although he would have liked to visit. Later, before I left for England, he sent round two fruit cakes he had made, one for us and one for Nurita.

Mrs Haga reminded me of our time living in Sky Mansion. I had been disappointed that none of the cooking/Bible Class had believed in Jesus while we were there.

'After you left,' she explained, 'Mrs Ishikawa, the Christian owner, continued the Bible Class. And do you remember the lady with the albino son?' she asked.

'Yes, very clearly,' I replied.

'She moved to another area, was baptized and joined a church.'

'I am sure you will remember the Miyahara family.' (see page 218)

'Yes, they were our next door neighbours, very friendly and with two little girls.'

'They had a time in America where they attended church and have also become Christians. They are back in Japan, living in Kokubunchi and regularly worshipping at a nearby Lutheran church. Why don't you phone her?'

She gave me the phone number; I was delighted with the warm, happy response I received from Mrs Miyahara rejoicing in her faith.

Pastor and Mrs Haga took us out to a meal of beef steak at 'Woodstock'. The pastor had always been expert on finding special places to eat. Here we sat at our table and ordered our steak, well-done, medium or 'raw'. The waiter brought us large, white, serviettes to avoid the splashes of oil when the steaks were placed in front of us on hot iron plates and further cooked with the hot iron utensil. It was a delicious meal: we were glad that Pastor Haga was able to enjoy his food again, recovered from the massive cancer operation that had removed his stomach.

The church had arranged for a meal in a restaurant with those we had known well twenty years previously. Knowing that I was particularly fond of tofu, they had arranged a feast of successive dishes all based on different kinds of tofu. We were seated at low tables, apparently in the traditional Japanese fashion but in fact we had low backed seats, our legs below the table – so many old friends – most of those mentioned in my previous description of Christian Homes, helpers in the cooking class at Sky Mansion, one younger woman who told us that my children's English class in the church had inspired her to study English, and become a Christian.

They gave us a present of deerskin spectacle cases.

At breakfast time on Sunday morning we watched a Christian broadcast on TV. This was normal for a Sunday morning. There is no restriction on religious broadcasting provided there is a sponsor.

We also watched the progress of an earthquake that had hit Hokkaido. The epicentre was in the sea just off the southern coast near to Kushiro. Pastor Watanabe's house and church had been damaged, but no lives lost.

The final anniversary celebration for the Koganei church brought in other people we had known. Each department of the church was called to the front in turn to sing. Doug was pulled in for the men's choir. I had always claimed to have no singing voice. During the service a number of people spoke of their connection with the church. Mr Kuroda (see page 244), the English professor, to whom we had been introduced through our friend in England, spoke of his association with us although from a different church. Mr Kawasaki, a student from Sapporo, had joined Koganei church. I hadn't remembered his name but was told all the students could because of the connection with motorbikes. A former friend from Hirosaki days was present. Mrs Imai from the cooking class had not been able to come – she and her husband were attending Pastor Tsutada's church but her daughter was a member of Koganei church involved in transworld evangelism.

The service was followed by a meal in the upstairs room which had been made large enough by removing partitions. We each received our boxed lunch. There were many speeches, Doug and I had both been allocated fifteen minutes each. I had great freedom speaking on the heritage we all had in the Koganei church. I also got to know Mr and Mrs Mikami, Gideon leaders in Japan. When I asked Pastor Haga about them he was enthusiastic. In his high school days Mr Mikami had brought him along to the meeting in Mrs Milikan's house. It was through him that Pastor Haga had come into faith.

At the end of the day I experienced the sentiment of the chorus 'My cup's full and running over,' but with the reminder of the little girl's version, 'My cup's full and so's my saucer.'

And so to bed.

OMF Japan Headquarters

The last lap of our journey was to the OMF Japan Headquarters in Ichikawa. When we had left Japan in 1986 our HQ was still in Sapporo. The property in Ichikawa had been owned by a Christian lady, Mrs Ukiya, whose son, a well-known Christian racing driver, had been killed in a crash. She established a museum and church in commemoration. She wanted everyone to know about Jesus Christ.

A Japanese translation of a Chinese account of the life of Hudson Taylor came into her hands. 'I would like to leave my property to this mission, the CIM, but does it still exist?' she asked. She discovered that OMF, working in Japan, was the same mission, so she gave the property to OMF. It became the OMF Japan HQ, Home Council premises, guest home, offices and church.

Pastor Haga drove us over to Ichikawa. Dorothea Langhans welcomed us with a big smile. We would not have known her, as it was nearly twenty years since we had welcomed her and her husband, Wolfgang, to language study in Sapporo. He was now very capably leading the team in Japan.

Gareth and Ruth Ayling were guest home host and hostess and had prepared everything for us. They gave us a meal in a local café where we exchanged news of our families. Gareth told us something of the problems of modern Japan. Outwardly it seemed very prosperous, new buildings, shops full of goods, but there was an underlying unrest. Many young people were shutting themselves away from society, living in one room in their house, and not speaking to anyone for as much as six months or more. Often failure to reach necessary grades for university entrance caused this withdrawal. They would have the TV in their room and obtain food from the kitchen when no one was around.

Gareth and Ruth also showed us round the Chapel of Adoration, a small sanctuary established by Mrs Ukiya, and introduced us to the daughter, whose generosity brought her to the verge of poverty. She gave us a warm welcome and later sent us a present of a round, carved wooden tray, which we still have.

The Mausoleum, a more imposing building also on the premises, enshrined Mrs Ukiya's ashes and her son's.

Jim and Mariana Nesbit had been our close associates in Sapporo, where Jim was treasurer and had become a member of the City Chamber of Commerce. He was a financial wizard, and had been a great help to Doug in mission administration. Jim was still treasurer, living in a tiny flat in Ichikawa because rents were so high. We had a meal with them in their kitchen cum dining cum sitting room. Mariana had been so successful in introducing women to Christ, in different groups, that she had worn herself out and was having to relax to recuperate.

Pastor Haga and the Koganei church had given much assistance in the setting up of the HQ. The Japanese Home Council (the body responsible for sending Japanese missionaries abroad) were meeting here the day of our visit; we joined them for lunch. Pastor Haga had been the first Home Council chairman; on return from Singapore, our friend Makino had taken over this responsibility and was currently acting chairman until a permanent appointment could be made. They told us of the small church in central Tokyo, run-down, in debt and needy, where he and Izu were now pastors. They were both always cheerful and a pleasure to meet again.

Emiko, whom we had known in her lonely situation in Koganei, was now happily working in the office of the Home Council, and no longer alone. It was Emiko who had supplied the tickets for us to go to the Kabuki Theatre.

I sat next to Pastor S from Sakae church, Sapporo. He had previously been pastor at Hanazono church, Hakodate. We had been involved in the start of both these churches. Pastor S told me of their growth. He was a man with a vision for the world (a bit like Pastor Haga).

Also present at lunch were Japanese missionaries on home assignment in Japan, or hoping to go abroad themselves.

Back in our guest room, Doug had just gone out of the door when the phone rang. A lady's voice said, 'This is Mrs Hatakeyama from Sapporo.'

I answered, 'Oh, I'm so sorry, my husband has just gone out.' I knew that Doug had asked that Pastor Mrs Hatakeyama would phone him.

'I'm not the Pastor Mrs Hatakeyama. I know her and have the same name but I married a Christian man, Mr Hatakeyama, and came to live here. I was in your Sunday School in Hakodate in 1960. Do you remember me? I was called Sato.'

'Yes, I remember that Sunday School very clearly (see page 129). There were four middle school girls who helped in teaching; and you were one of them.'

'After you left, I went to high school and Mr Baker baptized me. Now I am married with a family. My daughter has gone as a missionary to Cambodia working in an orphanage.'

When I put the phone down, I just worshipped my God, who had let me know this after more than forty years.

And finally . . .

Our send off was from Narita Airport; we left rejoicing, tired and happy. DD loved the place, Our health had held, the Japanese language had returned, we had remembered many people. I had been overwhelmed to see what God had done and was doing; the tremendous advances since we first arrived in Japan in 1952, and even since we had left in 1986 – magnificent new premises, churches established and growing, pastors appointed, Japanese missionaries going to other lands, plus a deep affection for us.

We had seen God's ways over many years. They had truly been immeasurably higher than ours.

Final Thoughts – the Epilogue

Relaxing in my comfortable mobile home in Whitley Bay, I was looking forward to a phone call from my old friend Win. She would buzz me when she arrived at the car park so that I could help her across the uneven grass to the caravan. Not that she didn't know the way, but with hip replacements and brittle bones she could not risk a fall. The fog horn still alerted sailors at sea but St Mary's Lighthouse was no longer needed to flash warning signals to ships now equipped with radar. As I set off to meet her, I mused, 'Are we like the lighthouse, no longer of use in our ninth decade?'

When we were settled with our cups of tea and coffee, enjoying each other's company, ready to reminisce about the adventures of our long lives, I asked the question, 'What do you think, Win? Is St Mary's Lighthouse of any use, now that she no longer flashes her warning signals?'

'Of course she is,' an astonished Win replied. 'She belongs to us. We see her night and day glistening in the sunlight now that she is repainted, and at night her floodlit stature produces a striking reflection on the sea.'

'How did she come to be preserved, repainted and floodlit? I don't remember the floodlighting years ago.'

'You were away in Japan when the changes were made. The National Lighthouse Authority ordered her destruction. We weren't having any of it. The whole local population was incensed and would not hear of such a spectacular and loved symbol of the town being destroyed. The North Tyneside Council with help rescued and transformed her.'

'So what's left – now that there is no longer a lighthouse keeper or homemade scones and cakes available at the little red cottages on the island,' I asked wistfully.

'Did you ever climb the 137 steps to the top?'

'Yes, I did, years ago, with the lighthouse keeper guiding and describing how the lighthouse worked. And ten years ago I climbed with Bethany on her sixth birthday. The view from the top to the Cheviots in the north and the mouth of the Tyne in the south, remains brilliant – the air is so clear.'

'Well, if you climb the 137 steps now you get a certificate and badge to prove it. (I couldn't manage it today but maybe you could.) But they have made a kind of museum inside. It's history, pictures, stories of the sea, illustrations of the birds, fish and rock pools — and a reminder of the heroism of Grace Darling of the nearby Longstone Lighthouse on the Farne Islands.'

'It may not be what it was — but it represents the past, present and future. Perhaps our lives are a bit like the lighthouse. The past gives us precious memories that we can't help talking about, our cycling tours, dips in the cold sea, glowing in the warmth of the Panama Café and our separate lives all over the world. We want to share our memories with our children, grandchildren, friends and colleagues.'

'That sounds like the end of your story but has anything new happened recently.'

'As a matter of fact it has. When wondering what next I had two links from my old College, Girton, Cambridge. The first was a telephone call from a first year history student asking about my life in Girton and subsequently. The aim was to ask for financial help towards the development of the College and to connect present students with the alumni.'

'Was he interested? Did you send any money?'

'Indeed he was. We spoke for over an hour on the telephone. He was intrigued by my story and I was chuffed that an eighteen-year-old student wanted to chat to an eighty-year-old woman.'

'What was your other link?'

'That was a bigger surprise. I received a letter sent to former students who had been in College in the war years between 1936 and 1946. There had been a gap in the College roll of those years. We were asked to write freely about our memories and experiences. It was an encouraging, friendly letter, not demanding but asking for a quick reply so that the record of those years would not be lost. I was there from 1943 to 1946 so, at eighty-one, must be amongst the youngest of the group.'

'Can you remember that time?'

'Yes, especially as I have been writing about them for this book. Win, as I look back over the years I recall many surprises, seeing how God has led me on time and again to the unexpected. God's thoughts and ways have been higher than mine.'

Is the circle complete or do I still ask 'what next'?